WORKING WITH
ORACLE®

WORKING WITH
ORACLE®

Jack L. Hursch, Ph.D.
and Carolyn J. Hursch, Ph.D.

TAB Professional and Reference Books

Division of TAB BOOKS Inc.
Blue Ridge Summit, PA

Notes:

1. *ORACLE* is a registered trademark of Oracle Corporation. Certain portions of copyrighted Oracle Corporation user documentation have been reproduced herein with the permission of Oracle Corporation.

2. IBM is the registered trademark of International Business Machines Corporation.

3. SQL*Forms and SQL*Plus are trademarks of Oracle Corporation.

FIRST EDITION

THIRD PRINTING

Printed in the United States of America

Library of Congress Cataloging in Publication Data

Hursch, Jack L.
Working with ORACLE.

Includes index.
1. Relational data bases. 2. ORACLE (Computer system) I. Hursch, Carolyn
J. II. Title.
QA76.9.D3H868   1987   005.75′65   87-14009
ISBN 0-8306-2916-5 (pbk.)

Questions regarding the content of this book
should be addressed to:

Reader Inquiry Branch
TAB BOOKS Inc.
Blue Ridge Summit, PA 17294-0214

TAB BOOKS Inc. offers software for
sale. For information and a catalog,
please contact TAB Software Department,
Blue Ridge Summit, PA 17294-0850.

Contents

Introduction

This book is intended as a supplement to the user's manuals supplied with an *ORACLE[1] Relational Database Management System*. The material presented here will amplify and illustrate that presented in documentation supplied by Oracle Corporation.
It assumes that:

1. You are about to install or have recently installed an *ORACLE* database system on a micro, supermicro, mini, or mainframe computer.
2. You are setting up a single-user or a multi-user system.
3. You are not necessarily a computer programmer, but are conversant with some common computing terms and concepts.

The viewpoint in this text is strictly "external," i.e., that of the user. The internal structuring of the data, and other such topics, are not treated here. However, the first eight chapters will be of more use to the administrative user than the new or casual user of *ORACLE*. The user whose main concern is day-to-day work with the database can (after reading the definitions in Chapter 1) go directly to Chapters 9 through 16 for hands-on instructions for creating tables, views, and indexes, and putting them to use. The contents of all chapters are outlined below.

Chapter 1 briefly discusses the characteristics of a relational database and then lists the necessary basic definitions of terms used through this text. Definitions of entities in individual chapters appear as needed.

Chapter 2 explains the programs and products that constitute the *ORACLE* database system as it is described in succeeding chapters. Chapter 2 also explains auditing, the data dictionary, the sort/merge utility, and the *ORACLE* context space.

Continued research and development by Oracle Corporation results in additional features and new versions of the database system. This book is based on Version 5.0. Wherever possible, the differences between Version 5.0 and earlier versions are pointed out. A table listing recently added features according to version number and linking these updates with features in earlier versions is included in Chapter 2.

The user interface to *ORACLE* is the Structured Query Language (SQL, pronounced "sequel") which was originally developed by IBM[2] . This is the data sublanguage with which the user sets up and maintains his *ORACLE* database system. SQL and Oracle Corporation's *SQL*Plus[3]*, a user-friendly interface, are described in detail in Chapter 3.

Chapter 4 is devoted to database design, a procedure that should take place before the database system is put into use. While the relational form of this database allows information to be retrieved regardless of how the data are entered, and thus new uses can be achieved without reprogramming, the usual and normal uses of the database should be planned for in advance. How the tables are set up, how many variables each table contains, and the backup provisions in any practical application are determined by the user.

At the same time, some experience with the database may be necessary before improvements are attempted. For a system already installed without extensive preplanning, or a system where the original purposes have enlarged or radically changed, redesign may not only be advisable, but may be necessary to take full advantage of *ORACLE* capabilities. Chapter 4, based on the mathematical principles underlying relational principles, will guide you to the most trouble-free design in such cases.

Chapter 5 discusses the need for a *database administrator* (DBA) in any system with more than one user. Not only for security reasons, but also for control, an administrative entity must be in charge of operating decisions that arise. Some of these will occur only sporadically; others may arise daily. A multi-user system cannot operate efficiently unless these decisions are under the control of a DBA. The actual running of the database is split up between two DBA designations, SYS and SYSTEM, and in larger installations these duties may be sufficiently heavy to engage two persons. Security facilities in *ORACLE*, as well as methods by which levels of access are granted to the users, are also set forth in Chapter 5.

In Chapter 6, the necessary short- and long-term space projections are discussed, as well as methods of allocating space. Detail is provided here, chiefly for the use of database administrators, regarding how the basic space specifications may be augmented as the database enlarges over time.

Depending upon whether or not your records are in computer-readable form, you have several options as to how you will transfer them into the *ORACLE* database. Chapter 7 explains these options in detail. It also deals with modifications to and the settings for computer parameters.

Chapter 8 explains the various types of locking systems provided by *ORACLE* and the locking modes within each system. Multi-user systems with a heavy volume of database use are faced constantly with the possibility of data being changed by one process as another process is using it. Preventing this problem is one focus of the locking system. In addition, there is the problem of long user waiting periods to gain access to the data in order to modify or update it. Such waits can be costly; therefore, in many cases the locking system can be used in share modes which provide limited access to some users while others are making necessary changes. The ultimate focus is to prevent deadlock, and in Chapter 8 methods of avoiding this are discussed.

Chapter 9 explains and illustrates the use of the SQL Data Definition Statements for creating and dropping tables, views, and indexes, and for altering tables by adding columns or changing their data type. The examples in this and succeeding chapters will provide a ready reference for a user without additional knowledge about the system.

Chapter 10 explains and illustrates the SQL Data Manipulation Statements for selecting, updating, deleting, and inserting records in tables, views, and indexes.

Chapter 11 shows how to use the clauses, functions, expressions, and operators which put the Data Definition and Data Manipulation statements to work. These terms provide the versatility inherent in *ORACLE*.

In Chapter 12, the DDL statements of Chapter 9 are combined with the DML statements of Chapter 10, in conjunction with the appropriate clauses, functions, expressions, and operators of Chapter 11. In this way, the steps necessary to create, maintain, and alter the *ORACLE* database are illustrated. Detailed examples are given.

Chapter 13 enlarges upon the basic usage of Chapter 12, showing more advanced methods for constructing SQL statements, and using conditional clauses in order to optimize the overall efficiency of the system. This chapter is an advanced treatment of the basic concepts, intended for the user who has had some experience with *ORACLE* and who would like to improve system performance by taking advantage of the fine points and less obvious features of *ORACLE*'s relational construction.

In Chapter 14, *ORACLE*'s *Report Writer* is described. This application consists of a Report Formatter (RPF) and a Report Generator (RPT). Together these two programs provide a way to generate custom reports and include in them information from the database. In a large installation, filing periodic data-oriented reports becomes almost completely automatic once *Report Writer* is set up.

Chapters 15 and 16 explain the use of *SQL*Forms,* another application supplied by Oracle Corporation. With *SQL*Forms* you can design forms to be used by terminal operators who have little or no knowledge of the database itself. The application is designed to make the filling out of the forms on the screen as much as possible like filling out paper forms. The operator, by using function keys, can merely enter the information requested by each field as it appears on the screen.

SQL*Forms also provides a check on various integrity constraints by the use of triggers which will or will not execute, depending upon whether or not the information has been entered accurately. They can be designed to move the screen automatically onto other fields, depending upon the information entered. This feature allows the form designer broad latitude in setting up custom forms to meet the specific needs of any installation. These forms do away with the need to have every end user of the system become highly informed on system features, since the naive operator can easily follow the screen instructions for filling out the forms.

The glossary provides a quick reference to all terms used in this book relating to databases in general and *ORACLE* in particular; an effort has been made to include an explanation of every possible term that might be new and/or puzzling to a user. This section should be especially helpful to the person without extensive experience in database terminology. Frequent and early reference to the glossary will probably be the fastest way to achieve comfort and security in the initially forbidding world of the database.

Because the user often needs precise information quickly and many texts are insufficiently indexed, the last few pages of this book are devoted to providing the user with heavily cross-indexed references to every subject and command covered in this text.

Chapter 1

The Relational Database

IN GENERAL, A DATABASE IS SIMPLY A LARGE COLLECTION OF STORED DATA FROM WHICH individual data items need to be retrieved quickly and easily from time to time, sometimes in combination with other data items.

There are several different types of databases. The exact number seems to depend on which expert opinion one subscribes to. Our research on this subject forces us to conclude that the correct answer lies somewhere between two and seven. Underlying these differences of opinion is the fact that while the basic mathematical distinction between major types is clear, many of the databases on the market combine characteristics from two or more types.

The sharpest distinctions for our purposes, are between *hierarchical* and *relational* databases. It will suffice to say here that for a hierarchical database the structure is predetermined and remains that way. Therefore it is necessary to load the data into the system in a way that will allow it to be accessed in an appropriate sequence according to how it will be used.

In a relational database, on the other hand, it is not necessary to know ahead of time how data will be used in order to enter it into the system. Its specific uses and combinations of uses may be largely determined after it is entered into the database. However, this feature should not be taken too literally if retrieval speed will be an important factor—and it almost always is. Sufficient advance planning on the makeup of the tables will speed up immeasurably the retrieval process in a relational database. At the same time, adding to and altering the tables is a relatively simple process—unlike the massive disruption necessary to change the structure of a strictly hierarchical database.

Fortunately for our purposes, *ORACLE* is a relational database, which may be defined as a collection of related tables—and nothing but tables. In a relational system, a table is a row of column headings with zero or more rows of data values.[1] Its ultimate uses do not all have to be established before entering the data.

In addition to being a relational database, *ORACLE* is set up to receive large quantities of data; therefore its use is appropriate for the large company or institution or other enterprise where it is necessary to keep track of large amounts of information with regard to inventories, suppliers, or other voluminous sets of details.

ORACLE will also work well with smaller quantities of data. If your system is now relatively small, but is expected to grow appreciably, *ORACLE* would be an appropriate choice of database manager. In contrast to a highly structured database system where extensive modifications beyond the control of the user are necessary to make changes, *ORACLE*'s simple commands allow the user to make additions, deletions, and modifications.

1.1 DEFINITIONS AND TERMINOLOGY

To insure that the material in the following pages is maximally useful to you, terms commonly in use in the computing field will be used. Where ambiguity still exists for a term or meaning, a meaning will be adopted here and then used consistently. In a few cases where a frequently used term in the field still has not been precisely defined, a new term will be chosen, defined, and then used throughout.

We have already defined a relational database as a database that is perceived by the user as a collection of tables, and nothing but tables.

1.2.1 Tables

In a relational database system we define a TABLE (which is also an *ORACLE* reserved word) as a row of column names, with zero or more rows of data values inserted under those column names.

1.2.2 Columns

A *column name* is the name that you, the user, give to represent the data values that will be entered under it. Each COLUMN of a table in a relational database system has a unique name in that table, and the columns are ordered from left to right, i.e., Column 1, Column 2 . . . Column *n*. (From a mathematical standpoint, this statement is not strictly true because in a relational system the columns are unordered. However, from the user's point of view, the order in which the column names are entered becomes the order in which you must make value entries in those columns unless you name the columns each time you enter a record.)

1.2.3 Rows

Rows may be seen as representing the RECORDS in a file, and we will use the terms "rows" and "records" interchangeably. The ROWS of a table in a relational database have the following properties:

- Each row of a table has only one value for each column of that table.
- All rows of a table have the same set of columns, although any row may have NULL values in specific columns, i.e., may have no value for those columns.
- Each row of a table must be unique; there can be no identical rows.

1.2.4 Data Values

An individual data value, i.e., that value found at the intersection of a column and row, will be defined here as a *datum*.

2

Some authors refer to the individual value at the intersection of a row and column as "data" and also refer to the entire set of entries in the table as "data." Because the word "data" is a plural noun, we will use it when we refer to more than one entry in the table. When we refer to an individual entry, we will use the word *datum*, the singular form of the plural noun "data."

Some authors of database texts call the individual value a "field" and some refer to the entire column as a field. We will call each individual value a datum, and the individual location in the column where that datum is placed, will be called a "field."

The designation of *field* as the residence of an individual data value is especially important in working with *SQL*Forms*, an application which is discussed in Chapters 15 and 16.

1.2.5 NULL Values

A *NULL value* is not necessarily equal to zero. It is simply a missing datum. Moreover, one NULL value is not necessarily equal to any other NULL value.

For some columns in a table, NULL values should not be allowed to occur. You can accomplish this by specifying "NOT NULL" when you create the column. This specification insures that a datum necessary for retrieval purposes will not be omitted when a record is entered into the database. Columns containing vital identifiers (such as Social Security numbers) which, if omitted, would cause a serious handicap to the whole operation, should be specified as NOT NULL. On the other hand, a column specified as NOT NULL will not accept a record with a missing value in that column with the promise that it will be filled in later. Therefore, judicious use of the specification is necessary. (Fortunately, there are ways to get around the latter problem; the Null Value Function (NVL), explained in Chapter 11, will come to the rescue.)

There are numerous references to NULL values in different situations throughout this text, since they can seriously affect the efficiency of the database both positively and negatively.

1.2.6 Base Tables

Base tables are usually referred to simply as "tables" or "real tables"; the full name "base tables" is used here to distinguish them from "virtual tables," which are discussed below.

A base table must have a name, which you must assign when you set it up using the CREATE TABLE command (explained in detail in Chapter 9.) A base table exists in its own right in the database, whether or not it will ever be retrieved in that form. A base table may be altered or dropped. This will result in the altering or dropping of all indexes and views defined on it.

1.2.7 Virtual Tables

A table that does not actually exist in its own right in the database, but looks to the user as if it does, is called a *virtual table*. For example, in answer to a query, a table may be produced which is only a part of a Base Table, such as a list of the names and salaries of all employees whose annual salary is under $50,000. That table as such may not exist in the database. However a "Base Table" showing all employees, their salaries, and a great deal of other information about them may actually exist in the database.

Therefore, the appropriate SQL command will produce a "virtual table" where only those name-and-salary combinations under $50,000 will be visible.

1.2.8 Views

A *view* may be considered a virtual table. It is a way of looking at some portion of the data that has been retrieved from one or more base tables. A VIEW is a named, derived table. It is a "window" into one or more base tables.

VIEWS allow for data independence. In multi-user systems, VIEWS allow the same data to be seen by different users in different contexts—all at the same time.

Forcing users to work only with VIEWS can provide automatic security for hidden data in the base tables. (This point is explained further in Chapter 5, where security is discussed.) It also may be faster and more efficient for end users to be able to bring up only the information they need in concise form, rather than to be presented with a huge base table full of information that they do not need (and perhaps should not see) each time they need to work with the database.

Especially in a large system, most users will be working with views, rather than base tables, most of the time.

1.3 NOTATION

The following notation will be used throughout. Wherever standard or common usage of notation has emerged within the field of computer science, that notation will be used.

- An asterisk (*) has its usual meaning in computer practice, i.e., "all cases fitting the description."

- An ellipsis (. . .) means "more of the same," e.g.:

      Column1, Column2, Column3, . . .

    means "any number of columns."

- Items to be typed in exactly as shown, commands, clauses, expressions, etc., that the user must enter exactly as represented in the text—will be shown in uppercase letters, e.g., CREATE. Items to be filled in from the user's own situation will be shown in lowercase italic letters, e.g., *tablename*. Thus,

      CREATE *tablename*

    means to type in the word "CREATE" and fill in the name of the table you want to create for your database.

1.4 ILLUSTRATIVE MATERIAL

A fictitious grocery chain called ABC Foods will be used to illustrate the practical use of the procedures being explained. Most examples will refer to this chain, its stores in different cities, its personnel, its suppliers, inventory, sales items, and delivery schedules. All names, numbers, products, and prices used under these headings are, of course, fictitious, and are being used here merely for the purpose of making the concepts and instructions clear.

---

[1]According to C. J. Date, *An Introduction to Database Systems*, Vol. 1, 4th Ed. (Menlo Park, Calif.: Addison-Wesley, 1986).

Chapter 2

What Is *ORACLE?*

ORACLE IS A RELATIONAL DATABASE MANAGEMENT SYSTEM (RDBMS) PRODUCED BY Oracle Corporation of Belmont, California, which also publishes a number of products designed to be used with the RDBMS. These products cover a wide range of user needs and user levels of expertise.

In addition, the RDBMS itself is occasionally revised and presented in a new version. This book is based primarily on Oracle Corporation's Version 5 of the RDBMS, but will wherever possible point out differences between Version 4 and Version 5. Table 2-1 shows the correspondence between product names in Version 4 and those in Version 5.

This chapter is concerned primarily with a description of the *ORACLE* products, rather than instructions for their use. Along with these descriptions you will find references to the instructional chapters that occur later in this book.

Beginning with Version 5, *ORACLE* product names indicate both the type and level of the product. A set of prefixes defines the level (as in "Pro" indicating that the product is intended for computer programmers) and a set of suffixes for the type of product (as in "Forms" for full-screen applications). The defining prefixes are shown below. The suffixes appear in the Version 5 product names shown in Table 2-1.

Easy Indicates products which are full-screen and menu-driven, and guide users through their work offering them choices via menus, and detailed on-line help and information. Intended for new or infrequent users of the *ORACLE* RDBMS, or persons who are not data processing professionals. Options are more limited than with SQL.

SQL Indicates products which are interactive or command-driven and therefore assume more comfort and expertise with the SQL language and *ORACLE* products. These are intended for users with fair experience with *ORACLE* SQL and the data.

Pro Indicates programming interfaces to an *ORACLE* RDBMS. These products

Table 2-1. Correspondence between Version 4 and Version 5 Product and Program Names.

V4 Program Name	V5 Product Name	V5 Program Name
ODS, ODL, AIJ, SGI, IOR EXP/IMP CCF	*ORACLE* RDBMS	ODS, ODL, AIJ, SGI, IOR, EXP/IMP CCF
HLI	*Pro*SQL*	HLI
UFI	*SQL*Plus*	SQLPLUS
IAG, IAP, FSF, CRT	*SQL*Forms*	IAG, IAP, FSF, CRT, IAD, IAC
PCC (for the C language)	*Pro*C*	PCC
(for Fortran)	*Pro*Fortran*	PCC
(for COBOL)	*Pro*COBOL*	PCC
RPT/RPF	*ORACLE Report Writer*	RPT, RPF

require programming knowledge as well as in-depth knowledge of *ORACLE*, and therefore are intended for programmers.

Table 2-2 lists the *ORACLE* database limits, some of which are subject to the capacity of your disk space. To use *ORACLE,* you will need disk space for

- The program itself
- Its temporary tables
- Your tables, views, queries, and reports.

Chapter 6 gives details on determining your space requirements.

The material in this book is directed primarily to end users, and therefore does not cover the entire range of *ORACLE* products. The following *ORACLE* programs and facilities, constituting the basis of the *ORACLE* system, are described in this chapter:

- *ORACLE* RDBMS (ODS, ODL, AIJ, SGI, IOR, EXP/IMP, CCF)
- *Pro*SQL* (HLI)
- *SQL*Plus* (SQLPLUS)
- *ORACLE Report Writer* (RPT, RPF)
- *SQL*Forms* (IAG, IAP, FSF, CRT, IAD, IAC)

In addition, the following special features of *ORACLE* will be described:

- The Audit Trail
- The Data Dictionary
- The *ORACLE* Sort/Merge Routine
- *ORACLE* Context Space

2.1 COMPONENTS OF THE *ORACLE* RDBMS

The *ORACLE* RDBMS consists of the following programs:

- *ORACLE* Display System (ODS)
- *ORACLE* Data Loader (ODL)
- After Image Journaling (AIJ)
- System Global Information (SGI)
- IOR Program
- Export/Import (EXP/IMP)
- Create Contiguous File (CCF) Utility

The *ORACLE* Display System (ODS). The *ORACLE* Display System (ODS) monitors the ongoing use of an *ORACLE* system. It provides many different screens displaying such information as which users are active, which locks they are holding, and how much activity has occurred in the database since the last warm start (IOR W). ODS is described in detail in Chapter 5.

The *ORACLE* Data Loader (ODL). The *ORACLE* Data Loader (ODL) loads raw data from operating files into existing tables in an *ORACLE* database. It is described in detail in Chapter 7.

After Image Journaling (AIJ). After Image Journaling is a program used to log all changes made to data in order to allow for recovery in the event of disk failure. It is described in detail in Chapter 5.

Table 2-2. ORACLE Database Limits.

Item	Limit
Tables in a database	No limit*
Rows in a table	No limit*
Columns in a table	254
Characters in a row	60,960
Characters in a character field	240
Digits in a number field	105
Significant digits in a number field	40
Range of values in a date field	1-JAN-4712 BC to 31-DEC-4712 AD
Indexes on a table	No limit*
Tables or views joined in a query	No limit*
Levels of nested subqueries	16
Characters in a name	30

* No enforced limits; practical limits may vary according to system configuration.

System Global Information (SGI). System Global Information (SGI) is a utility used by the database administrator (DBA). SGI describes the shared memory area used by *ORACLE*. It is described in Chapter 5.

IOR. The IOR program is used by the DBA to start or stop an *ORACLE* system, including the very first start (initialization) of the system. It is discussed in Chapter 5. It includes the INIT.ORA file which contains the system parameters used when starting a database system. A list of these parameters is in Appendix B.

Export/Import. Export/Import is a user utility for backing up and recovering archival storage. It is described in Chapter 7.

Create Contiguous File (CCF). The Create Contiguous File (CCF) is a utility used prior to initializing the database, to create the Database (DB) and Before Image (BI) files. It is discussed in Chapter 6.

2.2 PRO*SQL AND THE HOST LANGUAGE INTERFACE

In *ORACLE* Version 5, the product called *Pro*SQL* contains the Host Language Interface (HLI) program. HLI is a layer of subroutine call entry points into the *ORACLE* data storage space and Data Dictionary. It translates the SQL statements into machine language and executes them. All functions of *ORACLE* are accessible through the HLI. HLI is not described further in this book.

2.3 THE USER FRIENDLY INTERFACE (UFI)

The User Friendly Interface (UFI) exists through Version 4; Version 5 replaces UFI with *SQL*Plus*. The following detailed explanation is included here for Version 4 users because UFI is not treated anywhere else in this text. *SQL*Plus* is briefly described in Section 2.4 in this chapter, and in detail in Section 3.4 in Chapter 3.

ORACLE is both an interpreter and a compiler for SQL commands; the User Friendly Interface (UFI) is the interpreter.

2.3.1 Invoking UFI

You can invoke UFI from a terminal in any of the following five ways:

1. Type UFI after your system prompt. UFI will then prompt for *username* and *password.*

2. Type UFI and the *username* after the prompt. UFI will prompt for *password.*

3. Type UFI, the *username* and the *password* after your operating system prompt.

4. Type UFI, then specify a command file containing the *username* and *password.*

5. Type UFI, then specify that UFI should determine *username* from the operating system. This will connect to ORACLE as OPS$*username,* if defined, where *username* is your operating system username.

2.3.2 The UFI Editor

When a SQL statement is entered into UFI, it is placed in UFI's SQL buffer. It can then be changed with UFI's editor. The UFI Editor contains the following commands:

L or **LIST**	Lists the current SQL command.
L*n*	Lists the specified line of the current SQL command, and makes it the current line.
C/*old_text***/***new_text*	Replaces *old_text* in the line with *new_text*.
A.*text*	Appends the text to the current line.
I *text*	Inserts a new line after the current line.
I	Prompts for new lines following current line.
DEL	Deletes the current line.
/	Executes the current SQL statement.
RUN	Lists and executes the current SQL statement.

UFI commands which change formatting or the environment are not buffered, but executed immediately.

2.3.3 UFI Operating System Commands and Files

The SAVE command preserves the current SQL statement in an operating system file. The SAVE command will save the SQL statement to a file suffixed .UFI. A full file name may be specified with a period, e.g., SAVELIST.UFI. The SQL statement may be executed or read at a later time.

The SAVE APPend command adds SQL statements to the end of an existing file.

The GET command will list but not execute a save UFI file. The GET command puts the entire file into UFI's SQL buffer; therefore it should be used when the file contains only one SQL statement.

The START command is used to execute UFI command files. This command should be used when a file contains multiple SQL statements.

2.3.4 Controlling Display Format

The UFI COLUMN command formats column data for a UFI session. The syntax is:

COLUMN *column_name option(s)*

For example:

COLUMN STORENO HEADING STORES JUSTIFY CENTER

The options are shown in Table 2-3.

Table 2-3. Options for UFI Column Commands.

Option	Meaning
JUSTIFY L|R|C	Alignment of heading: LEFT, RIGHT, OR CENTER.
HEADING *str*	Column heading *str* is printed over the column.
NULL *str*	Character string to be displayed for null values in the column.
ON | OFF	Ability to turn off output format specification.
PRINT|NOPRINT	Specifies whether to print the column or not.
WRAP | TRUNC	Wrap or truncate data within the current column.

2.3.5 Environment Options

You may tailor the UFI environment by setting specific options. A listing of these options appears in Table 2-4. Use the SET command to change an option, and use the SHOW command to display an option. (The above settings remain in effect only during the current UFI session. Frequently used options may be set automatically by placing them in the LOGIN.UFI file.)

2.3.6 The UFI On-Line Help Facility

Type the word HELP beside the UFI prompt to bring up the HELP facility. This allows you to consult ORACLE documentation on line:

    HELP

Then type in the character string (or a partial string) of the command with which you need help, such as:

    DELETE

If only the first word of the string is entered, then all commands starting with DELETE (such as DELETE TABLE, DELETE VIEW, DELETE INDEX) will be referenced. However, if your question is with DELETE TABLE, type that command in to get specific help with deleting a table.

2.4 SQL*PLUS

*SQL*Plus* (pronounced "Sequel Plus") is an enhanced version of UFI which is described in Section 2.3 above. It is a procedural, interactive interface to ORACLE that includes enhanced report writing. It is invoked with the program SQLPLUS. SQL*Plus is described in Chapter 3, and referred to extensively throughout this text.

2.5 THE *ORACLE* REPORT WRITER

The *ORACLE Report Writer* consists of two programs, the Report Text Formatter (RPF) and the Report Generator (RPT). The *Report Writer* is a very powerful text processor.

It will produce formatted reports containing data retrieved from the database. It is discussed in detail in Chapter 14.

2.6 THE INTERACTIVE APPLICATION FACILITY (IAF)

The Interactive Application Facility (IAF) is replaced in Version 5 by *SQL*Forms*, which increases the ability of the IAF by adding two programs, IAD and IAC. *SQL*Forms* programs are treated in Section 2.7 below.

2.7 SQL*FORMS

*SQL*Forms* is an interactive facility used to create, display and edit forms. *SQL*Forms* is designed to facilitate the process of customizing forms, and to simplify their use. It is described in detail in Chapters 15 and 16.

*SQL*Forms* consists of the components listed below, each of which is described in the sections that follow:

IAG, IAP, FSF, CRT, IAD, and IAC

2.7.1 The Interactive Application Generator (IAG)

The Interactive Application Generator (IAG) is a component of *SQL*Forms*. It reads an input (INP) file and generates a form (FRM) file. IAG is executed after the Interactive

Table 2-4. UFI Environment Options.

Options	Meaning
LINesize *n*	Specifies the number of characters per line; default is 80.
NEWPage *n*	Specifies the number of line feeds at the top of a new page. A 0 value will generate a form feed; default is 3 lines.
NULL *set*	String to be used for printing NULL values. Character strings must be enclosed in quotes; default is blank.
NUmwidth *n*	Specifies an automatic display size for numbers; default is 10.
PAGESize *n*	Specifies the number of lines per page; default is 60 lines.
WRAP ON|OFF	Controls wrapping of data exceeding LINESIZE; excess will be wrapped or truncated. Default is wrap.
ECHO ON|OFF	On causes commands in a command file being executed to be displayed; default is OFF.
HEADING ON|OFF	ON causes the printing of a column heading; default is on.
PAUSE ON|OFF	ON causes UFI to print the string and wait for a carriage return before displaying the next page; default is OFF.
WORKsize *n*	Sets the size of the context area.
TERMout ON|OFF	Inhibits printing of output at the terminal when running a UFI command procedure. This command is ignored unless issued from a file.
SCAN ON|OFF	OFF suppresses scanning of SQL statements.

Application Converter (IAC) when control is returned to the main menu by the "Create a Form:" or "Modify a Form" function.

2.7.2 The Interactive Application Processor (IAP)

The Interactive Application Processor (IAP) is a component of *SQL*Forms*. IAP reads a form from a FRM file and runs it. It is executed by the "Run" option of the *SQL*Forms* main menu.

2.7.3 The FSF Component

FSF, a component of *SQL*Forms*, creates an INP file for a default form. It is executed by the "Default Form" part of the "Create a Form" option. FSF is not discussed further in this text.

2.7.4 The CRT Utility

The CRT utility, is a component of *SQL*Forms* (which is described in Chapters 15 and 16). *SQL*Forms* and some other *ORACLE* programs can operate with many different types of display devices. This device independence is achieved through the use of the CRT file, which tells the program what commands will make a specific type of display device perform various functions. The program for creating a CRT file is *ORACLE's* utility named CRT, which reads information about a specified device type from a group of ORACLE database tables. These tables are stored in the database under a username that differs with the host system. Your *ORACLE Installation and User's Guide* will tell you where they are stored in your system.

The CRT utility is not discussed further in this text.

2.7.5 The Interactive Application Designer (IAD)

The Interactive Application Designer (IAD) is a component of *SQL*Forms*. IAD creates or modifies a form in the database. It is executed by the "Modify a Form" option of the *SQL*Forms* main menu, and the "Custom Form" entry on the "Create a Form" option.

2.7.6 The Interactive Application Converter (IAC)

The Interactive Application Converter (IAC) is a component of *SQL*Forms*. IAC loads existing forms into the forms definition dictionary so that the forms can be modified by IAD, and it creates an INP file for forms for input to IAG. IAC is executed by *SQL*Forms* when control is returned to the main menu by the "Create a Form" or "Modify a Form" function.

2.8 THE AUDIT_TRAIL FEATURE

The auditing feature is new in *ORACLE* Version 5. It is primarily for security purposes. If enabled, it can be used to monitor user activity on the database. (By default, it is disabled.) It enables a DBA to improve and monitor the security of the system. It also allows users other than DBAs to audit successful or unsuccessful attempts to access tables or views owned by the user.

There are options available to both DBA and other users as to which actions are audited. The results of auditing are usually written to the table AUDIT__TRAIL, which is in the data dictionary. Complete details of the auditing feature are in Chapter 5.

2.9 THE DATA DICTIONARY

The Data Dictionary is a table consisting of rows and columns like any other table in the database. It contains tables automatically created by *ORACLE* at the time of installation, as well as all the tables and views created by users during operation of the system. Whenever you create a table, the Data Dictionary is automatically updated by *ORACLE* with the definition of that table.

The tables created by *ORACLE* in the Data Dictionary may change from one *ORACLE* release to the next. Therefore, to find the table definitions for the release you are using, you should consult the actual Data Dictionary at your site. The listing in Table 2-5 is for *ORACLE's* Version 5.

To see the tables you own (i.e., all those which you have created, and to which you have been granted access) in the Data Dictionary, the command is:

```
SELECT * FROM TAB
```

This will actually display the Data Dictionary view of the names and types of tables and views you have created.

To see the tables available to all users at your site, the command is:

```
SELECT * FROM DTAB
```

The "tables" displayed will actually be views from the table DTAB. The complete table itself is in the file CATALOG.ORA, which was created when the *ORACLE* system was installed at your site by using *SQL*Plus*. To see any one of the Data Dictionary views listed in Table 2-5, use the view name in a SELECT command.

The basic tables in the Data Dictionary are created automatically during an IOR.INIT, and belong to the database administrator (DBA) designated SYS. Only DBAs have access to these tables. The views in the Data Dictionary that belong to the DBA user designated SYSTEM are usually created at each site by using *SQL*Plus* to run the CATALOG.ORA file. (See Chapter 5 for the definition of DBA users SYS and SYSTEM.)

Data Dictionary tables are updated automatically by ORACLE. Views are not updated by *ORACLE*, since they will always show the most recent data.

A non-DBA user should almost never change tables created by *ORACLE*. This means that you should not DROP, ALTER, DELETE, INSERT, or UPDATE the data in them. The two major exceptions are described below.

Adding New Data Dictionary Tables or Views. To preserve the integrity of the system, the DBA SYSTEM should be the owner of these new items, or a third DBA should be created to own them.

Deleting From SYS.AUDIT__TRAIL. If auditing has been enabled, and a number of auditing options are being tracked, this table may rapidly grow very large. Therefore it might be convenient to delete periodically early audits from this table. But the file SYS.AUDIT__TRAIL should never be altered or dropped.

Table 2-5. Data Dictionary Views.

View	Description
DTAB	Tables and views in Data Dictionary.
AUDIT_ACTIONS	Audit action codes and their descriptions.
AUDIT_ACCESS	*ORACLE*'s AUDIT output relating to the user's current or most recent table access. For a DBA, *ORACLE*'s AUDIT output relating to all users' current or most recent table accesses.
AUDIT_CONNECT	*ORACLE*'s AUDIT output relating to the user's current or most recent session. For a DBA, *ORACLE*'s AUDIT output relating to all users' current or most recent sessions.
AUDIT_DBA	*ORACLE*'s AUDIT output relating to DBA-only operations; for DBAs only.
AUDIT_EXISTS	*ORACLE*'s AUDIT output relating to table accesses that failed with a "does not exist" condition; for DBAs only.
AUDIT_TRAIL	*ORACLE*'s AUDIT output relating to the user. For a DBA, *ORACLE*'s AUDIT output relating to all users.
CATALOG	Tables, views, and clusters accessible to user, excluding the Database Dictionary itself.
CLUSTERS	User's clusters.
CLUSTERCOLUMNS	Columns in user's clusters.
COL	Columns in user's tables.
COLUMNS	Columns in tables accessible to user.
DEFAULT_AUDIT	*ORACLE*'s AUDIT options for newly created tables. For a DBA, *ORACLE*'s AUDIT options relating to all users' tables.
EXTENTS	Data structure of extents within tables.
INDEXES	Indexes created by user and indexes on tables created by user.
PARTITIONS	File structure of files in partitions (for DBA only).
PRIVATESYN	User's synonyms.
PUBLICSYN	PUBLIC synonyms.
SPACES	Space definitions for creating tables and clusters.
STORAGE	Data and index storage allocation for user's tables.
SYNONYMS	User's synonyms and PUBLIC synonyms.
SESSIONS	Shows user's logons (if session auditing enabled by DBA).
SYSCATALOG	Tables, views, and clusters accessible to user.
SYSCOLUMNS	Columns in tables and views accessible to user.
SYSEXTENTS	Data structure of tables in system (for DBA only).
SYSINDEXES	Indexes, underlying columns, creator, and options.
SYSSESSIONS	Show all users' logons (if session auditing enabled by DBA).
SYSSTORAGE	Summary of database storage (for DBA only).

View	Description
SYSTABALLOC	Data and index space allocations for all tables; for DBA only.
SYSTABAUTH	Directory of access authorizations granted by or to user.
SYSTEM__AUDIT	Data about system resource utilization that *ORACLE* writes in response to the AUDIT command; for DBA only.
SYSUSERAUTH	Master list of *ORACLE* users; for DBA only.
TAB	Tables, views, and clusters owned by user.
TABALLOC	Data and index space allocation for all of user's tables.
TABLE__AUDIT	*ORACLE*'s AUDIT options relating to the user. For a DBA, *ORACLE*'s AUDIT options relating to all users.
VIEWS	Text of the subquery in the CREATE VIEW command that created each view in the database.

2.10 THE *ORACLE* SORT/MERGE ROUTINE

The *ORACLE* Version 5 Sort/Merge routine sorts incoming data internally into several sets of ordered runs, then merges these runs into a sorted result. It improves performance on operations such as CREATE INDEX, SELECT DISTINCT, ORDER BY, GROUP BY, and certain joins; it does this by avoiding the creation of temporary tables (and consequent disk activity) if enough internal work area is available to accomplish the sort/merge.

The following INIT.ORA parameters relate to the sort/merge routine:

```
SORT__AREA
SORT__FINAL__RA
SORT__MERGE__RA
SORT__POOL__SZ
SORT__SPCMAP__SZ
SORT__READ__FAC
```

Two work areas relate to the sort/merge routine:

internal This size is set by the INIT.ORA parameter SORT__AREA__SZ. Increases in the parameter will increase the System Global Area (SGA) size and may improve performance.

external This area is used for storage of runs before and during the merge. External work area is allocated via, and managed like, temporary tables. Maximally, an external work area of twice the size of the column(s) being sorted may be needed to accomplish the final merge pass.

2.11 THE *ORACLE* CONTEXT SPACE

The *ORACLE* context space is the buffer used to contain the SQL statement being executed. If the statement is a query, then the context space will also contain one row of the result and the headings for the result.

In *ORACLE* Version 5, context space is automatic; *ORACLE* extends the context space when necessary. In previous versions, this was handled through an error message which required the user to extend it. Therefore, in systems using versions after Version 4, the user generally will not have to be concerned about context space. A brief summary of how this space is allocated follows.

When a context area is created, an initial area (the *primary extent*) is allocated. If a size is specified in the OOPEN command, it is used. If not, then the parameter CONTEXT_SIZE, specified in the INIT.ORA at the last warm start, is used. If CONTEXT_SIZE was not specified at the last warm start, then the system constant is used. This is 4K bytes in most systems.

When space is needed in a context area and not enough has been allocated, an additional area is allocated, called a *secondary extent*. The target size for this area is the size specified in CONTEXT_INCR in INIT.ORA, usually 4K if this parameter is not specified. If this won't result in a large enough area for the current requirement, however, then a sufficiently large area is allocated. This secondary extent cannot be specified in the OOPEN call.

This process continues as required, either until the operating system refuses to provide any more storage or until the maximum number of content extents is reached. This is a system constant which cannot be set in INIT.ORA. It is currently set at 50.

When storage is allocated to a context area, it is available for parsing subsequent statements. It is not freed until the cursor is closed. It may be reset to its original size by closing and reopening it.

2.12 RESERVED WORDS

Reserved words are keywords used by *ORACLE,* which are not available to the user for use as names of tables, columns, or views. If you should use a reserved word as the name of a table, column or view, you will get an error message to the effect that the word you used "is not a valid name." However, you may use a reserved word for a name if you enclose it in double quotes, e.g., "ASSERT."

A current list of reserved words appears in Appendix A. New versions of *ORACLE* sometimes add words to this list. Therefore, you should check the documentation you received with the version you have purchased to be certain that no new words have been added. (The list in Appendix A is correct through Version 5.)

Chapter 3

SQL and *SQL*Plus*

T HE STRUCTURED QUERY LANGUAGE SQL (PRONOUNCED "SEQUEL") IS THE INTERFACE
between the user and the *ORACLE* database. It was originally defined by a group at
the IBM Research Laboratory at San Jose, California[1]. It is both an interactive query
language and a database programming language.

SQL*Plus (pronounced "sequel plus") is an interactive, command-driven interface
to *ORACLE,* used for querying and report writing. It will be described starting in Section
3.4 in this chapter. It was developed by Oracle Corporation, and first appears in *ORACLE*
Version 5. It replaces the User Friendly Interface (UFI) of earlier *ORACLE* versions.

3.1 TYPES OF SQL STATEMENTS

SQL consists of four main types of statements: Data Definition Statements (DDS),
Data Manipulation Statements (DMS), Queries, and Data Control Statements (DCS). The
first three types are used by all users to create and maintain the database; the fourth type,
Data Control Statements (DCS), are used mainly by the database administrator. The four
types are described below.

Data Definition Statements (DDS). The Data Definition Statements (DDS) such as
CREATE TABLE, CREATE VIEW, CREATE SYNONYM, ALTER TABLE, DROP
TABLE, DROP VIEW, DROP SYNONYM, and DROP INDEX are used to set up and
maintain the database. The syntax and use of these statements is explained in Chapter 9.

Data Manipulation Statements (DMS). The Data Manipulation Statements (DMS)
such as INSERT, DELETE, and UPDATE are used to change the data in the database.
The syntax and use of these statements is explained in Chapter 10.

Queries. To retrieve data in any order or combination you must use a "query." Queries
always begin with the reserved word SELECT, followed by the desired information, and
the names of the tables or views containing it. Queries do not change the data. Syntax
and examples of queries occur principally in Chapters 10 and 11, and are used in Chapters
12 and beyond.

Data Control Statements (DCS). The Data Control Statements (DCS), such as

GRANT CONNECT, REVOKE, COMMIT, ROLLBACK, LOCK TABLE, and AUDIT control access to the data and the database, and determine how, when and by whom, data manipulations can occur. Descriptions of the use and syntax of GRANT CONNECT, REVOKE, and AUDIT appear in Chapter 5 on the duties of the database administrator. The LOCK TABLE and all other locking commands are in Chapter 8. COMMIT and ROLLBACK are explained in Chapter 12 where the full use of ORACLE commands and their connecting terms is illustrated.

3.2 DATA TYPES

SQL supports the following data types in *ORACLE*:

CHAR   Columns can contain alphabetic characters, digits, and all special characters. CHAR data are stored in variable length strings of ASCII or EBCDIC values. Length of a CHAR column is specified at table creation; the maximum is 240.

DATE   Date fields can contain only valid dates from January 1, 4712 B.C. to A.D. December 31, 4711. When you display a date field, it appears in the standard format of DD-MON-YY. (Further information on date functions is in Chapter 11.)

LONG   The long data type has more than 240 characters. It is a special variant of CHAR. A column with LONG datatype can store variable-length character strings up to 65,536 characters. You are limited to one long data type per table.

NUMBER   NUMBER columns can contain only the digits 0 through 9, and an optional negative sign. You have the option of specifying a maximum width and number of decimal places for a number field by using NUMBER(w,d) where w is the width and d is the number of decimal places.

RAW
LONG RAW   New in *ORACLE* Version 5, these types are used for byte-oriented data that are to go uninterpreted by *ORACLE*. RAW is similar to CHAR data, and LONG RAW is like LONG except that no assumptions are made about the meaning of the bytes. Intended for binary data or byte strings, e.g., to store graphics character sequences.

In addition to *ORACLE* data types, the SQL commands:

```
CREATE TABLE . . .
CREATE CLUSTER . . .
```

will also accept data types from IBM's products *SQL/DS* and *DB2*, and will internally convert them to *ORACLE* data types as shown in Table 3-1. Table 3-2 shows all SQL commands and gives a brief description of each. The use of these commands is explained in detail in Chapters 9 through 13.

SQL/DS Datatype	ORACLE Datatype
SMALLINT	NUMBER
INTEGER	NUMBER
DECIMAL(m,n)	NUMBER(m,n)
FLOAT	NUMBER
VARCHAR(n)	CHAR(n)
LONG VARCHAR	LONG
GRAPHIC	no corresponding datatype
VARGRAPHIC	no corresponding datatype
LONG VARGRAPHIC	no corresponding datatype

Table 3-1. Conversion of SL/DS Datatypes to ORACLE Data Types.

Table 3-2. Summary of SQL Commands.

Command	Description
/* . . . */	Comment within or before a SQL command.
ALTER PARTITION	Adds a file to a database partition.
ALTER SPACE	Alters a space definition.
ALTER TABLE	Adds a column to, or redefines a column in, an existing table.
AUDIT	Makes *ORACLE* audit use of a table, view, synonym, or system facility.
COMMIT	Makes permanent the changes made to the database since the last COMMIT.
CREATE CLUSTER	Creates a cluster which may contain 2 or more tables.
CREATE INDEX	Creates an index for a table.
CREATE PARTITION	Creates a new partition in the database.
CREATE SPACE	Creates a space definition which may then be used to define the space allocation properties of a table.
CREATE SYNONYM	Creates a synonym for a table or view name.
CREATE TABLE	Creates a table and defines its columns and other properties.
CREATE VIEW	Defines a view into one or more tables and/or other views.
DELETE	Deletes row from a table.
DROP	Deletes a cluster, index, etc. from the database.
GRANT	Creates user IDs, assigns passwords, grants *ORACLE* and table and view access privileges to users.
INSERT	Adds new rows to a table or view.
LOCK TABLE	Locks a table, enabling a user to share access to it while preserving its integrity.
NOAUDIT	Partially or completely reverses the effect of a prior AUDIT com-

Command	Description
	mand, or of auditing options in the default table; makes *ORACLE* stop auditing use of a table, view, or synonym.
RENAME	Changes the name of a table, view, or synonym.
REVOKE	Revokes database or table access privileges from users.
SELECT	Performs a query; selects rows and columns from one or more tables.
UPDATE	Changes the values of fields in a table.
VALIDATE INDEX	Checks the integrity of a table index.

3.3 *SQL*PLUS*

*SQL*Plus* is a program developed by Oracle Corporation for working with the *ORACLE* database. With it you can:

- Create tables in the database.
- Store information in the tables.
- Change information in the tables.
- Retrieve information in a form you choose.
- Perform calculations on information you retrieve.
- Combine information you retrieve in new ways.
- Maintain the database.

The *SQL*Plus* command language is easy to write and read, yet powerful enough to serve the needs of users with some database experience.

The *SQL*Plus* program accepts *SQL*Plus* commands from your keyboard, executes them through *ORACLE*, and formats the results according to your specifications. Table 3-3 contains a summary of *SQL*Plus* commands and their descriptions.

Like *ORACLE* itself, *SQL*Plus* can run on many different kinds of systems. For information specific to your host computer, see the *ORACLE Installation and User's Guide*, published by Oracle Corporation for your equipment.

To start *SQL*Plus*, enter

SQLPLUS

beside your operating system prompt, and press [Return]. *SQL*Plus* will then prompt you for your user name and password. The *SQL*Plus* prompt will then appear: SQL>. *SQL*Plus* will accept both SQL and *SQL*Plus* commands.

3.3.1 SQL Command Syntax in *SQL*Plus*

All SQL commands must end with a semicolon (;). You may enter your command on a single line, or on as many lines as you wish, as long as individual words are not broken up between one line and the next. If your command is longer than one line, *SQL*Plus* will prompt you for the next line by entering a 2 (for line 2), then a 3 (for line 3), etc.,

Table 3-3. Summary of SQL*Plus Commands.

Command	Description
@	Runs a command file.
#	Ends a sequence of comment lines begun by a DOCUMENT command.
$	Executes a host operating system command line without leaving *SQL*Plus*. Equivalent to HOST.
/	Runs the command in the SQL buffer.
APPEND	Appends text to the end of the current line in the current buffer.
BREAK	Specifies what events will cause a break, and what action SQL is to perform at a break.
BTITLE	Makes SQL display a title at the bottom of each page of a report.
CHANGE	Changes contents of the current line of the current buffer.
CLEAR	Clears break definitions, current buffer text, column definitions, etc.
COLUMN	Specifies how a column and a column heading should be formatted in a report.
COMPUTE	Performs computations on groups of selected rows.
CONNECT	Logs you off *ORACLE* and back on with a specified user name.
DEFINE	Defines a user variable and assigns it a CHAR value.
DEL	Deletes the current line of the current buffer.
DESCRIBE	Displays a brief description of a table.
DISCONNECT	Commits pending work to the database and logs you off *ORACLE*, but does not terminate *SQL*Plus*.
DOCUMENT	Begins a block of documentation in a command file. (Not valid in programs.)
EDIT	Invokes the host system's standard text editor on the contents of the current buffer or a file.
EXIT	Terminates *SQL*Plus* and returns control to the operating system.
GET	Loads file into the current buffer.
HELP	Displays information about a *SQL* or *SLQ*Plus* command.
HOST	Executes a host operating system command line without leaving SQL. Equivalent to "$".
INPUT	Adds new lines after the current line in the current buffer.
LIST	Lists lines of the current buffer.
NEWPAGE	Advances spooled output to the beginning of the next page. An obsolete command.
PAUSE	Displays a message, then waits for you to press Return.
QUIT	Terminates *SQL*Plus* and returns control to the operating system. A synonym for EXIT.
REMARK	Begins a remark in the program.
ROLLBACK	Rolls back (discards) changes made to the default database since changes were last committed.

Command	Description
RUN	Displays and runs the command in the SQL buffer.
SAVE	Saves the contents of the current buffer (a program or SQL command) in the database or in an operating system file.
SET	Sets a system variable to a specified value.
SHOW	Displays the setting of a system variable or of a *SQL*Plus* property such as the current release number.
SPOOL	Manages spooling (copying) of displayed output to a system file and system printer.
SQLPLUS	System command. Starts *SQL*Plus*.
START	Executes the contents of a command file.
TIMING	Does performance analysis on SQL commands and *SQL*Plus* programs.
TTITLE	Makes SQL display a title at the top of each page of output.
UNDEFINE	Deletes the definition of a user variable.

until you conclude the command with a semicolon. Words in a SQL command must be separated by at least one space.

Whether or not you use upper- or lowercase characters in making up your SQL command is sometimes significant in *SQL*Plus*. Case will make a difference when you enter:

- A CHAR value (a sequence of characters that *SQL*Plus* is to process).
- A username.
- A password.

If you enter a command telling *SQL*Plus* to display the CHAR value "Annual Report" as a heading, this is different from "ANNUAL REPORT" and from "annual report." In expressing a CHAR value, you *must* use upper- and lowercase in exactly the form you wish the data to appear. The same is true for passwords and usernames; upper- and lowercase are not interchangeable.

Case will not make any difference when you enter:

- The name of a table, column, or other database object.
- The name of a reserved word.

For example, "EMPLOYEE," "Employee," and "employee" are all the same table in the database. Likewise, reserved words such as SELECT and FROM can be written in any mix of cases, i.e., "SELECT," "Select," "select," or even "SEleCt," all function identically.

3.3.2 *SQL*Plus* Command Syntax

*SQL*Plus* command syntax is slightly different from SQL command syntax. Usually a *SQL*Plus* command is entered on a single line. However, if you reach the end of the line without finishing the command, you may continue on the next line. Do not press [Return]; instead, enter a hyphen (-) at the end of every line except the last. You should only press [Return] when you have finished the entire command—no matter how many lines it takes—but you must enter a hyphen at the end of every line that is not the end of the command. Moreover, a *SQL*Plus* command does not have to end with a semicolon, although you may put one there. But you must end the command with a [Return].

Editing SQL Commands with *SQL*Plus*. The editing commands are especially useful in correcting typing errors, or in modifying a query you have entered. Some editing commands are listed in Table 3-4 that can be used to examine, change, or rerun a SQL command without reentering it. If you make a mistake in entering a command, use [Backspace] to erase it, and enter it over again.

If you have already pressed [Return], then [Backspace] will not remove an error. In that case, if the mistake was in a SQL command, use the editing commands shown in Table 3-4. If the mistake was in a *SQL*Plus* command, reenter the command correctly.

When you enter a SQL command, *SQL*Plus* stores it in the buffer, and it stays there until you enter another command. This stored command is called the "current SQL command."

All of the editing commands except LIST and RUN affect a line in the buffer. This line is called the "current line," and is marked with an asterisk when the current command is listed.

For example, if you want to display the contents of the SQL buffer, enter:

LIST

beside the SQL prompt (SQL>). *SQL*Plus* will then return the following (in which the *SQL*Plus* prompt numbers are shown so that we can exhibit the asterisk beside the line number).

```
SQL> LIST
  1   SELECT   *
```

Table 3-4. Some SQL*Plus Editing Commands.

Command	Abbreviation	Purpose
APPEND	A	Add text at the end of a line.
CHANGE	C	Change text in a line.
CLEAR BUFFER	CL BUFF	Delete all lines.
DEL	(none)	Delete a line.
INPUT	I	Add a line.
LIST	L	List all lines in the SQL buffer.
LIST n	L n	List a specified line.
LIST m n	L m n	List lines from m to n.
RUN	R	Rerun the current SQL command.

```
2  FROM  EMPLOYEES
3* WHERE  SALESMAN  =  432
```

The asterisk after line number 3 means that line 3 is the current line. If you enter a CHANGE command at this point, the change will affect that line.

Any semicolons that you entered at the end of the original command are not listed when *SQL*Plus* displays the contents of the buffer because the semicolon is not stored (even though you must use it when you enter the SQL command). The LIST command did not need a semicolon when you entered it because it is a *SQL*Plus* command rather than a SQL command.

If you make a mistake (for example, in entering a column name), you will get an error message, indicating the line containing the mistake. Suppose you mistakenly try to SELECT from STRENO instead of STORENO, the error message would look like this:

```
SELECT STRENO
       *

ERROR at line 1: ORA-0704: invalid column name
```

In this message, the asterisk shows where the error is, i.e., in the mistyped column name STRENO. Now, instead of retyping the entire command, you can correct the mistake by editing the command in the buffer, like this:

1. Use the LIST command followed by the line number to display the line containing the error, and make it the current line.

2. Use the CHANGE command to correct the mistake. You will need to enter the following three items separated by slashes:

    a. The word CHANGE (or the letter C)
    b. The sequence of characters containing the error
    c. The sequence of characters you want to insert to make the change.

To change STRENO to STORENO, edit the misspelled column as shown below. (*SQL*Plus* prompts are shown at the left to make the process clear.) First, enter LIST and the line number you want to change:

```
SQL> LIST 1
```

When the following line appears on the screen:

```
1* SELECT STRENO
```

enter this:

```
SQL> CHANGE / STRENO /STORENO/
```

and the corrected line will appear:

```
1* SELECT STORENO
```

The CHANGE command will find the first occurrence of the designated character sequence in the current line and will change it to the new sequence.

After changing a command, you can use the RUN command to put it on the screen again. Just enter

```
RUN
```

and the complete, corrected command will be shown on your screen and executed.

Inserting a New Line. To add a new line to the buffer, or to insert a line between existing lines, use the INPUT command. After doing so, you may want to again use the RUN command in order to see and execute the revised version of the original command.

Appending Text to a Line. If you want to add text to the end of a line in the buffer, use the APPEND command. First, display the line you want to change with the LIST command. Then enter APPEND followed by the text you want to add. If the text you are adding begins with a blank, separate the word APPEND from the first character of the text by two blanks (one to separate the command from the text, and one to go into the buffer with the text).

Deleting a Line. Use the DEL command to delete a line in the buffer. Display the line you want to delete with the LIST command, and then enter DEL. This makes the following line of the buffer (if any) the current line. You can delete several consecutive lines by making the first of them the current line and then DELeting each one consecutively.

Storing and Printing Results. You may want to store the results of a query in a file so that you can edit them with a word processor before printing them, or so that you can include them in some other document. To store them in a file and also display them on the screen, enter

```
SPOOL file.LIS
```

All information displayed on the screen after you enter this command will be stored in the file you have specified before the period. (If there already is a period in the filename you specify in the SPOOL command, you cannot use the .LIS suffix.) *SQL*Plus* will continue to spool information to the file you designated until you stop it by entering

```
SPOOL OFF
```

To print query results instead of just stopping the spooling, instead of SPOOL OFF enter:

```
SPOOL OUT
```

*SQL*Plus* will stop spooling and will copy the spool file's contents to your host computer's printer.

Help Messages. *SQL*Plus* has a great many HELP panels showing available commands and how to use them. For a display of all SQL and *SQL*Plus* commands, just enter

HELP

For a display about a specific command, enter the word HELP followed by the name of the command, as follows:

HELP SELECT

Error Messages. If *SQL*Plus* detects an error in a command, it will display an error message. Often you will be able to detect the error from the content of the message and correct it. If not, look the message up in Oracle Corporation's publication, *Error Messages and Codes,* to find the cause of the problem and how to correct it.

Interrupting the Display. If you want *SQL*Plus* to pause after each screen of a long report being displayed, you may use the SET PAUSE command. Enter

SET PAUSE ON [*text*]

and fill in any *text* (such as "Press Return to continue") you want displayed before the pause. After each PAUSE, *SQL*Plus* will wait for you to press [Return] before continuing to scroll. To get rid of this pause, enter

SET PAUSE OFF

and press [Return].

Stopping a Display. To stop a multipage display before it comes to the end, press the Interrupt key. This key varies among operating systems, but in most systems you can accomplish an Interrupt by pressing Control-C (^C). *SQL*Plus* will then stop the display and return to the prompt. Pressing [Interrupt] will not stop a parsing operation once it is in progress.

Leaving *SQL*Plus*. When you have finished working with *SQL*Plus* and wish to return to the operating system, enter

EXIT

Running Other Programs. You can execute a host operating system command while you are in *SQL*Plus*, as for example, if you want to look at the contents of the host operating system directory. To do this, enter the *SQL*Plus* command HOST followed by the host command. For example, in DEC VMS or MS-DOS this is:

HOST DIR *.SQL;

When the host command has finished running, the *SQL*Plus* prompt will reappear.

Executing a Command from a File. To retrieve a query from a file and run it in a single step, use the START command, followed by the name of the file:

```
START filename
```

You don't need to add the .SQL suffix in this case.

Including *SQL*Plus* Commands in a Command File. When you store the current SQL command in a file using the SAVE command, the *SQL*Plus* commands you entered are not stored with it. When you retrieve this command file later, you will have to reenter the *SQL*Plus* commands if you want the same result.

There is a way to store the *SQL*Plus* command file along with the SQL commands, however. To accomplish it, use the SET command to establish a current buffer that is not the SQL buffer. The command to do this is:

```
SET BUFFER name
```

where *name* is any word that obeys the usual rules for naming a *SQL*Plus* object. Then all edit commands will operate on the new current buffer instead of the SQL buffer.

Now use the *SQL*Plus* editor to place your *SQL*Plus* commands and the SQL command together in your new current buffer. Save the commands with SAVE, and run them with START.

Using the Host System's Text Editor. If you wish to use your host system's text editor rather than the *SQL*Plus* editing commands, you can do so by entering:

```
EDIT
```

This will edit the contents of the current buffer. If you tell the text editor to save edited text, that text will be saved back into the current buffer.

You may edit the contents of a specific file by entering:

```
EDIT filename
```

A .SQL file suffix will be assumed for the file. If this is not the suffix you want, you must state your *filename.suffix* specification on the EDIT command line. If you save the command file with the text editor, it will be saved back into the same file.

Using SQL and *SQL*Plus*. Details of using SQL and *SQL*Plus* for creating tables and other database objects, and for querying and maintaining the database, are in Chapters 9 through 13.

---

1. D.D. Chamberlin and R.F. Boyce "SEQUEL: A Structured English Query Language," *Proceedings of the 1974 ACM SIGMOD Workshop on Data Description, Access, and Control* (May 1974). See also Chamberlin, et al: "A Summary of User Experience with the SQL Data Sublanguage," *Proceedings of the International Conference on Databases, Aberdeen, Scotland* (1980); and "A History of System R and SQL/Data System," *Proceedings of the 7th International Conference on Very Large Databases* (September 1981).

Chapter 4

Database Design

THIS CHAPTER DISCUSSES THE BASIC CONCEPTS INHERENT IN THE PROCESS OF DATABASE design, shows some normal forms, and presents a practical method for putting your database into third normal form. The chapter ends with a list of the steps necessary for achieving a database design that will help avoid anomalies.

You doubtless know what data you want to keep in your database and how you intend to use those data. However, you may not yet have considered the details of data organization. For example, if you intend to list your employees in your database, do you want to distinguish them by name or by Social Security number? Perhaps it would be better to use Social Security numbers, because someday you may have two employees with the same name.

Similarly, if your organization is divided into departments, do you want to distinguish the departments by names or numbers. Do you want a table for each department? If so, do you want to keep employees' salaries in that table? If you have telephone numbers for distributors in a table, are some telephone numbers missing?

Questions like the above come under the topic of "integrity constraints." In order to set up your database, you will need to write down all possible integrity constraints that apply to your situation and your data.

ORACLE provides a tool called *SQL*Forms* for building applications (see Chapters 15 and 16). Using *SQL*Forms*, you will employ "triggers" to check and maintain integrity constraints. There are also other ways of enforcing integrity constraints that are built into *ORACLE*. For example, when you create your tables, you will be able to specify that certain columns are not NULL. This will force all of your employees who use the database to fill in a value for such columns when they enter data. When you create indexes you will be able to specify UNIQUE so that the column or columns on which you create indexes cannot be the same in two different rows. Thus, when you create tables, create indexes, or build your application with *SQL*Forms*, you will need to refer to your list of integrity constraints.

This chapter will present an outline of how to set up a database. It may be that your planned database is so complicated that you will need to hire a consultant to design it for you. Even if this is the case, by working through the steps outlined below, you will be in a much better position to discuss your data with a consultant if you do use one. If your database is not too large or too complicated, you may be able to design it yourself.

4.1 RELATIONAL DATABASE THEORY

This section provides only a brief introduction to relational database theory and database design theory; to carry these topics any further would be beyond the scope and purpose of this book.

The design of databases has always been and still is more an art than a science. However, it has been empirically established that the advantage of relational over other kinds of databases is that mathematical theory can more easily be applied to relational databases than to other types of databases. The advantage of applying mathematical theory is that it provides a degree of organization, as well as the foundation upon which to build a database design.

Research on relational database theory currently is a very active area of mathematics and computer science. Expertise in relational database design involves keeping up with the latest theory, methods, and algorithms, and is highly specialized. That is why, if you have a very complicated database to design, you will probably want to consult a specialist.

4.2 ATTRIBUTES, TUPLES, COLUMNS, ROWS, AND TABLES

The definitions that appear in Chapter 1 hold for this chapter. However, in order to link the concepts presented here with those in the current literature on database design, the synonyms used in that context will be presented along with their more mathematical definitions. After the tie is established in the following sections, the more familiar terms (i.e., columns, rows, tables) will be used in the latter part of this chapter as well as in the balance of the text.

Attribute is a general term for describing a collection of similar things. For example, the attribute ''fruit'' can serve to describe a collection of apples, oranges, plums, and pears. Another example of an attribute is ''employee names,'' which is a general term under which the name of every past and present employee in your organization can be listed.

Given an ordered set of attributes, a *tuple* is a collection of things, in the same order as the attributes, one each from the collection of things described by each attribute. For example, if the ordered set of attributes is

1. fruits 2. birds 3. employee names 4. salaries

then a corresponding tuple would be:

apples robins John Jones, $10,000

The $10,000 need not be the salary of John Jones. $10,000 is merely a salary amount. The tuples that you will be concerned with will be the rows in your tables. The members of the tuple (the attributes) will be the columns in your tables. A table is a collection of tuples all having the same columns.

Given an ordered set of columns, a *relation* or *relation scheme* is a collection of related tuples (usually more than one). In a relational database, the values in the tuples will usually be related. A relation can be any set of tuples where the values in the tuples are selected from the columns.

A *relational database* is a collection of relations. In a relational database the sets of relations are called *tables* and the tuples in the tables are rows. For our purposes, the attributes are the columns in the tables.

4.3 FUNCTIONAL DEPENDENCY

Functional dependency is the ability of one or more column(s) to uniquely determine one or more other columns. For example, "employee" uniquely determines "salary"; an account receivable uniquely determines the amount receivable from that account. It is convenient to use a mathematical symbol, $->$, for the term "determines." Thus, employee $->$ salary. It may take two or more columns to uniquely determine another column. In that case we may write:

column A and column B $->$ column C

Any number of columns may be on either side of the $->$ sign.

A more precise definition of functional dependency is the following: Given a relation R and two subsets X and Y of attributes of R, then Y is said to be "functionally dependent" on X if the values of X uniquely determine the values of Y. In other words, once you know the values of all the attributes in the set X, you know uniquely the values of all the attributes in the set Y.

4.4 SETTING UP THE TABLES

Given that you have a collection of data that you want to put in a relational database, the first and most important problem in "designing the database" is to decide what will be in each table. In database language, what you have is a collection of related columns and some data values for those columns. The question is: What is the best way to assemble those data in tabular form?

At this point you should make a preliminary list of the tables you will want in your database. Each table should confront a main topic such as employees' salary information, accounts receivable, supplier information, inventory, or some other large category representing an important topic for your specific installation. Write down the names of the columns you want to put in each table.

A table should contain more than one column. For example, if you want to set up a table called Employees, it might include your employees' names, their addresses, phone numbers, Social Security numbers, salaries, employment dates, birthdates, job titles, duties, and possibly some other information about them. Initially, you may put too many columns in one table; breaking the tables down will be discussed in a later section.

4.5 ANOMALIES

Let's say you have a great deal of information regarding your employees, such as employee's name, employee's salary, employee's children. Should we have a table including those three attributes? If an employee has five children then there would be five rows in the table—one for each of the five children. However, each of the rows would have the same salary in it. This is an unnecessary repetition of the salary, and is called *redundancy*. This kind of redundancy is an example of what is called an *anomaly* in database theory. (Tables in a relational database also cannot have multiple entries in the same row or column. This fact is more technically stated as, "The database is not in first normal form." Normal forms will be discussed in Section 4.7.1 below.)

Redundancy is not the worst anomaly that can occur. For example, if you have a parts store and your database is not correctly designed, you may get a retrieval that tells you that you have parts in stock that you don't really have. If a database is poorly designed, it is possible that you will lose data or even retrieve data that don't exist. Loss of data frequently results from what is known as the *deletion anomaly*. For example, if you have a table listing suppliers and parts, and that is the only table where the suppliers appear, then deletion of all parts from a certain supplier will result in losing that supplier from the database. (Back to the phone book!) On the other hand, let's say you have a table containing suppliers' names, their addresses, and their phone numbers, and another table listing information about the parts offered by each supplier. Then you will not lose the information about a supplier even if you temporarily list no parts supplied by that supplier in your parts table.

Probably everyone these days has been a victim of the *update anomaly*. How many times have you tried to call your bank to see why they don't have some fact about you correct and been told that it is because it "fell out of the database." If some company repeatedly fails to use your correct address after you have repeatedly supplied it, it could be because of an update anomaly in their database.

Another type of update anomaly occurs when you have the supplier's address and the parts he supplies in the same table. Say that the supplier changes his address. Then, when that supplier starts supplying another part and it is added to the database, you will have the same supplier in the database with two different addresses. To avoid this, you would have to search the database for every occurrence of that supplier and change his address everywhere it occurs. Not very efficient. On the other hand, if the supplier's address occurs in one table where the supplier's name occurs only once, then you only need to change the address once. Parts are added to a separate table, which contains only the supplier's name or a coded number.

A more complex anomaly is caused by the *join*, which is used in retrieval in relational databases. The uses of joins are discussed in detail in Chapter 12, but to exhibit certain points in the balance of this chapter, they will be defined and illustrated here.

4.6 JOINS, PROJECTION, AND DECOMPOSITION

In this section, one (presumably large) table will be decomposed into two smaller tables by a method called *projection*. Then the two smaller tables will be joined back into one table. Small tables are used here to clearly illustrate the point that the equijoin (although a useful and legitimate procedure) may not restore the same table you started out with, i.e., that some data in the resulting join are false.

Given that you have a table with tablename "T," consisting of three columns called "A," "B," and "C," and values in those columns as shown below:

Table T

A	B	C
1	2	3
1	2	4
1	3	3
2	5	3

To decompose this table "by projection" into two tables, called "Table R" and "Table S," where Table R contains columns A and B, and Table S contains columns A and C, we do the following:

1. Copy all data from Columns A and B into Table R, and all data from Columns A and C into Table S, as follows:

Table R	
A	B
1	2
1	2
1	3
2	5

Table S	
A	C
1	3
1	4
1	3
2	3

2. Delete duplicate rows from each of the two resulting tables, Table R and Table S. This gives the following decomposition:

Table R	
A	B
1	2
1	3
2	5

Table S	
A	C
1	3
1	4
2	3

If, at some time in the future it is considered advisable to reunite these two tables R and S, into one large table T, the join would proceed as follows:

1. Combine the first row of Table R with every row in Table S where Column A in R has the same value as Column A in S.
2. Continue combining rows according to rule 1 stated immediately above, until all rows have been combined in this way.

The resulting join is:

	Table T	
A	B	C
1	2	3
1	2	4
1	3	3
→ 1	3	4
2	5	3

Note that Table T has all the rows it originally had, but it now has an extra row. The fourth row down consists of false data that were not in the original table. This is an example of how an equijoin may produce the *join anomaly*—data that do not actually exist in the database.

To illustrate the join anomaly in another way, suppose we have two tables one with suppliers and types of shirts supplied and another with supplier and color of buttons on their shirts. If supplier X supplies "gala" shirts with only green buttons and "groupie" shirts with red buttons, then the join of the two tables will indicate that "gala" shirts come with both green and red buttons, which is false. Thus, the table containing style of shirt and button color should *not* be broken into two tables, one with supplier and style of shirt, the other with supplier and color of buttons supplied. On the other hand, if a supplier supplies all of his shirts with all the colors of buttons, then the breakdown into two tables is correct. The latter case (i.e., the fact that the shirt comes with all colors of buttons) is an example of a *multivalued-dependency*, which will not be discussed in this text, but which you may pursue by consulting the references shown at the end of this chapter.

4.7 DESIGNING YOUR DATABASE

Much of relational database theory has been devoted to methods for deciding how the data should be arranged in tables. While the outcome has not been definitive in the sense that it is always possible to decide upon the undeniably best method of arranging data in tables, it is sufficiently developed to give rules of thumb which will provide a satisfactory design. Much of the rest of this chapter will explore the theory far enough to give you a feeling for the theory of database design.

4.7.1 Normal Forms

This section will present some definitions that are necessary to an understanding of the various *normal forms*. The reason for using normal forms is that, if the tables in your database satisfy the conditions of these normal forms, you will be less likely to run into anomalies when your database is in use. Generally, the way to attain a normal form is to break down, or *decompose* one table into two or more tables. In so doing, however, the join anomaly mentioned above must be avoided.

4.7.2 Join Dependency, Fully Dependent, Prime vs. Nonprime

At this point, you should write down the functional dependencies, as discussed in Section 4.3 above, for each table. It is important to realize that your entire database is based on these functional dependencies, and therefore, a functional dependency must hold true in all possible states of your database.

In writing down dependencies you should ask yourself, "Will this be true for all of my data?" For example, you may assign each supplier a number, which will then uniquely determine the supplier's name, address, and phone number. But, when you stop using that supplier (because he has gone out of business, for example) do you assign that number to another supplier, just as a number on a football jersey may be assigned to another player in another season? Or do you retire the number? If you reassign the number, then any search back through your records will confuse the data on the new supplier with that of the old one.

If you decompose a table T into many subtables by projection, then you are assuming a join dependency, i.e., that the join of the tables that you decomposed T into will always return to you the original values of T.

A column A is said to be *fully dependent* on a set X of columns if and only if A is functionally dependent on X and A is not functionally dependent on any proper (not = X) subset of X. The following example illustrates the concepts of functional dependency, fully dependent, and prime vs. nonprime.

Given that you have a table consisting of the four columns shown below:

Fruit Suppliers A

1.	2.	3.	4.
Name of Supplier	Order #	Type of Carton	Fruit Supplied

Then:

- Column 4 is functionally dependent on the combination of Columns 1 and 2.
- Column 3 is functionally dependent on Column 1.

Using the table "Fruit Suppliers A", "Type of Carton" is dependent but not fully dependent on "Name of Supplier" and "Order #" because it is dependent (and fully dependent) on "Name of Supplier" alone.

4.7.3 Keys

Given a table R, let Y be all the columns in R. Then if X, a subset of Y, is such that Y is functionally dependent on X, X is said to be a *superkey*. If X is a superkey and no subset of X is a superkey, then X is said to be a *key*. "Superkey," then, just means larger than or equal to a key.

A column is said to be a *prime column* if and only if it is in some key of R. Otherwise the column is said to be *nonprime*.

Now consider the following example:

Fruit Suppliers B

1.	2.	3.	4.
Supplier	Order #	Fruit Carton	Reception #

where "Order #" is the number on the order made up by the supplier, and "Reception #" is the unique number we give to the fruit carton when we receive it. Then the superkeys are:

1. Supplier, Order #
2. Reception #
3. Supplier, Order #, Fruit Carton
4. Supplier, Order #, Reception #
5. Supplier, Order #, Fruit Carton, Reception #
6. Supplier, Reception #
7. Order #, Reception #
8. Fruit Carton, Reception #
9. Supplier, Fruit Carton, Reception #
10. Order #, Fruit Carton, Reception #

The only keys are Columns 1 and 2, because all others have 1 or 2 as a subset, and no subset of 1 or 2 is a superkey. Then "Supplier," "Order #," and "Reception #" are prime, and "Fruit Carton" is nonprime.

4.7.4 Candidate Key, Primary Key, Foreign Key

The designation of *primary key* for our purposes follows that used by C. J. Date,[1] who calls a set of columns in a table a *candidate key* if the set satisfies the following two properties:

1. At any given time, no two rows in the table have exactly the same values in all of the columns in the set.
2. All of the columns in the key are necessary to make the key unique.

Date's definition of candidate key is equivalent to our definition of key.

Date then arbitrarily selects a primary key from the candidate keys for that table. He points out that every table has at least one candidate key. (If there are any keys left over after the primary key is selected, Date calls these the *alternate keys*.) A *foreign key* is a set of columns which corresponds to a primary key in some other table.

Keys are used to tie your database together so you can insert into it and retrieve from it. You will want each table to have a primary key, preferably involving as few columns as possible.

For example, Social Security number is a good primary key. It is always advisable to use a number rather than a text string for a primary or foreign key. If you use a name for a primary or foreign key, then any change in the name will result in a loss of data. Inclusion of a middle initial, or even a difference in the number of blanks between first and last name, can result in data loss.

Any text string which might be misspelled also will lose data. For example, it would be unwise to key on addresses. An entry of "First Ave" would not be tied to an entry of "1st Ave." It may be necessary to generate a number to use for a key. For example, if you have a street name like "Madison Ave.," when "Madison Ave." is first inserted into the database, a unique number should be generated to correspond to it.

In order to maintain integrity of a database, the columns of a primary or foreign key must never be allowed to be null. (See the definition of NULL in Chapter 1.) Furthermore, the columns corresponding to a primary key must be unique in the table in which they occur. One way to enforce this is to create a unique index on the columns of every primary key.

A table may have any number of foreign keys from none to many. In order to maintain integrity in the case of a foreign key, the columns involved in the foreign key should be designated NOT NULL in the CREATE TABLE statement. Since retrieval frequently will be based on a foreign key, an index should be created on the concatenation of the columns in the foreign key. This should not be a "unique" index.

4.7.5 First Normal Form

A table is said to be "in first normal form" (1NF) if and only if the members of the columns are not sets containing more than one member. For example, if one of the columns is the set of children of the employee, then the table is not 1NF.

4.7.6 Second Normal Form

A table is said to be "in second normal form" (2NF) if, and only if, every nonprime column is fully dependent on each of the table's keys.

For example, the table of Fruit Suppliers A, shown above, would not be in 2NF as it stands because Column 3, a nonprime column, is not fully dependent on the key, Columns 1 and 2. It is only dependent on Column 1. To put it in 2NF, it is necessary to decompose it as follows:

Fruit Suppliers (a)

1	3
Name of Supplier	Type of Carton

Fruit Suppliers (b)

1	2	4
Name of Supplier	Order #	Fruit Supplied

The two tables above, Fruit Suppliers (a) and Fruit Suppliers (b), are now in 2NF because Column 3 is fully dependent on Column 1 in Fruit Suppliers (a), and Column 4 is fully dependent on Columns 1 and 2 in Fruit Suppliers (b).

4.7.7 Third Normal Form

A relation is said to be "in third normal form" (3NF) if and only if it is 2NF and its nonprime columns are functionally independent, i.e., there are no functional dependencies of Y on X where Y X, and X and Y are nonempty collections of nonprime columns.

For example, the decomposition shown in Section 4.7.2 above, of the Fruit Suppliers A table, is now in 3NF because it was shown in Section 4.7.6 to be in 2NF, and it meets the additional condition for 3NF, namely that its nonprime columns (Columns 3 and 4) are functionally independent.

A method will be given in Section 4.7.10 for achieving 3NF.

4.7.8 Boyce Codd Normal Form

A functional dependency of Y on X is said to be *trivial* if and only if X is a subset of Y.

A table R is said to be in *Boyce Codd Normal Form* (BCNF) if and only if whenever Y is nontrivially functionally dependent on X, then X is a superkey of R.

4.7.9 Normalizing the Database

A relational database is said to be in one of the normal forms if and only if every table in the database is in that normal form.

There are a number of normal forms, but as their rank increases, their usage becomes increasingly difficult and not always profitable at this point in the state of the art. Therefore, no use will be made here of normal forms higher than 3NF except to exhibit one important relationship between normal forms:

- *It can be shown that* 4NF => BCNF => 3NF => 2NF => 1NF, *where* => *means "implies," 4NF means Fourth Normal Form, and BCNF means Boyce Codd Normal Form.*

This expression means that whenever a higher order normal form is achieved, it can only be done so by achieving every lower-ranked normal form.

4.7.10 Attaining Third Normal Form by Decomposition

Here is a demonstration of a method for decomposition into 3NF, starting with a simple example and then going to a more complex example. The algorithm can be found in Maier[3] and Chang[4], and is known as the *decomposition algorithm.*

Suppose we have a key column X in a table T with two other columns Y and Z. If we have the functional dependencies $X->Y$, and $Y->Z$ and Y and Z are nonprime, then T is not in third normal form because Y and Z are not independent. If we then decompose T into tables U and V such that U is the projection of T on X and Y, and V is the projection of T on Y and Z, the resulting tables are in third normal form. Of course, this is trivially so because tables with only two columns must be in third normal form.

In this case, the decomposition removes the dependency of nonprime attributes, since Y becomes a key for table V (and thus is no longer nonprime) and neither of the resulting tables has dependent nonprime columns. Furthermore, the join of U and V is T.

The method may be generalized to more complex tables to decompose them into third normal form tables. To take it one step further, assume T is a table with a key column K and additional columns Y, A, B, and C, with the functional dependencies $K->Y$, $Y->A$, $Y->B$, and $Y->C$, so that Y, A, B, and C are nonprime and A, B, and C are mutually independent. Then T may be decomposed into tables U and V, where U is the projection of T on K and Y, and V is the projection of T on Y, A, B, and C. Once again, the tables U and V are in third normal form and T is the join of U and V. Y is a foreign key in U and a primary key in V.

To carry the method another step further, assume T and the functional dependencies are as above, and that T contains three more columns G, H, and I, such that G, H, and I are nonprime, and independent of Y. Then the decomposition of T into U and V, where:

U is the projection on K, Y, G, H, and I
V is the projection on Y, A, B, and C

is such that V is in third normal form and the join of U and V is T. However, U is not in third normal form unless G, H, and I are independent. If they are not, then decompose U into two more tables, and by repeated decomposition you will eventually reach third normal form, and joins will not produce false data.

Note that in the above decompositions, Y always becomes a key in one of the new tables. It should be selected as a primary key in that table, and thus it becomes a foreign key in the other table of the decomposition.

This decomposition can have some disadvantages. There is another method of reaching third normal form, that of *synthesis*. Synthesis has its own difficulties, namely, there is no guarantee that the join of the set of tables produced by synthesis is equal to the original table. Thus, a retrieval after synthesis may produce false data. The problems connected with decomposition and synthesis, as well as the higher normal forms, are beyond the scope of this book. For more information concerning decomposition, synthesis, and higher normal forms, see the references at the end of this chapter.

4.7.11 Summary of Database Design Steps

For the most efficient design of your database with the lowest probability of anomalies, follow the steps outlined below:

1. Make up a few large tables of related information for the information you want to put in your database.

2. For each resulting table write down the functional dependencies for that table.

3. For each table determine the keys. If your database is very complex, it may not be possible to find all keys within a reasonable period of time, or even whether or not a certain column occurs in some key. Determining the keys, therefore, may require a judgment call.

4. For each table, select a candidate key that (a) is most meaningful to you, and (b) has the smallest number of columns. Designate this key as the primary key.

5. Successively decompose the tables until most are in third normal form. This will result in selecting your primary and foreign keys in all of the tables.

6. Take a close look at the results. If the resulting keys are not very meaningful, or if there is still a lot of redundancy, you will want to repeat the process of decomposition, making a different set of judgments as to which decompositions to perform. It may be that you will prefer some intermediate decomposition. (It is not necessary for all of the tables to be in third normal form.)

7. Enforce your integrity constraints on keys by specifying NOT NULL on columns containing the designated primary and foreign keys.

8. Create unique indexes on the primary keys and nonunique indexes on the foreign keys.

9. Reinforce your functional dependencies and constraints by the use of triggers and host-language exits in the applications that you build with *SQL*Forms*.

10. You may also want to build additional application programs to check your constraints and your database integrity.

For more extensive treatment of relational database theory, and database design, see the texts referenced in the footnotes. The treatments by Date (1 and 2) are relatively simplistic and consist largely of a number of rules of thumb. The book by Maier (3) is more extensive and mathematical in nature, covering much of what was known up to the date of publication. The book by Yang (4) is even more mathematical.

1. C.J. Date, An Introduction to Database Systems, Vol. 1, 4th Edition (Menlo Park, Calif.: Addison-Wesley, 1986).
2. C.J. Date, *A Guide to DB2* (Menlo Park, Calif.: Addison-Wesley, 1984).
3. David Maier, *The Theory of Relational Databases* (Rockville, Md.: Computer Science Press, 1983).
4. Chao-Chih Yang, *Relational Databases* (Englewood Cliffs, N.J.: Prentice-Hall, 1986).

See also: J. D. Ullman, *Principles of Database Systems* (Rockville, Md.: Computer Science Press, 1982); and Gio Wiederhold, *Database Design* (New York: McGraw-Hill, 1983).

Chapter 5

The Database Administrator

A NY SYSTEM WITH MORE THAN ONE USER MUST HAVE A DATABASE ADMINISTRATOR
(DBA). (In a single-user system, that user performs the DBA functions as well as
all others.) Initially the DBA's most pressing function is to supervise the design of the
tables to be used, so that redundancy is kept at a minimum and efficiency is maximized.
This function of database design is discussed in Chapter 4.

Another important function of the DBA is allocating space for the database objects.
Since this is a large topic in itself, and involves other users besides the DBA, space
projections and allocations are dealt with in Chapter 6.

After the installation of the database and its applications, the DBA is responsible for
the functions described in sections 5.2 through 5.7 in this chapter.

5.1 TYPES OF DBAs

ORACLE allows for two types of DBAs, *SYS* and *SYSTEM*. Their functions are slightly
different.

The DBA SYS owns all of the tables in the data dictionary. These are critical to the
operation of *ORACLE*, so the SYS account should be used rarely. When *ORACLE* is first
installed, the DBA SYS is enrolled with the password "CHANGE_ON_INSTALL,"
which should be changed as soon as the *ORACLE* system is initialized to whatever password
the DBA SYS will be using. The command to do this is:

GRANT CONNECT TO SYS IDENTIFIED BY (*newSYSpassword*);

The DBA SYSTEM owns all the data dictionary views. These are less critical to the
operation of *ORACLE* than the tables owned by the DBA SYS, but it is also recommended
that they should be changed rarely. *ORACLE* is installed with the DBA called SYSTEM
identified by the password "MANAGER." This password should be changed immediately

after installation to whatever password the DBA SYSTEM will be using. The command to do this is:

GRANT CONNECT TO SYSTEM IDENTIFIED BY (*newSYSTEMpassword*);

The DBA called SYSTEM also owns some tables and views that are created by various *ORACLE* utilities. These should not be altered, and user data should not be stored in them. Table 5-1 contains a list of such tables and views; this list does change with different versions of *ORACLE*, however. You should consult the list in the *ORACLE Database Administrator's Guide* for the version you are installing. (The list in Table 5-1 is for *ORACLE* Version 5.0.)

5.2 ENROLLING AND DROPPING USERS

Once the *ORACLE* system is designed and installed, enrolling and dropping users is one of the DBA's most frequently used functions. The DBA can give other users privileges with regard to the *ORACLE* database, and can revoke or change those privileges. Each user must enter the system with a username and password. Only the DBA can enroll users. He accomplishes this with the SQL command:

GRANT *privilege* TO *username*

There are three types of privileges, which are listed below in the order of increasing privilege:

CONNECT

Table 5-1. Tables and Views Owned by DBA SYSTEM.

Export/ Import	HELP	CRT Utility	SQL*Forms	SQL*Menu
EXPTAB	HELP	CRT	FIELDS	DMU__MESSAGE
EXPVEW		CRTBOX	IAPAPP	DMU__OUTSEQ
		CRT__TYPE	IAPBLK	DMU__SEQNAME
		ESC	IAPFLD	DMU__FUNKKEYS
		FUNCTIONS	IAPMAP	TERMINAL__INFO
		GOTO__LRC	IAPSQLTXT	DMU__COMMAND__TYPE
		LORC	IAPTRG	WORK__CLASS
			ITEMS	USER__INFO
			MAP	MENU__INFO
			MENU	OPTION__HELP
			MESSAGES	PARAMETER__INFO
			SCREEN	PARAMETER__MENU
				MENU__OPTION
				DMU__APPLICATION

RESOURCE
DBA

The new user is granted one or more access privileges, with the following type of command:

GRANT CONNECT, RESOURCE TO *username*
IDENTIFIED BY *password*;

If the user is being admitted to the system for the first time, the IDENTIFIED BY clause must be used. On the other hand, if the user has already been granted the CONNECT privilege, and is now being given an additional privilege such as the RESOURCE privilege shown above, the IDENTIFIED BY clause can be omitted. The command would then be:

GRANT RESOURCE TO *username*;

5.2.1 The CONNECT Privilege

Every user must have at least the CONNECT privilege, and each such user must have a username and a password. These are then stored in the Data Dictionary. Each time a user logs on, the username and password are checked against the dictionary for validity. Users having only the CONNECT privilege may:

- Access *ORACLE*.
- Look at other users' data by using the SELECT command if SELECT access has been granted.
- Perform the data manipulation operations INSERT, UPDATE, and DELETE on other users' tables if access to these tables has been granted.
- Create views and synonyms.

Users who have only the CONNECT privilege cannot CREATE any tables, clusters, or indexes.

5.2.2 The RESOURCE Privilege

A user with RESOURCE privilege has all the privileges granted to a CONNECT user, and can:

- CREATE database tables, indexes, and clusters.
- GRANT and REVOKE privileges on the tables, indexes, and clusters he has created.
- Use the AUDIT command to control auditing of access to tables, indexes, and clusters he has created. (See Section 5.7 on Auditing.)

5.2.3 The DBA Privilege

A user with DBA privilege has all the privileges granted by CONNECT and RE-

42

SOURCE, and in addition may:

- Access any user's data, and perform any SQL statement upon it.
- GRANT and REVOKE users' database access privileges.
- Create PUBLIC synonyms (available to all users).
- Create and alter partitions.
- Control system-wide auditing and table-level auditing defaults.
- Perform full database exports.

5.2.4 Automatic Logins

The DBA may also grant automatic logins to certain users, tying their *ORACLE* IDs to the system IDs. Users enrolled this way do not need to type in their *ORACLE* username or password when logging in to *ORACLE*.

The syntax used to grant automatic logins is the same as for granting database privileges, except that the prefix OPS$ occurs directly before the user's name. The OPS$ signifies to *ORACLE* that this is an automatic login username. (Since this application may not be the same for all systems, refer to your documentation for the specifics on your equipment.) It is set up as follows:

GRANT CONNECT TO OPS$<*opsys__id*> IDENTIFIED BY *password*;

For example, to enroll a user whose system ID is HAGAR, a DBA would enter:

GRANT CONNECT TO OPS$HAGAR IDENTIFIED BY HORRIBLE;

After this GRANT is entered, a user who is logged onto the operating system as HAGAR does not need to enter an *ORACLE* username and password. Instead, he can log in as OPS$HAGAR.

The username is the whole character string OPS$HAGAR. Therefore all objects (tables, views, indexes, etc.) created by this user are prefixed by this name. For another user to reference a table PARIS, owned by OPS$HAGAR, he would have to enter:

SELECT * FROM OPS$HAGAR.PARIS;

5.2.5 Changing Privileges and Dropping Users

Only the DBA can drop users or change the privileges or passwords of other users. The DBA can do this at any time. (However, the user himself can change his own password.)

The command to drop a user is the SQL statement REVOKE CONNECT FROM, as follows:

REVOKE CONNECT FROM *username*;

Since CONNECT is the lowest level of privilege, when it is revoked the user has lost all privileges of connecting to *ORACLE*, and therefore is dropped.

If, however, the DBA wishes to revoke only part of a user's privileges, he may revoke selectively. The following command allows the user to retain all the CONNECT privileges, but removes that user's RESOURCE privileges:

REVOKE RESOURCE FROM *username*;

When a user's privileges are revoked, the tables that user owns remain in the Data Dictionary even though the user's name does not. The DBA (and all other users who have been given access to them) can still continue to access these tables originally owned by a (now) dropped user.

The DBA also can increase a user's privilege by using the GRANT statement followed by the higher-ranked privilege, as shown in Section 5.2 above.

5.2.6 Changing Passwords

The DBA can change the password of any *ORACLE* user. Any user also may change his own password at any time. This is done simply by using the GRANT CONNECT command and inserting the new password, as in the following:

GRANT CONNECT TO *user* IDENTIFIED BY *newpassword*;

5.2.7 The "User" Called PUBLIC

When *ORACLE* is installed, it automatically sets up a group user called PUBLIC. Every subsequent user enrolled by the DBA is a member of the PUBLIC group.

Granting PUBLIC Access to Tables or Views. When you create tables or views that will be of interest to many users, instead of naming each user who may access them, it is more efficient to simply GRANT access to PUBLIC. The command to do so looks like this:

GRANT SELECT ON *tablename* TO PUBLIC;

Every user who has access to *ORACLE* may see all Data Dictionary tables, and all tables where the owner has granted access to PUBLIC.

The PUBLIC Synonyms. Only a DBA can create PUBLIC synonyms. The DBA may create PUBLIC synonyms on tables, views, or even on other synonyms. All PUBLIC synonyms are then available to all *ORACLE* users.

A *synonym* abbreviates the amount of typing necessary to select a table or view. For example, if users must frequently access a SYSTEM file of rates, the DBA may create a synonym for that file as follows:

CREATE PUBLIC SYNONYM SYSTRATES FOR SYSTEM.SYSTRATES;

Then a user can simply type SYSTRATES instead of having to type SYSTEM.SYSTRATES every time he uses the file containing rates.

To find out what PUBLIC synonyms exist, you must enter the command:

SELECT * FROM PUBLICSYN;

44

5.3 THE BEFORE IMAGE (BI) FILE

The Before Image (BI) file contains the database blocks before they are changed in case a user starts to make a change, and then for some reason cannot, or does not want to, complete it. For example, if in the course of updating, you have insufficient information to complete a transaction, it may be preferable to leave the table in its original condition. You may then want to use the ROLLBACK WORK command. This will rewrite the blocks from the BI file back into the database.

During the time you are doing the updating or other transaction, the BI file will hold the blocks. Any other user wishing to query that table will read blocks from the BI file so that they will see a consistent (non-changing) view of the data. The blocks stay in the BI file until you have entered a COMMIT for the transaction.

Only the detached process Before Image Writer (BIW) writes to the BI file. It copies blocks from the BI file to the System Global Area (SGA). Entries in the BI file are overwritten when they are no longer needed. For example, when a transaction is COMMITted, that block entry is no longer needed.

The Before Image Screen of the *ORACLE* Display System (ODS) (See Section 5.4.3 in this chapter for other aspects of the ODS) can be used to monitor space usage in the BI file.

The Before Image Display shows how many blocks of the BI file are in use or available. In the BI file, blocks are used sequentially as needed. When the last block is used, *ORACLE* starts reusing blocks, beginning with the first. Each time it goes through the BI file, *ORACLE* has made one pass.

BI blocks are allocated as needed. Thus, blocks for one transaction are interspersed with blocks for other transactions. When you COMMIT a transaction, the blocks you were using in the BI file are freed for reuse. However, no blocks are really available for reuse unless the blocks before it are free. For example, if transaction A has blocks 1 and 2, and transaction B has blocks 3 and 4, blocks 3 and 4 will not be freed for reuse until both B and A transactions are committed.

The Before Image Display will show you the Before Image Status in terms of:

- Used Blocks
- Low Block
- High Block
- Head Block
- Tail Block

These block names are described in the next few paragraphs.

Used Blocks. This status indicator shows the number of BI blocks actually in use by transactions. If this is zero, no ongoing transactions require blocks in the BI file. This number does not indicate where those blocks are in the BI file; blocks in use may be contiguous or fragmented. If they are contiguous (as they would be, for example, from only one transaction), then all remaining blocks are currently available. If fragmented, then some blocks are not currently being used but are not yet available for reuse.

Low Blocks, High Blocks. These are first and last blocks of the BI file allocated to this instance. Unless the screen display is for an *ORACLE* instance running an *ORACLE* cluster, these values will represent the entire BI file.

Head Block. The Head Block indicates the last block allocated to a current transaction.

The value of the Head block is updated every time another BI block is required.

Tail Block. The Tail Block indicates the earliest block allocated to a current transaction. The Tail Block's value is updated only when more space is required which runs into the current Tail Block; thus it is only updated when another pass is made in search of available blocks. Obviously, this value is most meaningful when it has just been updated.

To determine how many blocks are available, use the following formula:

$$(\text{Tail Block} - \text{Head Block}) = n$$

If n is positive, then n blocks are available; if n is negative, then add (High Block $-$ Low Block) to n to get the number of blocks available.

Sometimes the Used Blocks will show a zero in the display, yet the Tail Block will show a much higher number than the Head Block. This usually means that all blocks are available for reuse, but the Tail Block has not yet been updated because there have been no further requests for space.

5.4 THE DBA TOOLS

There are several *ORACLE* utilities which are of interest only, or primarily, to the DBA. These are:

IOR   A program that is used to start *ORACLE* for the first time after installation, as well as succeeding times. IOR is also used to shut down *ORACLE*.

INIT.ORA   A file that contains the parameters of the user's operation.

ODS   The Display System Utility which monitors the ongoing use of an *ORACLE* system.

AIJ   The After Image Journal, a backup program which will allow recovery after a system failure.

SGI   The utility that displays the size of the System Global Area (SGA) generated by a parameter file.

In addition, there is an auditing facility that allows the DBA (and under certain conditions, other users) to monitor specific uses of the database.

The principal features of these utilities are described in the sections that follow.

5.4.1 The IOR Command and Parameters

Usually the DBA is the sole user of the IOR program. If misused, the IOR can be destructive to the database, so very few users should have access to it.

IOR is used to start *ORACLE* the very first time, and to start and stop the *ORACLE* system thereafter. Every time IOR is used in this way, it reads the INIT.ORA file and configures the system global area (SGA) according to the parameter settings in INIT.ORA (see Section 5.4.2 for further details on INIT.ORA).

The syntax of the IOR command is:

```
IOR { WARM | SHUT | CLEAR |INIT [ NOCONFIRM ] } [ DBA ] [ PFILE= <filename>][ SHARED ]
[ LIST ]
```

The arguments in the above command can be abbreviated to one letter, as in IOR W for IOR WARM. They are defined as follows:

INIT	Initializes the database and starts the *ORACLE* detached processes. This is called a "cold start."
WARM	Restarts an *ORACLE* database by starting the detached processes.
SHUT	Checks for ongoing activity by database users and shuts down *ORACLE* when all users have logged off *ORACLE*.
CLEAR	Clears *ORACLE* of all current users and shuts it down, without waiting for users to log off. Because a CLEAR only terminates the background processes, user processes must be stopped at the operating system level.
PFILE	Names a file, formatted like INIT.ORA, listing parameters used to start *ORACLE*. By default this file is INIT.ORA.
LIST	Requests that IOR show the parameters in the parameter file that would be used to start *ORACLE* (either the default file, or one designated with PFILE). Can be used alone, in which case it takes no other action. Can also be used with I, W, S, or C.
NOCONFIRM	Is used with INIT option to request that IOR not prompt for confirmation that the database is to be initialized.
DBA	Is used with either INIT or WARM to restrict logins to DBA users only until the next IOR W.
SHARED	Is for shared-partition systems only (as for VMS clusters with more than one user running an *ORACLE* cluster) and entered with the WARM argument, to indicate that the user is starting the database in a shared mode.

Initializing IOR.INIT. This option initializes the database files and starts the detached processes. Any user data existing in the database files is lost, since an IOR I restores the database and before image files to their original empty state. The initialize option is rarely used. Its two main purposes are to move up to a new version of *ORACLE* and to reconfigure operating system files.

After you enter IOR.INIT, a prompt appears for confirmation of your intention to initialize. You must respond with the word YES in uppercase letters. To suppress this prompt, you may use the option NOCONFIRM.

If you use the initialize option on a database containing user data, be sure to first export and back up the DB and BI files. Any user data in the database files when an IOR I is run will be lost.

IOR.INIT restores the database to a single-partition system. If you need to recreate other partitions, you must do so before importing your data. (See Chapter 6 for details on partitions, including how to create them.)

Warm Starting (IOR WARM). For all but the first start, a warm start is the normal method of starting an *ORACLE* system. A warm start opens the database and the BI files, so these must be online and accessible to the user doing the warm start. It also starts the detached processes ARH, BIW, BWR, and CLN if you are working with a multi-user system. (See Section 5.4.3 in this chapter for information on ARH, BIW, BWR, and CLN.)

A warm start rolls back any outstanding transactions and drops all temporary tables. Therefore, you should never abort an IOR WARM once it has started.

When you invoke IOR W, it will display the size of the following SGA components:

- Number of bytes of fixed data
- Number of bytes of variable data
- Before Image buffers
- Database buffers

Normal warm start messages like the following may appear:

n temporary tables deleted

instance n recovered

When the warm start is complete, you will see the message shown below. Users will not be able to log into *ORACLE* until this message appears:

ORACLE WARM STARTED

Shutting Down *ORACLE* (IOR SHUT). The IOR SHUT prevents new users from logging in to *ORACLE*, but does not affect users currently on. It waits for all current users to log off, then shuts down the database. If a new user attempts to log on, he or she will see the message:

ORACLE shutdown in progress

In this way, all pending transactions are completed or rolled back before shutdown. During a shutdown, messages may appear at the terminal issuing the shutdown, such as

IOR: 5 users still active

When a shutdown is complete, the message appears:

IOR: ORACLE shutdown complete

At this point the detached processes are stopped, and the database and the BI files are closed.

5.4.2 The INIT.ORA Parameter File

Every time you warm start or reinitialize *ORACLE*, it reads a file of parameters that specify characteristics of its operation. This is called the INIT.ORA file by default. You may rename it if you wish. Where *ORACLE* expects to find this file is dependent upon the operating system.

The INIT.ORA file identifies files used by *ORACLE* and controls resources directly affecting *ORACLE* performance. For example, it contains the parameters which must be given values or names to start the system, and those that determine the number of entries stored in the SGA. By adjusting the right parameters, you can change the size of the SGA and improve *ORACLE*'s performance. Oracle Corporation supplies you with a sample INIT.ORA file on the release tape, containing suggested parameter values that are appropriate for most installations. However, after your system is operating for a while and you are familiar with *ORACLE*, you may want to change some of these parameter values.

The distributed values of the INIT.ORA parameters may be different from the default values. These distributed values are listed in the *Installation and User's Guide* for your operating system. The default values are built into the code, and will be used on your system if you do not insert new parameters into the INIT.ORA file.

A complete list of the INIT.ORA parameters, along with a description of each and a list of default values, appears in Appendix B.

Variable INIT.ORA Parameters. Some of the INIT.ORA parameters simply name items; others set limits that will affect performance. For example, the setting for TABLES sets the size of the tables cache (in memory); therefore it determines how many table definitions can be cached at one time. If a definition is in memory, performance will be better than if it is not.

The parameters shown below are called *variable parameters*: the size of the SGA depends on their values. These are the most important parameters to adjust when tuning a system. For example, a higher value for BUFFERS usually improves performance; a lower value only slows work, but does not prevent it.

The following variable parameters affect performance, but do not impose limits:

BUFFERS
COLUMNS
TABLES
TABLENAMES

On the other hand, some variable parameters set capacity limits; for example, if PROCESSES is 10, then the 11th process attempting to log on will not be able to do so. The following variable parameters are called *capacity parameters*:

TABLE_ACCESSES
TABLE_HANDLES
ENQUEUES
OPEN_CURSORS
PROCESSES
TRANSACTIONS
USERS

Increasing the size of variable parameters may improve your system's performance, but it will also increase the size of the SGA. In virtual-memory operating systems, an oversize SGA may decrease performance efficiency if it is repeatedly swapped in and out of memory. Operating system parameters controlling virtual memory working areas should be set with SGA size in mind.

You may receive error messages that a parameter is too low or that you have reached its maximum. If this occurs repeatedly, you can shut down *ORACLE*, increase the relevant INIT.ORA parameter, and restart *ORACLE*. Alternatively, you can wait until the system is less busy and then retry the operation.

Which parameters will benefit your system most is dependent on several database characteristics, such as how your data are arranged, and how many users or programs are active at any one time. Therefore, improving system performance requires a knowledge of your system, as well as an understanding of what the variable parameters control.

The list of the INIT.ORA parameters in Appendix B includes an indication of the effect of each parameter on the SGA.

5.4.3 The *ORACLE* Display System (ODS) Utility

(The following sections are not relevant to single-user systems.)

The *ORACLE* Display System (ODS) is used to monitor use of the database. Different screens may be selected to find out which users are active, what locks they are holding, how much activity has taken place in the database since the last warm start (IOR W), and the contents of the Before Image file. Specifically, ODS will tell you:

- Which users are currently using *ORACLE*.
- What *ORACLE* programs they are using.
- What tables they are accessing.
- What locks they are holding or waiting for.
- The current status of the before image file.
- Logical and physical I/O activity.

With ODS you can also send "snapshot" display screens to a file for later evaluation of trends in *ORACLE* use and trouble spots.

Invoking ODS. The command ODS will bring up a screen logo, and then a screen showing the display options available. These are exhibited in Table 5-2.

The ODS Log File. You can save what appears on ODS screens by creating a log file and storing the screen displays there. To do this, enter the Open command to the prompt for display type (see Table 5-2). You may fill in a specific filename, or use the default filename, which is ODS.LOG. To close this file, return to the display menu and enter the Close command.

The ODS Display Screens. The following sections contain descriptions of the ODS display screens. While all of the displays are of interest to DBA's, other users will be most interested in the Before Image Display and the Locks Display.

The Before Image Display. The Before Image Display shows how many blocks of the Before Image file are in use or available. Details of the Before Image Display appeared in Section 5.3.1 above.

The I/O Display. The I/O Display is a graphic display, but it may be run on systems that do not support graphics. It may not be an accurate view of the precise distribution patterns. It is a histogram of the percentage contribution of each *ORACLE* process to the total amount of logical and physical I/O during the specified period. Each *ORACLE* process is identified by a user ID (*uid*) or a process ID (*pid*).

The Locks Display. If you have many locks, you can have the Locks Display page

Table 5-2. The ORACLE Display System Options.

Command*	Description of Display
Help (or ?)	This list of options.
BI	Before Image file statistics.
CLose	Close the log file.
CYcle <n>	Set the update interval to *n* seconds.
Exit	Exit from ODS.
Io	System I/O distribution on per-user basis.
Locks (0)	Lock and Enqueue list (0=all locks).
Open <filename>	Open the log file.
Process [VMS:]	Process, user, terminal, and image stats.
Process [VM:]	VM summary information.
Summary	Summary of *ORACLE* system activity.
Table	Tables accessed by each user (D=RBA in DEC).
User <first_pid> <last_pid>	Detailed user stats.

*Responses can be abbreviated to the first 1 or 2 characters. The chosen display will appear on the terminal screen. Enter E(xit) to exit to operating system. To change or reset the display cycle interval, enter CY(cle) and specify a cycle time in seconds as a command argument. Valid cycle range is between 1 and 600 seconds. You can change the interval between displays. Use your system's interrupt sequence to return to the ENTER DISPLAY screen.

through all of them by invoking it with a zero argument, like this:

    L 0

The Locks Display returns a listing of all active locks, and the number of users. It also indicates whether the locks are shared, shared wait, exclusive, or exclusive wait. (A complete description of each of these types of locks appears in Chapter 8, which is devoted entirely to *ORACLE* locks.) Each lock in the display represents one enqueue entry in the SGA.

The Process Display. The Process Display shows information (specific to the operating system) about users currently logged into *ORACLE*. Processes 2 through 5 are always Buffer WRite (BWR), Before Image Write (BIW), Cleanup (CLN), and Asynchronous Read Ahead (ARH).

Running the Process Display on your operating system may require certain privileges. Check your operating system guide if a complete display of all processes does not appear. With some systems, lacking the necessary privileges means that only information about your own usage will appear on the screen.

The Summary Display. The Summary Display monitors activity on the entire database during a set time interval. It shows the following:

Log reads	The number of logical blocks read from the blocks found in the cache buffer pool.
Phy reads	The number of physical disk blocks read.
Log writes	The number of modifications to cache buffer blocks.
Phy writes	The number of physical disk blocks written.
DML commits	The number of data manipulation commits.
DML rollbacks	The number of data manipulation rollbacks.
DDL commits	The number of Data Dictionary commits.
DDL rollbacks	The number of Data Dictionary rollbacks.
Deadlocks	The number of deadlocks detected system-wide.

The summary display also shows the number of detached process errors in the BWR, BIW, CLN, and ARH.

The Table Display. The Table Display shows the name of each table in the table cache, but not all tables currently being accessed. It shows the Relative Block Address (RBA) of the beginning of the table, the number of read (RD) cursors and update (UPD) cursors for each user of each table. The RBA's can be displayed in decimal or hexadecimal numbers. The RBA default is decimal, but the hexadecimal display may be useful to relate the RBAs in the display to the RBAs shown in the Locks Display.

The User Display. The User Display for one, all currently active, or a range of processes, can be invoked by entering any of the following:

U
U *<pid>*
U *<first_pid>* *<last_pid>*

where *pid* = process identification.

The information displayed varies slightly for each of the background processes, ARH, BIW, BWR, and CLN, but includes the following counters:

Log reads	The number of logical blocks read from the blocks found in the cache buffer pool.
Phy reads	The number of physical disk blocks read.
Log writes	The number of modifications to cache buffer blocks.
Phy writes	The number of physical disk blocks written. This value will always be zero except for BWR.
DML commits	The number of data manipulation commits.
DML rollbacks	The number of data manipulation rollbacks.
DDL commits	The number of Data Dictionary commits.

DDL rollbacks	The number of Data Dictionary rollbacks.
Deadlocks	The number of deadlocks detected system-wide.
Timeouts	The number of posts received while a process was waiting for resources; a high number does not indicate a problem.
DeadT	A counter indicating the number of times a routine wanted to do deadlock detection while it was performing a rollback. Processes do not do deadlock detection during rollbacks because they do not require additional enqueues. Therefore it is rare that DeadT is incremented. However, if a process doesn't release a lock needed by the process doing a rollback, then DeadT could steadily increase.
current operation	The operation currently being performed by *ORACLE* for this process. It may differ from the statement invoked by the user, e.g., a user doing a DROP TABLE might show a current operation of DELETE because the rows must be deleted before dropping the table.
User cursors	The number of currently open cursors invoked explicitly by this process.
ORACLE cursors	The number of recursive cursors currently opened on behalf of this process by *ORACLE*. Recursive cursors are cursors which *ORACLE* opens for administering the database, e.g., to update the Data Dictionary as tables or users are added or dropped.

The display also shows "cleanups tried" and "cleanups succeeded." If the value for "cleanups tried" does not equal the value for "cleanups succeeded" after a few cycles through the screen, you should perform an IOR SHUT or CLEAR and an IOR WARM.

5.5 AFTER IMAGE JOURNALING (AIJ)

After Image Journaling (AIJ) provides for recovery of a database after a failure such as a head crash on the disk drive(s) containing the database. Applying the Journal is called a *roll forward recovery*. The journal is a physical record of all changes to the database that can be applied to a backup copy to produce an exact copy of the lost data.

Before you use AIJ, you must:

- Periodically back up your valid copies of the database. This backup should consist of image copies of all the database files and the Before Image files.
- Discard any journal file generated prior to the backup.
- Include the appropriate parameters in the INIT.ORA file. (See Appendix B for a listing of these parameters.)

5.5.1 What AIJ Does

AIJ is a set of sequential disk files written one at a time. As it grows and a journal file is filled, the next file is opened for writing. If the database is heavily modified, as for example, if many DML statements are written, the AIJ can grow large. For this reason, each filled journal file is usually copied to tape to make room for further journaling. This can be done in the background by the operator or by a user-written procedure, so that *ORACLE* may run continuously. The journal may be a fixed set of preallocated files, or a series of files of a specified size created by *ORACLE*.

To be sure that journal files are applied in the same order in which they were written, a sequence number is written into the header of each journal file. AIJ will check the header of each journal file before applying it. The journal sequence number is stored in the database, and will start at 1 when you give the IOR I command to initialize the database. From then on, each subsequent journal file will use the next higher number. The sequence number is never reset during operation. The only time the sequence may be altered is by the AIJ utility during a roll forward recovery. In this case, the sequence will resume after the last journal file applied by the AIJ program.

After a system failure, the AIJ is applied to a valid backup copy of the database. To apply the journal, you must use the stand-alone AIJ utility before *ORACLE* is restored. The AIJ will read each file in the journal and update the database with any blocks that were part of committed transactions. Any outstanding transactions at the time of the failure will be ignored. When the journal application is complete, and the Before Image file is cleared, *ORACLE* may be restarted.

5.5.2 Enabling AIJ

To enable AIJ, do the following:

1. Add the AFTER_IMAGE parameter line to the INIT.ORA parameter file.

2. You may adjust the INIT.ORA parameter AI_WARN_PCNT if you wish.

3. Include the INIT.ORA parameter FILE_SIZE if you are using dynamic journal file creation.

4. Back up the database. It must have been shut down cleanly; if not, warm-start it and shut it down before backing it up.

5. Warm-start *ORACLE*. Journal writing begins with the first empty file in the journal file list. After that, a new file is opened whenever the current file is full, or a journal write error occurs, or *ORACLE* is restarted.

As each journal file is opened, a message to the operator console indicates the start of a new journal file. Journaling remains active until *ORACLE* is restarted with journaling disabled or a fatal journal-writing error occurs, such as an out-of-space condition.

There are two ways to create the journal. In the first, the journal is written to a fixed set of preallocated files. When each of these files is filled, the operator or a background process must copy it to tape and refresh it using:

```
AIJ INITIALIZE=fn
```

The file can then be reused by AIJ. *ORACLE* goes through the list of files specified by the AFTER_IMAGE parameter line(s) in a circular pattern. If that file has not yet been refreshed, *ORACLE* will keep trying the next file until it finds one, or until it makes the complete cycle with no success. In this case, journaling is aborted.

In the second way, journal files are created dynamically by *ORACLE*. The size of each file is specified by the AI_FILE_SIZE parameter. *ORACLE* uses the directories or files specified in the journal file list sequentially. This way of creating the journal cannot be used on operating systems that do not support this type of file allocation (IBM VM/CMS does not).

5.5.3 Journaling and the INIT.ORA Parameters

There are three INIT.ORA parameters that relate to AIJ:

```
AFTER_IMAGE
AI_FILE_SIZE
AI_WARN_PCNT
```

To enable journaling, the AFTER_IMAGE parameter must be present in INIT.ORA, and it must list one or more journal filenames. This list can be in any one of several forms, the simplest being a list of filenames separated by commas. If the first letter of the first filename is not alphanumeric, then it is used instead of a comma between the rest of the filenames. This provides for the situation where filenames have embedded commas.

If the list of filenames exceeds one line, you can use multiple AFTER_IMAGE lines as long as these lines immediately follow each other.

The following four examples show different ways of specifying the same list of journal files:

1.	AFTER_IMAGE	FILENAME1,FILENAME2,FILENAME3
2.	AFTER_IMAGE	\ FILENAME1 \ FILENAME2 \ FILENAME3
3.	AFTER_IMAGE	\ FILENAME1 \ FILE NAME2 \ FILENAME3
4.	AFTER_IMAGE AFTER_IMAGE AFTER_IMAGE	,FILENAME1 ,FILENAME2 ,FILENAME3

The AI_FILE_SIZE parameter can be used only on systems supporting dynamic file allocation. When it is used, *ORACLE* creates the journal files and sets their size in *ORACLE* blocks. To set the size for dynamically created journal files to be 4000 *ORACLE* blocks, for example, just fill in the number of blocks after the parameter:

```
AI_FILE_SIZE  4000
```

To avoid conflict, journal files are given unique names derived from the journal sequence number and name given in the AFTER_IMAGE parameter line. Journal file names are in the form:

SQN*nnnnnn*.AIJ

where *nnnnnn* is a six-digit number between 000001 and 999999. *ORACLE* creates these dynamic files in the directory(s) specified by the AFTER_IMAGE parameter line(s). Directories are used in the order they appear in the AFTER_IMAGE lines.

The parameter AI_WARN_PCNT specifies the point where *ORACLE* sends a message to the operator console advising that the current journal file is getting full. The message is the percentage of space used. To set this percentage at 80 percent, for example, just fill in that number after the parameter name:

```
AI_WARN_PCNT  80
```

5.5.4 The AIJ Command and Parameters

AIJ operation may be modified by several command line parameters, some of which can be passed on the command line, some read from the IOR parameter file, and some answered at the terminal. The syntax for AIJ is:

AIJ [*parameter1*] [*parameter2*] [*parameter3*]

All parameters are optional, and they are separated by a space, not by a comma. These parameters are named and described in Table 5-3.

5.5.5 Applying the After Image Files and Invoking AIJ

AIJ must never be run unless *ORACLE* is shut down.

Journal files are processed in two passes. The first pass collects statistics and builds a list of noncommitted transactions and eliminates them from the journal application. The second pass modifies the database, applying all blocks remaining after Pass One.

After checking the AIJ parameters, AIJ opens the primary database file and displays the names of the extents (but this does not happen if NO_APPLY was specified on the command line).

Next, AIJ performs Pass One on the journal files, requesting the name of each successive journal file and scanning for uncommitted transactions. After reading the last file, you will see a filename prompt. You should enter an empty line to end Pass One. AIJ then displays a summary of the data found in the journal, including a list of transactions that were never completed. Each uncompleted transaction is on a single line showing the transaction ID (*tid*) and the journal block number of the first and last block seen for the transaction. The journal block number is the journal sequence number and the block number within that file.

AIJ does not continue if there were no completed transactions, or if the NO_APPLY option was specified on the command line. Otherwise, at this point it goes on to Pass Two and opens all database extents. Then the entire journal is reread using the same filenames given in Pass One, and the database is updated with the journal blocks containing committed transactions (Pass Two may take a while). As in Pass One, the name of each journal file is displayed when processing begins on the file. When processing is complete, AIJ displays the number of *ORACLE* blocks in the file which were actually applied.

After all journal files have been processed, the journal sequence number is updated in the database. AIJ then closes the database extent files and terminates with a completion message.

Table 5-3. Names and Descriptions of AIJ Parameters.

Name	Description
DATABASE=*filespec*	Name of the primary database file. If not specified, AIJ looks in the IOR parameter file for the matching parameter (see PFILE).
DEBUG={1|2|3}	Used only for debugging or reporting detailed statistics, this parameter controls the amount of information output to the terminal about the journal blocks being read. Normally omitted. 1 means only display commits and rollbacks. 2 means a line for each journal block. 3 means continue past certain fatal errors.
FIRST_SQN=*nnnnnn*	Journal sequence number of the first journal file to apply (a number between 1 and 999999, inclusive). It must identify the first journal file created after the database backup occurred. If not specified, AIJ uses the sequence number found in the database. This parameter should normally be omitted. If incorrectly specified, it may damage the database.
INITIALIZE=*filespec*	Used to refresh an AIJ journal file which has been filled and copied to tape. This option initializes the specified file so that it may be reused by AIJ.
NO_APPLY	The presence of this parameter inhibits the second pass of AIJ, when the journal is actually applied. It can be used if you wish to simply gather statistics on the journal and database activity.
PFILE=*filespec*	Alternate IOR parameter file in which to search for the DATABASE parameters. Ignored if both are specified on the command line. If not specified, default is INIT.ORA.
UNTIL=*timespec*	Date and time up to which to apply the journal. All transactions committed after this time are ignored. Format of the time specification is: *mm/dd/yy-hh:mm:ss.mmm* millisec (0-999) seconds (0-59) minutes (0-59) hours (0-23) year (0-99) day (0-31) month (0-12)

5.5.6 Messages Returned to the Operator's Console

There are a number of errors that may occur during journaling. For a complete list of the error messages, their interpretation, and the effects of these errors, refer to the documentation supplied with your specific installation.

5.6 THE SYSTEM GLOBAL INFORMATION (SGI) UTILITY

With the System Global Information (SGI) utility, the DBA can test the size of the SGA generated by different parameter files. In the SGI display, the size is broken down according to fixed data and variable data. The SGA required size differs according to the settings for the different parameters.

The syntax to invoke SGI is:

SGI [PFILE=*parameter_file*] [LIST] [DETAIL]

where:

parameter_file	is the name of a parameter file for an *ORACLE* system. If not specified, INIT.ORA is assumed. If a file other than INIT.ORA is specified, its contents should be in the same format as INIT.ORA.
LIST	displays the settings in effect for the parameter file (specified or assumed). This display is the same as that resulting from IOR LIST. Either the distributed value for each parameter or the value indicated in the specified parameter file appears. (Values from the parameter file are marked with an asterisk.)
DETAIL	displays the total size, in bytes, that specific parameters or groups of parameters require.

The default listing from SGI gives the name of the parameter file and a summary of the bytes used in the SGA.

SGI's DETAIL option breaks down the total SGA size into bytes required by specific parameters. However, caution is advised in drawing conclusions about the number of bytes required by each parameter: The number of bytes required varies by operating system, and some sizes include an overhead number of bytes per parameter. (Dividing total size by number of units thus will give the wrong unit size.)

Despite the fact that you cannot easily determine the unit size of a parameter, the SGI DETAIL option will allow you to see which parameters have more effect on SGA size. This relative information will allow you to have somewhat better control over the eventual size.

5.7 AUDITING

In Version 5.0, new auditing features are introduced that are not contained in prior versions of *ORACLE*. The following description of the auditing facility is based on Version 5.0.

By using auditing, the DBA can monitor user activity on the *ORACLE* database. Any user who owns a table or view also can use auditing to monitor the successful or unsuccessful use of his data objects by other users.

5.7.1 Enabling Auditing

Auditing is not automatic; it must be enabled. This must be done when the system is started during an IOR INIT or IOR WARM, as follows:

1. Set the parameter AUDIT_TRAIL in the INIT.ORA parameter file to a nonzero integer (zero turns auditing off).
2. Warm-start the *ORACLE* system using the edited INIT.ORA file.

After steps 1 and 2 above, the DBA and other users can use the SQL AUDIT statements to choose which actions to audit.

The descriptions of audited operations are written to the Data Dictionary audit trail table, SYS.AUDIT_TRAIL. This table can be used like any other table. It is discussed under Section 5.7.3 below.

5.7.2 Monitoring Audit Activity

Once auditing is enabled, any user who owns a table or view may use it to:

- Choose auditing options by using SQL statements.
- Audit successful/unsuccessful attempts to access his tables or views.
- Select specific types of SQL operations to audit, such as DELETE only, SELECT only, or INSERT, UPDATE only.
- Control the level of detail recorded in the audit trail (SYS.AUDIT_TRAIL).

The DBA may use auditing for all the purposes listed above, and in addition he may use auditing to:

- Monitor successful/unsuccessful attempts to log on or off *ORACLE*.
- Monitor successful/unsuccessful attempts to GRANT or REVOKE privileges.
- Enable or disable writing to the audit trail table (SYS.AUDIT_TRAIL).
- Set default auditing options for database tables.

5.7.3 The Audit Trail Table SYS.AUDIT_TRAIL

The audit trail table, SYS.AUDIT_TRAIL, gives descriptions of all audited operations. It is in the Data Dictionary, and can be queried like any other table.

To enable auditing, the parameter AUDIT_TRAIL in the INIT.ORA parameter file must be set to a nonzero integer. Then warm-start the system using the INIT.ORA file.

5.7.4 Auditing Tables and Views

For any given table, view or synonym, the only users who can enter an AUDIT command are the object's owner and the DBA. The syntax of the AUDIT command is:

```
AUDIT { <t_option> [, <t_option>] | ALL }
ON { <tablename| DEFAULT }
[ BY { ACCESS|SESSION } ]
[ WHENEVER [ NOT ] SUCCESSFUL ]
```

where <t_option> is:

```
ALTER | AUDIT | COMMENT | DELETE | GRANT | INDEX
INSERT | LOCK | RENAME | SELECT | UPDATE
```

where the grant option means that both the GRANT and REVOKE statements on the giv-
en table should be audited; where *tablename* is the name of a view, base table, or synonym
denoting a view or base table; and where ALL means all options applicable on the
tablename. For example:

```
AUDIT ALTER, RENAME, UPDATE ON JONES.EMPLOYEE
    WHENEVER SUCCESSFUL;
```

For base tables, all auditing options apply. For views, the options that apply are
AUDIT, COMMENT, INSERT, DELETE, GRANT, LOCK, RENAME, SELECT, and
UPDATE.

The BY clause determines how often (and how many) rows are written to the audit
trail. This is necessary because some operations, such as DML commands, occur much
more frequently than others, such as GRANTs. The BY options are:

BY SESSION—A missing BY clause is equivalent to BY SESSION.

BY ACCESS—Each operation specified is audited by inserting one or more rows
in the audit trail. For a DML operation, all audit trail rows are written or updated
at the completion of the operation's parse phase.

WHENEVER SUCCESSFUL—means that each operation specified should be
audited only when it is successfully completed.

WHENEVER NOT SUCCESSFUL—means that each operation specified should
be audited only if it does not successfully complete.

If you do not include a WHENEVER clause, both successful and unsuccessful completions
will be audited.

The NOAUDIT statement specifies which options on a table no longer should be
audited. This statement's syntax is like that of the AUDIT statement except that it has
no BY clause. The designated activity is terminated regardless of whether it is BY ACCESS
or BY SESSION.

```
NOAUDIT { <t_option> [, <t_option>] . . . | ALL }
    ON { <tablename> | DEFAULT }
    [ WHENEVER [NOT] SUCCESSFUL ]
```

5.7.5 System Auditing Options

Levels of auditing can also be specified for DBA operations and other operations that
do not apply to database tables. The same AUDIT statement is used to specify these system
auditing options:

```
AUDIT { <s_option> [, <s_option>] . . . | ALL }
    [ WHENEVER [NOT] SUCCESSFUL ]
```

where *<s_option>* is:

```
CONNECT | DBA | NOT EXISTS | RESOURCE
```

For example:

```
AUDIT CONNECT, DBA WHENEVER SUCCESSFUL
```

The main difference between the table AUDIT and the system AUDIT statements is in the operations that are audited. In the system AUDIT statements, each option defines a class of database operations:

CONNECT—means *ORACLE* logon and logoff.

DBA—means system-wide GRANT, REVOKE, AUDIT and NOAUDIT statements; CREATE/ALTER PARTITION; CREATE/DROP [PUBLIC] SYNONYM.

NOT EXISTS—means all references to objects which result in the ''. . . does not exist'' error message. This does not include security violation errors even though such errors appear the same to the user.

RESOURCE—means CREATE/DROP TABLE, VIEW, SPACE, SYNONYM CREATE/ALTER/DROP CLUSTER;

The system NOAUDIT statement specifies which system operations should no longer be audited. Its syntax is the same as that of the AUDIT statement.

5.7.6 Auditing the Data Dictionary

The Data Dictionary contains several tables relating to auditing. To see them, enter:

```
SELECT * FROM DTAB WHERE TNAME LIKE '%AUDIT%';
```

This will produce the list shown in Table 5-4.

The table AUDIT_ACTIONS lists all possible actions that can be audited along with their numeric codes. The code rather than the action name is used in the other tables that record auditing information.

To see what your current auditing settings are, SELECT the dictionary table TABLE_AUDIT. To see what entries your auditing settings have produced, select the AUDIT_TRAIL table. To see what options you have chosen for your own tables, you can use a query like:

```
SELECT *
FROM TABLE_AUDIT
WHERE CREATOR = 'my_name';
```

And to see what system auditing options are in effect, refer to (if you are a DBA) the SYSTEM_AUDIT table.

Table 5-4. Data Dictionary Tables Related to Auditing.

Table Name	Description
AUDIT_ACCESS	Audit entries for access to user's table/views; DBA sees all.
AUDIT_ACTIONS	Maps auditing action numbers to action names.
AUDIT_CONNECT	Audit trail entries for user logon/logoff.
AUDIT_DBA	AUDIT trail entries for DBA activities; for DBA use only.
AUDIT_EXISTS	Audit trail entries for objects which do NOT EXIST; DBAs only.
AUDIT_TRAIL	Audit trail entries relevant to user (DBA sees all).
DEFAULT_AUDIT	Default table auditing options.
SYSAUDIT_TRAIL	Synonym for sys.audit_trail; for DBA use only.
SYSTEM_AUDIT	System auditing options; for DBA use only.
TABLE_AUDIT	Auditing options of user's tables and views; DBA sees all.

5.7.7 The USERENV Function

The USERENV is used to insert records into the audit trail. This allows you to obtain information about a specific *ORACLE* session. USERENV takes a literal string as a parameter, and returns a string or number as its value, depending on its parameter.

The syntax for invoking USERENV is:

```
SELECT USERENV('TERMINAL'), USERENV('SESSIONID'),
   USERENV('ENTRYID')
FROM DUMMY
WHERE ROWNUM <2;
```

TERMINAL means the operating system terminal identifier. This is returned whether or not auditing is enabled via the INIT.ORA. Specification of the terminal ID will vary with the operating system. SESSIONID means user auditing session identifier. This is only returned if auditing is enabled via INIT.ORA. Finally, ENTRYID means the next available audit_trail table entry number for the current session. This is only returned if auditing is enabled via INIT.ORA.

The USERENV can be used to add a comment row to the audit trail. It can also be used for constructing views that restrict access to users logged into certain physical terminals.

Chapter 6

Space Projections
and Allocation

THIS CHAPTER IS INTENDED CHIEFLY FOR THE DATABASE ADMINISTRATOR (DBA), BUT also will be useful for other primary users of the database. It explains how data are stored, starting with the general picture of the database and proceeding down to storage of specific types of data.

6.1 THE DATABASE FILE

Every database consists of at least one partition, the SYSTEM partition. Other partitions may be added and may be named according to the user's choice. In a newly installed database, the file named in the INIT.ORA file under the DATABASE parameter will be the SYSTEM partition.

A *partition* is a logical unit containing at least one file. Files can be added to a partition as required. The maximum number of files per database (total of all files in all partitions) is system-dependent. These may reside anywhere in the operating system. Refer to the *Installation and User's Guide* for your operating system to find the maximum for your operation.

A single partition may contain many tables. A table may span any number or all of the files in a partition, but a table cannot span partitions. To use any partition other than SYSTEM, a table must be created in that partition. An index is stored in the same partition as the table for which it was created.

6.2 THE SYSTEM PARTITION

The DBA can add files to the SYSTEM partition at any time. Initially, the following items reside in the SYSTEM partition:

- Data Dictionary tables
- Temporary tables
- Online help tables, if loaded (approximately 250 *ORACLE* blocks)

With careful customizing, a user can install a system where the listed items do not reside in the SYSTEM partition.

When estimating the size of the SYSTEM partition file, you must allow room for the above items, as well as any user data that will be entered.

Partitions and files must not be dropped. They can, however, be added by persons with DBA authority. In *SQL*Plus* they are added with a SQL statement. To add a file to the SYSTEM partition, you only need enter:

```
ALTER PARTITION system_partition_name
ADD FILE filename
```

because the SYSTEM partition is already created.

To add a file to a new partition, you must first create the partition by entering:

```
CREATE PARTITION partition_name
```

Then, since a partition is merely a logical entity, you must immediately add a file to it by entering:

```
ALTER PARTITION partition_name
ADD FILE filename
```

The specification of the filename is system-dependent. See the *Installation and User's Guide* for your system to determine the exact file specification.

Spelling of the filename is important. If *ORACLE* doesn't find the exact filename at the next warm start, the following error message will appear:

```
UNRECOVERABLE RECURSION ERROR
```

If this occurs, the database must be reinitialized. Oracle Corporation recommends that you do a full database file backup or export before adding a partition.

If you are running a shared-partition system (e.g., *ORACLE* instances on a VAX Cluster) then you must start the database without the SHARED option before adding or altering a partition. After adding or altering a partition, restart *ORACLE* by entering:

```
IOR WARM SHARED
```

Do not add the same file twice.

6.3 THE CREATE CONTIGUOUS FILE (CCF) UTILITY

The CCF exists for certain operating systems to "clean out" and allocate blocks for Database and Before Image files. (See Chapter 5 for a discussion of Before Image files.) If your system has it, you should use CCF for every file to be used in *ORACLE* before naming it in the INIT.ORA file or adding it to a partition. Use CCF only to create new files, not to work on existing files. The CCF syntax is:

CCF *filename, size*

where *filename* is the file's name (this may be a logical assignment on operating systems supporting logicals), and *size* is the number of *ORACLE* (512-byte) blocks to be allocated.

6.4 AVAILABLE SPACE IN PARTITIONS

When a partition fills up, you will see:

OUT OF SPACE IN PARTITION

There are two queries a DBA can use to find out the current use of space in the database. One query the DBA may use is:

```
SELECT SPM$ PID, SPM$ ENDBLOCK — SPM$ STARTBLOCK + 1
FROM   SYS.SPACEMAP
```

This will show the partition ID numbers (the SYSTEM partition is number 1) and the number of free blocks between the startblock and endblock (i.e., in each set of contiguous free blocks).

The response the DBA will receive from *ORACLE* will look like this:

SPM$ PID	SPM$ ENDBLOCK−SPM$ STARTBLOCK+1
1	1800
1	295
1	68
1	120

By adding all the numbers of free blocks in all partitions, you will get the total number of free blocks.

The second query the DBA can use is:

```
SELECT AVG(SPM$ ENDBLOCK — SPM$ STARTBLOCK + 1) "AVERAGE"
       MIN(SPM$ ENDBLOCK — SPM$ STARTBLOCK + 1) "MINIMUM"
       MAX(SPM$ ENDBLOCK — SPM$ STARTBLOCK + 1) "MAXIMUM"
       COUNT (*) "HOWMANY", SPM$ PID "PARTITION"
FROM   SYS.SPACEMAP
GROUP BY SPM$ PID;
```

This query will show the average size of space available by partition. The units are blocks. The response the DBA will receive from *ORACLE* will be in this form:

AVERAGE	MINIMUM	MAXIMUM	HOWMANY	PARTITION
1650	1	4758	3	1

Too little total space (for your installation) means that you need to add a file to the database or store some tables offline till you need them again. (But keep in mind that when you do bring these tables back in, you may need to add space.)

A few large sets of free blocks are preferable to many small sets. A database with many small sets of free blocks is said to be *fragmented*. This condition usually means that it is time to reorganize to make space for larger sets. You can do this by a full database export, respace, and import, or by selectively copying and dropping tables (or sending them to be archived).

6.5 SPACE DEFINITIONS OF TABLES

A table is the basic unit of data storage in your database. Each table is created with a name and a named set of columns. In addition to a name, each column must have a specified datatype and width.

When you create a table, *ORACLE* automatically reserves space for your later input of data into that table, as well as for its indexes. These two reserved spaces are called the table's *segments*. The initial size, and the later growth of the data and index segments, is controlled by the space definition you use in creating the table. The data and index segments consist of *extents* of data blocks.

These table space definitions give you control over a table's future use of database space and the maximum storage it can use. Space definitions also control the storage of a table into a specific partition. If you do not specify a space definition, then the table uses the default space definition built into *ORACLE*. The space limit applies to all table data and all indexes (not each index) created on that table.

Every table requires two data blocks and one index block of overhead. The first data block is the *extent block,* containing space information such as the start address of each extent currently used by the table, the last block, and how many blocks are in the extent. The start address of this first data block coincides with the TAB$RBA for that table's data.

The second data block duplicates Data Dictionary information such as definitions. Storing this information here avoids repeated use (and consequent locking) of the Data Dictionary for frequently used checks.

The index block of overhead is an extent block like the one described above for data.

Each column of a table has two bytes of overhead. One byte stores the column identification number. The second byte stores the number of bytes of column data. NULL columns do not require overhead, since no part of a NULL column is stored.

Each row of a table has at least four bytes of overhead. Two bytes store the row's total length and two bytes store the row sequence number, i.e., the order in which the row was inserted into the block. A row in a clustered block requires an additional byte of overhead to indicate the table number. This gives a row from a clustered block a total of five bytes. (The row sequence number is not the same as either the ROWID or the ROWNUM. The row sequence number is a part of the ROWID, but ROWID is not stored and may change over time. See Section 6.11 in this chapter for a discussion of ROWID. ROWNUM is a reserved keyword in SQL.)

The row sequence number is specific to the block. Each block has a row with a row sequence number of 1 unless the first row of that block has been deleted. There are no duplicate numbers within the same block, and once assigned to a row, the row sequence number for that row never changes. Row sequence numbers assigned in a block are never reused even if the row is deleted.

One space definition can be used by more than one table. The creation of the space definition is independent of the creation of the table. To create both at once, name the space definition when you issue the CREATE TABLE command, as in:

```
CREATE TABLE SUPPLIERS (CITY CHAR(25), STATE CHAR(20))
SPACE smallspace;
```

where *smallspace* is an existing space definition. The default space definition values are shown in Table 6-1, and the descriptions of the parameters of a space definition are shown in Table 6-2.

For example, when a table is created using the default space definition, five blocks are set aside for the table's data, and five for its indexes (See the parameters INITIAL under DATAPAGES and INDEXPAGES in Table 6-1.) When the number of rows has grown so that these five blocks are occupied, the extent allocates 25 more blocks to the table (See the parameter INCREMENT under DATAPAGES in Table 6-1)

6.5.1 Listing Current Space Definitions

Any user may query the Data Dictionary to see what space definitions are currently defined. These definitions are in the view SPACES. There should always be at least one definition there, called TEMPTABLE.

6.5.2 The Space Definition TEMPTABLE

Your system is initialized with a default space definition for temporary tables. These are contained in the view SPACES under TEMPTABLE.

By default, temporary tables are in the SYSTEM partition. The space definition for TEMPTABLE can be changed to increase or decrease space allocations or to put it in

Space Definition	Default Value
DATAPAGES*	INITIAL 5 INCREMENT 25 MAXEXTENTS 9999 PCTFREE 20
INDEXPAGES**	INITIAL 5 INCREMENT 25 MAXEXTENTS 9999
PARTITION	SYSTEM

Table 6-1. Default Space Definition Values.

* The blocks making up the data segment.
** The blocks making up the index segment.

Table 6-2. Descriptions of Parameters of a Space Definition.

Parameter	Description
INITIAL	Number of blocks in the first allocation of blocks. Made for data and indexes separately. At time of table creation enough contiguous blocks must be free for both allocations. Minimum allowed for both data and index initial extents is three blocks.
INCREMENT	After the blocks in the initial extents are filled, and when user data or indexes require more space, another set of blocks is allocated. INCREMENT determines how many more blocks will be allocated.
MAXEXTENTS	Indicates how many times *ORACLE* can allocate an incremental extent. MAXEXTENTS should be set very high unless you really want to impose a limit. Increasing MAXEXTENTS after it has been set, is arduous. While default is 9999, the actual maximum is operating system-dependent. (On VAX/VMS the maximum is about 475 extents; on MS-DOS it is about 110). Refer to your *Installation and User's Guide* to find your system's maximum. Default maximum is set at 9999 so that if tables and data are exported from one system and imported to another, the maximum number of extents is not held to the lower limit of the two systems.
PCTFREE	Indicates what percent of the logical block size (minus 32 bytes of physical overhead) will be reserved for updates made to the data. The minimum PCTFREE parameter is 1; maximum is 99.
PARTITION	To specify that the table use any other than SYSTEM the alternate partition's name must be specified here.

a different partition, but it should *never* be dropped. If TEMPTABLE should be dropped, errors would occur in response to queries requiring the creation of temporary tables. Temporary tables are discussed further in Section 6.13 in this chapter.

Only a DBA can drop or alter the TEMPTABLE definition.

6.5.3 How to Create a Space Definition

Any user with at least RESOURCE privilege may create a space definition. The syntax is:

```
CREATE SPACE [DEFINITION] space_name
   DATAPAGES (INITIAL n,
      INCREMENT n,
      MAXEXTENTS n,
      PCTFREE n)
   INDEXPAGES (INITIAL n,
```

INCREMENT *n,*
MAXEXTENTS *n*)
PARTITION *partition_name;*

You may choose any name for a space definition, but it might be most useful to associate it with the table for which it is to be used.

You do not need to specify every parameter under DATAPAGES or INDEXPAGES; any parameters left blank will be defined as the default value shown in Table 6-1. If you leave the PARTITION blank it will be the default, which is the SYSTEM partition.

The creation of the space definition does not allocate any space. Space is allocated when a table or cluster is created, and then it is allocated according to the space definition for that table or cluster. In general:

1. Fewer large extents are preferable to many small extents.

2. Updates can widen rows. If some columns are left NULL, updating will increase the space because NULLs take no space. Therefore, the PCTFREE parameter should take this into consideration.

3. The MAXEXTENTS parameter should not be specified unless there is some good reason for setting a ceiling on the amount of space a table can use.

4. Enough logically contiguous blocks must be allowed so that the initial data and index extent can be formed when the table is created. Logically contiguous blocks will also be needed for incremental data or index blocks.

6.5.4 Determining the Number of Data Segments

There is a general formula recommended by Oracle Corporation for estimating the initial number of data blocks in the space definition of a single unclustered table. It makes use of the following variables:

INPUT:

R	Number of rows in the table
C_i	Average length of *i*th item
N_i	Fraction of *i*th column with NULL value
F	Percent free in each block (PCTFREE parameter)

ORACLE-SPECIFIC (based on operating system and *ORACLE* version):

K	Column length indicator	(VAX=1)
I	Column ID number	(VAX=1)
L	Row length	(VAX=2)
Q	Row sequence number	(VAX=2)
S	*ORACLE* logical block size	(VAX=2048,VM=4096)
H	*ORACLE* header info per block	(VAX=76)

CALCULATED RESULTS:

BR	Average number of bytes per row

RB   Average number of rows per ORACLE BLOCK
SUMi Sum taken over all values of i
B   *ORACLE* logical blocks required for table

The formula is computed as follows. First, calculate the average bytes per row:

$$BR = SUM i \; [(1 - Ni) * (Ci + K + 1)] + L + Q$$

Second, calculate the average rows per block:

$$RB = \text{integer portion of } \frac{(1-F) * (S-H)}{BR}$$

Third, calculate the number of blocks (Use B as the INITIAL parameter for DATAPAGES):

$$B = \frac{R}{RB}$$

6.5.5 Calculating the Number of Index Segments

Calculating the space required for indexes is difficult. It is dependent on:

- The number of distinct values in the indexed column(s).
- How different one value is from the next.
- How many columns are indexed.
- The length of the indexed columns.
- The percent of NULLs.
- Whether the index is created compressed or noncompressed.
- Whether the index is created before or after the table's data are loaded.

A rule of thumb is that about 20-30 percent of the space necessary for the table is required for indexes.

The formula used to estimate the number of blocks needed for indexes uses the following variables:

R   Number of rows in the table
S   Block size for your machine (usually 2048 or 4096)
H   Header bytes per block (usually 76)
KL   Estimated key length:

> = 10 for compressed indexes
> = 16 + (number of columns in key) + (sum of lengths of columns in key)

The formula is:

$$B = 1.1 * \frac{R}{\left(\dfrac{(S - H) * .75}{KL} \right)}$$

70

The .75 is the approximate percentage of an index block in use. This factor also assumes a PCTFREE of 25. If you are calculating the blocks for an existing table created with the default space definition, use .80 instead of .75.

6.5.6 Calculating Space Requirements for Clusters

(For a complete discussion of clusters, see Section 13.3 in Chapter 13.)

Allow, if possible, one logical cluster block for each unique cluster key. If more data are associated with the key than will fit in one logical block, additional data will be placed in chained blocks, which may defeat the purpose of clustering.

PCTFREE is meaningless for clusters. Index segments for clusters should be allocated so that they contain all indexes for all tables in the cluster, as well as the cluster key.

6.6 LOGICAL FORMAT OF DATA BLOCKS

Each data block has its own overhead, which includes pointers to chained blocks and a time stamp indicating when the block was last used.

The size of an *ORACLE* logical block is dependent on your operating system. On many systems it is either 2048 bytes or 4096 bytes; on some others it is 1024 bytes. *ORACLE* requires 76 bytes of block overhead; 44 bytes are used for the header of the *physical data block*, and 32 bytes for the header of the *logical data block*.

There may be several logical cluster blocks per physical block. If there are two logical blocks per physical block, the overhead is 108 bytes per physical block (44 + 32 + 32), and so on.

6.7 HOW SPACE IS USED

When a table is created, space is immediately allocated for the initial data and index segments. As rows are inserted in the table, they will fill the initial data extent. As indexes are created on the table, these will fill the initial index extent. Three Data Manipulation Language (DML) operations affect data in the data blocks: (DML commands are discussed in detail in Chapter 10.)

INSERT
UPDATE
DELETE

These DML commands also affect the index blocks because indexes must be updated continually to reflect new data. The first CREATE INDEX statement begins to fill the first index extent for that table. Succeeding CREATE INDEX statements will take up extents as they are needed. A DROP INDEX command will release index blocks which can then be used by other indexes on the same table.

6.7.1 Inserting Rows

Rows are inserted in a table in sequence. The first row is stored in the first block of the first extent. Succeeding rows are inserted in the first block until that extent is full. Only complete blocks are inserted in an extent; a row cannot span extents. Therefore, if a complete row or an updated row cannot fit into one extent, the entire row goes into the next extent.

Column data cannot span blocks either, except for LONG data.

The 2048 bytes (for most systems) of the *ORACLE* block, minus the overhead per data block (76 bytes for unclustered data blocks on most systems) and the PCTFREE specified in the space definition (default = 20 percent of the logical block size), constitute the initial space available.

When sufficient rows have been inserted to fill all blocks in the table's first extent, *ORACLE* allocates the first *incremental* extent. When insertions fill that extent, *ORACLE* will allocate the next data extent, and so forth.

Space reserved for updates by the PCTFREE parameter in the space definition is not available for insertion of new rows.

If a clustered block runs out of space during insertion of new rows with that cluster key, the new rows are written to a *chained block* (chained blocks are discussed in Section 6.8 below).

6.7.2 Updating

Updated data are written to the same block that contained the row before it was updated, using space in the following order:

1. Available space in the block including space reserved by PCTFREE.
2. Space in a block "chained" to the current block.

Data remaining in the data block are compressed as changes are made to the data values. This leaves free space at the end of the block. As rows are deleted or updated, row numbers may not remain in order. Depending on the sequence of insertions and deletions, rows with higher row sequence numbers may appear before rows with lower row sequence numbers.

6.8 CHAINED BLOCKS

A *chained block* is a physical block that is added to a logical block. One logical block may consist of multiple chained blocks. *ORACLE* keeps track of block addresses in the headers of the data blocks by noting the next block's address, the previous block's address (including chained blocks, if any), and the original data block address. The chained block may or may not be in the same extent as the other blocks.

Chained blocks are used to insert a row larger than an *ORACLE* block, update a row that cannot fit in the current data block, and to insert into clustered data that will not fit entirely in the logical block for that cluster key.

Retrieval of chained data is slower than searching for data which is physically sequential, so you should include an adequate amount of updating in your estimate of PCTFREE when you create the space definition. This is especially important when loading into a table where many columns are initially NULL, but will be filled in later.

If all data in a chained block are deleted, the chained block is then available for reuse by that table.

6.9 DELETIONS

If one row in a block is deleted, that space can then be used for updates to remaining rows. If all rows are deleted, the empty block may be reused by that table or cluster.

When a table or cluster definition is dropped, the data block defined on it is then returned for general use by the database.

6.10 REGAINING SPACE

Once an extent is allocated for use by a table's data or index, it will always appear in the Data Dictionary. It is not released until the table is dropped. If all rows of a table are deleted, however, then that block is available for reuse by the table or cluster. Also, if all data in an index block are deleted, the block remains allocated for indexes on that table until the table is dropped. If all data in chained blocks are deleted, then all chained blocks except for the header block become available for reuse.

Therefore, even though the view STORAGE may show all extents for a specific segment "in use," there still may be room to add more data because you cannot tell how full an extent is. It is only when a table is dropped, that all blocks become free space to be used by other tables or indexes.

6.11 ROW ADDRESSES: ROWID

The address of every row in the database is defined by the ROWID. That address can be retrieved in hexadecimal form by a SQL query using the reserved word ROWID. The information returned will locate the row by partition, by block, and by position of the row in the block.

ROWIDs are stored in a logical—not physical—column, which sometimes can be accessed like table columns, i.e., used in SELECT or WHERE clauses, but:

- A ROWID is not guaranteed to be constant for any row over time. The physical location of a row may change due to updating, or exporting and reimporting.
- A ROWID is not stored in the database. It can be referenced like other data, but it is not actually a column of data. Therefore, you cannot UPDATE, INSERT, or DELETE a ROWID.

The usefulness of a ROWID lies in the fact that:

- It is the fastest means of accessing a specified row.
- It can be used to determine how many blocks of storage a table requires.
- It can be used to obtain row-level locks.

6.12 USING A SPACE DEFINITION

If you want to associate a table with a space definition, name the space definition in the CREATE TABLE command as follows:

```
CREATE TABLE tablename (column1, column2)
SPACE spacename;
```

where *spacename* is an existing space definition.

If no space definition is named, the table will be placed in the default space definition. When this table is created, *ORACLE* allocates two separate sets of blocks for the table's DATAPAGES and INDEXES. As the table grows, it will follow space guidelines set by the space definition even if the definition is subsequently dropped or altered.

6.12.1 Specifying a Partition when Creating a Table

To specify a partition for a table other than the SYSTEM partition, you must first identify (CREATE if necessary) a space definition which specifies the desired PARTITION name. Then you use the SPACE option to name the space when the table is created.

The following example shows the creation of a new space definition INCOME, specifying the partition ACCOUNTING.

```
CREATE SPACE DEFINITION INCOME
    DATAPAGES  (INITIAL 200,
        INCREMENT 100,
        MAXEXTENTS 999,
        PCTFREE 25)
    INDEXPAGES  (INITIAL 80,
        INCREMENT 100,
        MAXEXTENTS 999,
        PCTFREE 25)
    PARTITION ACCOUNTING;
```

Now, we create a table SALES, using space INCOME, so that space will be allocated from the ACCOUNTING partition:

```
CREATE TABLE SALES (acct_no number, acct_name char (35))
SPACE INCOME;
```

6.12.2 Altering Space Definitions

If you change the allocation for an existing space definition, this will only impact tables created after the change. It will not affect tables created under the old space definition. You can change any parameter by specifying it in the command. Any parameter not specified stays unchanged. The syntax resembles that for CREATE SPACE DEFINITION.

```
ALTER SPACE spacename
    DATAPAGES (INITIAL n,
        INCREMENT n,
        MAXEXTENTS n,
        PCTFREE n)
    INDEXPAGES (INITIAL n,
        INCREMENT n,
        MAXEXTENTS n)
    PARTITION partition_name;
```

6.12.3 Dropping Space Definitions

Any user with at least RESOURCE privilege may drop a space definition. The syntax is:

DROP SPACE *space_name*;

Users can use or drop any definition except TEMPTABLE. Only the DBA can drop or alter the TEMPTABLE definition.

6.12.4 Exceeding Maximum Extents

If a table exceeds the maximum extents, you have several alternatives. (Altering the space definition will have no effect because the extents are already set for that table.) You may do any of the following:

1. (a) Create a table with the same structure, but give it a different name and a larger space.

   (b) Load the new table with the data from the table that has exceeded its space definition. To do this, use the following syntax:

   CREATE TABLE *temporary_table*
   AS SELECT * FROM *old_filled_tablename*
   SPACE *bigger_space*;

2. Drop the table that has run out of space.

3. RENAME the new table with the name of the table you dropped.

As an alternative, if space in the database is at a premium, you might want to take the following steps:

1. Export the table that has run out of space.
2. Drop the table's definition.
3. Create a space definition with higher limits or parameters.
4. Create the table specifying the new space definition.
5. Import the table, specifying IGNORE CREATE ERRORS (because the table will already exist when Import tries to create it.)

6.13 TEMPORARY TABLES

Your database often needs to create temporary tables to complete transactions. You will never directly see, create, or use this type of temporary table, but the following operations may require them.

- CREATE INDEX
- ORDER BY
- DISTINCT
- GROUP BY
- UNION, INTERSECT, or MINUS

- unindexed joins
- certain correlated subqueries

No temporary table is created by *ORACLE* if the sorting operation (such as ORDER BY) can be done in memory, or if the system optimizer finds some other way to perform the operation.

There are no temporary tables when a database is initialized or warm-started. As temporary tables become needed, *ORACLE* creates as many as necessary. After a statement no longer needs the temporary table, the temporary table becomes available for reuse by another statement.

An INIT.ORA parameter TEMP_TABLES determines the number of temporary tables maintained by *ORACLE* after a warm start. For example, if the parameter TEMP_TABLES is set to 20, but at some point 25 are in use, then the first 5 to become free will be dropped. Thus, *ORACLE* continues to maintain only 20, the amount set by the parameter.

Your system is initialized with a default space definition for all temporary tables. These can be seen in the view SPACES as the space definition named TEMPTABLE. Only users with DBA authority should create and/or modify temporary table space definitions. The syntax for the space definition for temporary tables is:

```
CREATE SPACE DEFINITION TEMPTABLE
    DATAPAGES  (INITIAL 20,
        INCREMENT 100,
        MAXEXTENTS 240,
        PCTFREE 1)
    INDEXPAGES  (INITIAL 20,
        INCREMENT 100,
        MAXEXTENTS 240)
    PARTITION SYSTEM;
```

Indexpages are defined, but they are not used for temporary tables. By default, temporary tables are created in the SYSTEM partition. The definition of temporary tables can be changed, but it should never be dropped.

Chapter 7

Loading and Moving Your Data

THIS CHAPTER DESCRIBES HOW THE TWO UTILITIES *ORACLE* DATA LOADER (ODL) AND Export/Import work. ODL is used to load data from operating system files into an *ORACLE* database. Export/Import moves data to and from *ORACLE* databases.

7.1 THE *ORACLE* DATA LOADER (ODL)

The *ORACLE* Data Loader (ODL) loads data records from external files into the *ORACLE* database. It will handle and understand most formats. The requirements for the raw data to be loaded are:

1. The file(s) may be in any record format defined by the operating system.
2. The records must be fixed-length except for the last column.
3. The last column in the record may be of variable length.
4. All columns of the table in the source record need not be loaded.

7.1.1 Invoking ODL

Any user with CONNECT access to the database can run ODL, but to load a specific table, he must also either own it or have been granted INSERT access to it by its owner.

All you need to do to invoke ODL is to enter the command ODL with the appropriate arguments. The information needed to execute ODL is specified on the command line.

ODL does not create any tables, so the tables to be loaded must already be in existence. ODL requires a minimum of two files: the ODL Control File and at least one data file. After ODL starts to run, it will create a Log File, and, if needed, a Bad File. These four files are explained in Sections 7.1.3, 7.1.4, 7.1.5, and 7.1.6 below.

ODL also requires the *ORACLE* username/password of the owner of the table (or synonym) that you intend to load. This is called a UID. ODL will prompt for this UID if it is not supplied on the command line.

7.1.2 ODL Command Line Options

Each of the command options takes an integer as an argument. The options are as follows:

B Indicates the number of bytes to be used for bind arrays and input buffers; default is 16K. You may want to increase this if you are loading very wide tables. The maximum number depends only on your equipment's available memory. You will use the letter B and a number to specify this option, e.g., [−B20].

C Is the instruction to commit after a specified number of records have been loaded. Default is to commit after every 100 records. You will use the letter C followed by a number to tell ODL to commit after every n records, like this: [−C100]. Use the following rule:

   $n > 0$ means commit after n successful inserts.
   $n = 0$ means commit only after the whole table is loaded.

E Tells ODL how many errors (i.e., bad records) to allow before ODL should stop loading data. Default is 50; that is, unless you specify otherwise, ODL will stop loading the data after encountering 50 errors. Use the letter E followed by a number, like this: E20. Use the following rule:

   $n > 0$ means to allow n errors before stopping
   $n = 0$ means load the data regardless of errors.

L Is the number of records that you want ODL to load (after skipping any that you specify with S—see below). If no L number is specified, ODL will continue loading until it gets to the end of the file. Follow the rule:

   $n > 0$ means load n records
   $n = 0$ means load the entire file (same as default).

S Is the number of records to be skipped before loading the remaining records in the data file. Default is to skip none.

The syntax for the ODL command that invokes all of these options looks like this:

   ODL *control_file log_file* [uid] [−B#] [−C#] [−E#] [−L#] [−S#]

For example:

   ODL eggcont.ct1 egglog.log john/denver −S25 −E10

This example will read the EGGCONT control file, and the EGGLOG file will contain information about the data to be loaded. ODL will skip 25 records before loading the rest of the records in the data file, and ODL will stop loading if it encounters 10 errors. Because the COMMIT option is not specified, a COMMIT will be performed after every 100 records by default.

7.1.3 The ODL Control File

The ODL Control File contains instructions for accomplishing the load-in. You must name the Control File in the ODL command. The Control File names the data file(s). *ORACLE* has no default for the file extension or file type of the control file; therefore

⌐name in the ODL command. The Control File must contain
ᵣent, the DEFINE SOURCE statement, and the FOR EACH
ed below.

⌐ Statement. The DEFINE RECORD statement describes
es. It must:

e loaded.
e record to be loaded.
with each field.
ᵒf each field in the record.

⌐ RECORD statement looks like this:

⌐name
l⌐type [,LOC (*field⌐loc*)])
⌐type [,LOC (*field⌐loc*)]);

name you give to your raw data records, and *field⌐name*
ᵥw data field. The *field⌐type* argument defines the data type
⌐GER or CHAR, along with the size in bytes enclosed in
⌐han defaults. The acceptable sizes and defaults are shown in
ᵐn is defined as NUMBER and the raw data field is the ASCII
ᵧ, then the data type should be CHAR. *ORACLE* handles the
ᵤat.

t is the position of the field in the raw data record, which must
ₑr) a minus number (− number), or a number without a plus
ⅼ in parentheses. The first position of each record is column
). A sign in front of the number indicates the position relative
A minus sign signifies a position toward the beginning of the
s a position toward the end of the record. An integer without
ⁱon from the beginning of the record. The default position is
end of the previous ᵣᵢₑₗᵤ ᵥr the beginning of the record for the first field. For example:

```
DEFINE RECORD REC1 AS
    FLD1 (CHAR (8)),
```

Table 7-1. Acceptable Machine Sizes and Defaults for Data Types.

Data Type	Sizes	Machine Defaults			
		RSX-11M	VAX/VMS	IBM/CMS	UNIX
FLOAT	8, 4	8	8		
INTEGER	4, 2, 1	2	4		
CHAR	1 through 240	1	1		

```
FLD2 (CHAR (16)),
FLD3 (FLOAT, LOC (−2));
```

The DEFINE SOURCE Statement. This statement defines the input media (e.g., file or tape) and the record contained within this source. The syntax is:

```
DEFINE SOURCE  src-name
    FROM  filename [, filename, . . . , filename]
    LENGTH  length
    CONTAINING  rec-name;
```

where *src-name* is a symbolic name used to identify the source, and *filename* is the filename of your operating system file containing the raw data. You may concatenate multiple files for input by listing the filenames separated by commas.

LENGTH is the raw data record length. You should specify the maximum record length; records longer than the length you specify will be truncated. ODL can handle variable length records as long as the last column is the one varying, or all columns after the variable column are NULL. Finally, *rec-name* is the name used to define the record in the DEFINE RECORD statement. For example,

```
DEFINE SOURCE SRC1
    FROM FILE1, FILE2
    LENGTH 80
    CONTAINING REC1;
```

The FOR EACH Statement. The FOR EACH statement reads each of your raw data records and inserts it into the table you specify. It is actually a standard SQL INSERT statement preceded by the phrase FOR EACH RECORD. The phrase NEXT RECORD is required at the end of the SQL statement to terminate the insert loop. It looks like this:

```
FOR EACH RECORD
INSERT INTO tablename (column__name, column__name . . .)
VALUES (fieldname, fieldname, . . .)
NEXT RECORD;
```

where *tablename* is a table or synonym you own.

Any of the following may be specified as data to be inserted:

1. The name of a field in a raw data file.
2. A character string.
3. A number consisting of either a string of digits or a special notation, such as a scientific or statistical notation.
4. NULL
5. The GENSEQ function which will generate a new integer for each record.

The format is:

```
GENSEQ(initial__value,increment__value)
```

For example:

> (GENSEQ(200,10), . . .)

which specifies that the first value is 200 and each succeeding value will be incremented by 10.

7.1.4 Raw Data Files

The raw data file (or files) contains the data that are to be loaded in. These files are named in the control file. The ODL will read the raw data, and load it into the *ORACLE* table named in the control file, using SQL INSERT statements.

One ODL control file can refer to one or more data files. Data files may be in any record format defined by the operating system, but must conform to the following:

1. Records can be fixed or variable length.

2. Each physical record in the file corresponds to a new logical record.

3. The first record that ODL is to read must be valid or ODL will terminate. In other words, if you tell ODL to skip the first 10 records, then the 11th record must be a valid one.

4. Each field in the record must be fixed length except the last field. The last field may be variable length, but if so, then data values must be padded with blanks before being inserted into the table.

5. Not all fields of the source record have to be loaded. Any columns may be skipped depending on the instructions in the control file.

6. Data columns of the source record need not correspond to the columns of the table, but they must correspond to the DEFINE RECORD and FOR EACH . . . INSERT statements in the control file.

7. The data types supported are character strings, binary integer numbers, and floating point numbers. Through Version 5.0, ODL will not accept packed decimal numbers.

Refer to the *ORACLE Installation and User's Guide* for your operating system for possible additional details about raw data files.

7.1.5 The Log File

While ODL is running, it will create a log file. It will then write into that log file the number of records read, loaded, or rejected, and the error messages it receives. You must specify the log file's name when you invoke ODL. There is no default file extension, or filetype, so you must explicitly designate one. But do not use a file extension or filetype of BAD because ODL automatically uses BAD as the extension or filetype of your bad filename.

All ODL messages are written to the log file. In addition, the following statistical messages will be written to the log file:

- Number of bytes allocated
- Number of records read
- Number of records skipped
- Number of records loaded
- Number of records rejected
- Number of errors

When an error occurs during record processing, it will produce the following message:

```
RECORD <#> REJECTED
```

where # is the relative number of the record being processed.

7.1.6 The Bad File

If the raw data file contains bad records (i.e., records with invalid data such as CHAR data to be loaded into a NUM column), ODL will put these into a Bad File and continue loading the records with valid data. A record is rejected when it does not correspond to the definitions in the control file. However, if the first record to be loaded is bad, ODL will terminate. The bad records in such a file can be corrected and loaded later.

The Bad File is named automatically by ODL. The letters BAD are attached as an extention or filetype to the name you give to your log file. For example, if you name your log file STATS, then ODL will name the Bad File STATS.BAD.

The number of bad records that ODL will tolerate is specified in the argument contained in the command line when ODL is invoked. (See Section 7.1.2 above.)

7.1.7 ODL Error Messages

Three different types of errors can occur during ODL processing. These are control statement errors, ODL fatal errors, and ORACLE errors. Each type is discussed below.

Control Statement Errors. The error messages in response to control file errors include information to help locate the error in the control file statement. Three different formats are used. Format 1 is:

```
<message> ON LINE # COLUMN #—
```

where the message will be one of the following:

```
Number too large
String too large
Bad number
Missing exponent
Identifier too large
Illegal character
Quoted literal not ended
```

Table 7-2. Control Statement Errors, Format Three.

Symbol	Message
<*rec_field*>	Field name is ambiguous.
<*rec_field*>	Field is improperly aligned.
<*rec_field*>	Inconsistent *rec_field* definition.
<*rec_field*>	Field location too negative.
<*rec_field*>	Bad location field expression.
<*rec_field*>	Inconsistent location field.
<*rec_field*>	Unsupported field length.
<*source*>	Source from clause is missing.
<*source*>	Source length clause missing.
<*source*>	Multiple sources not supported.
<*source*>	Bad source length clause.
<*rec_name*>	Record too large for source.
<*rec_name*>	Multiple records not supported.
<*table*>	Table col/field count mismatch.
<*table*>	Multiple tables not supported.
<*symbol*>	Not a record field.
<*symbol*>	Undefined record field.
<*symbol*>	Previously defined.
<*symbol*>	Record name expected.
<*symbol*>	Undefined record name.

Format is <*symbol*> : <*message*> ON OR ABOUT LINE _____

Format 2 is:

SYNTAX ERROR LINE # ON INPUT *symbol*—

where *symbol* identifies where the error was detected. Finally,
Format 3 is:

<*symbol*>: <*message*> ON OR ABOUT LINE #—

where <*symbol*> and <*message*> are as shown in Table 7-2.

Fatal Errors. Fatal errors occur because of an internal problem or because a resource, such as memory, is exhausted. The format is:

ODL FATAL ERROR : <*message*>

where <*message*> is

    Out of parse stack space
    Out of heap space
    Out of table space

For the messages "Out of heap space" and "Out of table space," the error can be corrected by linking ODL with more memory.

There is also a set of fatal messages which can occur if other errors exist before the fatal error. These are:

    excsub : invalid kind
    Illegal insert field definition
    defsyn : unknown type
    unreachable code - optional length
    unreachable code - default length

These will usually disappear when the original error is corrected.

ORACLE Error Messages. *ORACLE* error messages have the following format:

<call> ERROR : <message>

where *call* is the name of the *ORACLE* interface subroutine which failed, and *message* is the *ORACLE* error message as listed in the *ORACLE Error Messages and Codes Manual* included in the documentation you received with your software.

7.2 EXPORT AND IMPORT

The Export utility copies data in a database to a backup file. The Import utility restores exported data back into an *ORACLE* database. These two utilities can be used to:

1. Store *ORACLE* data (table definitions, table data, grants, synonyms, view definitions, indexes) in an operating system file independent of an *ORACLE* database.
2. Free space in the *ORACLE* database.
3. Store obsolete or temporary data.
4. Move data between *ORACLE* databases.
5. Convert data from ASCII to EBCDIC and vice versa.
6. Move data from an older *ORACLE* database to a newer version.
7. Move data from one owner to another.

Export files cannot be edited, however, nor used by ODL, *Pro*SQL*, or *Pro*ORACLE* programs due to the fact that they are stored in a special compressed format.

Only the DBA can export or import tables of data belonging to any user. Users other than the DBA may only export database objects that they own.

Both Export and Import attempt to continue after encountering an error. If an error occurs during inserting of a row in Import, the bad row is printed and the rest of the table

Table 7-3. Information Exported by Each Export Mode.

Mode	Will Export	Will not Export
Users	table definitions table data clusters indices first-level grants	views synonyms
Tables	table definitions table data	views synonyms grants indices clusters
Full DB	table definitions table data clusters indices grants views synonyms space definitions	objects belonging to SYS

is imported; the same is true of Export. If a fatal error occurs while importing or exporting a single table, processing continues on the next table. If a DDL error occurs, processing continues.

When Export is compiled at installation time, the Export module notes whether it is on a native ASCII or EBCDIC machine. When exporting occurs, all export files are automatically written accordingly. When Import attempts to bring an exported file back into the database, it recognizes whether a translation is necessary, and if it is, Import performs it.

7.2.1 Export

A user must have either RESOURCE or DBA authority to use Export. By using Export, you may write data from an *ORACLE* database to an operating system file for either permanent or temporary storage. Later the data may be returned to your *ORACLE* database by using Import.

Export is easy to use: it will simply ask you a few questions, then proceeds based on your answers. The first question will ask what mode of export you wish to use. The amount and type of information you can export depends on the database access privileges you have been granted. A DBA can export in Full Database Mode; other users may only export in the Users Mode or the Tables Mode. Table 7-3 shows the export possibilities in each mode.

7.2.2 The Export Command

The syntax of the Export command is:

EXP

or

EXP *username/password*

All users will then be asked the first three questions below. Starting with Question 4, the answers will depend on which mode you select. Where appropriate, default answers are shown by Export along with the question. At any time, you can end your input by entering period-[Return]. The questions which will appear on your screen after you issue the Export command are described below.

Enter array fetch buffer size (default is 4096)?> Your answer to this will determine the size available to buffer rows. Export uses the array fetch program interface call to speed performance. The default may be adequate. If zero is entered, only one row is fetched at a time.

Export filename? This is the name of the output file to be created by Export. If you enter a filename only, the file extension or filetype of the export file will be DMP.

Mode of Export? Your answer to this depends on what type of database access privileges you have. If you have DBA authority, you may choose any one of the three modes: User, Tables, or Full Database. If you do not have DBA authority, you must reply with either the User or Tables Mode. From here on, your answers will depend on the export mode you chose under this question.

Export Grants? If you answer Yes, the grants you export will depend on whether you are in full database mode or users mode.

Export the rows? If you answer Yes, table definitions as well as data in the tables will be exported. If you answer No, then only the table definitions will be exported.

Compress extents (Y/N): Y The default is Yes. If you default or specify Yes, then data for each table exported in this session will be compressed into one initial extent when imported.

User to be exported? If this prompt appears, then the current exporter may enter the name of the next *ORACLE* user whose objects should be exported. If this is to be the end of an exporting session, then the current exporter should indicate "no user" by entering a period.

Table name? If this prompt appears, Export is asking for the name of the next table to export. Table names can be entered with or without the prefix of their owner's name. If you do not enter a prefix, then Export assumes you are the exporter or owner of the last table exported in this session. For example, if you are a DBA and you are exporting in Tables mode, then Export assumes that you are exporting all tables in this session until another username is specified.

7.2.3 Import

Any user who has RESOURCE and CONNECT access, and access to an export file, can use Import. If the user who has only RESOURCE access attempts to import, he will receive an error message. The user importing a file need not be the user who exported that file.

The Import utility will read data from Export files into an *ORACLE* database. All of the data exported can be imported back, or you may import only selected parts of it. Tables, clusters and space definitions are automatically created, and space definitions can be automatically resized to accommodate tables that have grown into several extents.

If Import encounters a bad row, it will print that row and continue. If a fatal error occurs while a table is being imported, Import will abandon that table and go on with the next table.

Any user with CONNECT and RESOURCE access to the database and access to an export file can import. The importing user need not be the owner of the Export file.

7.2.4 The Import Command

Like Export, Import is an interactive utility. It will ask you questions, and will then proceed based on your answers. The syntax of the Import command is:

IMP

or

IMP *username/password*

The information imported will depend on what is in the Export file you wish to import, and your answers to the Import prompts. The prompts are as follows.

Enter insert buffer size (default is 10240, minimum is 4096). While the default will be adequate for most tables, you may need to increase it for tables with many long columns.

Import file < default file >. If you want to import some file other than the default file named inside the brackets, enter the full name of the file you want to import. You don't have to be the *ORACLE* user who exported the file, but you do need to have current access to it.

List contents of import file only? (Y/N):N> Answering Yes here will allow you to see what is in the export file, for example, to check whether or not it contains a certain table in which you are interested. Import will then ask more questions to find out if you want to see the whole export file or only parts of it. Depending on what you answer, Import will display the Export file at your terminal, and terminate without performing the Import. The default, or a No answer, will cause Import to continue with prompts regarding what you want to import.

Ignore create errors due to object existence? (Y/N) Y > If you answer Yes (the default), Import will import rows of data, even if it cannot create the table. This option is useful when, for example, you want to use a certain space definition or cluster, and therefore want to create the table before invoking IMP. If you answer No, Import will not attempt to import rows if the CREATE TABLE fails.

Import of entire import file requested? Y/N Y> By default, or if you answer Yes, Import will import every table that was exported. No other prompts will appear and Import will terminate after importing the entire file. If you answer No, Import will ask you for a username, then for tables belonging to that user to import. This will allow you to choose which tables are to be imported from the Export file.

Import the rows? (Y/N): Y> If you answer Yes, or default, Import will import the data rows. If you answer No, Import will run the data definition statements, such as CREATE TABLE or CREATE SPACE, but will not import the actual table data.

7.2.5 Importing Pre-Version 5 Export Files

The *ORACLE* Version 5 Import will accept a Version 4 Export file, but it will not import files exported in Version 3. If you are importing from Version 4, note that selective import of individual tables cannot be done with export files produced by Version 4, but import of an entire user works correctly. Since Version 5 does not support ALTER CLUS-TER, clustered tables are imported in unclustered form. To compensate for this, you can create tables in clusters before the import, or create a table and copy the data into the cluster after the import.

Chapter 8

Locks

ORACLE HAS A WIDE RANGE OF SECURITY FEATURES; SOME OF THEM, SUCH AS THE DBA'S ability to GRANT and REVOKE specific levels of access to the database, the DBA's ability to change user's passwords, and the ability of an individual user to change his own password, have already been covered in Chapter 5.

In addition, there are locking procedures designed specifically for security purposes, and other locking procedures designed to prevent a heavily used database from deadlocking.

All of the security features, especially the locks described below, are much more important in a multi-user than in a single-user system, such as MS-DOS. While MS-DOS has locking capacities just as any other system does, no waits or deadlocks will occur due to simultaneous use, as in multi-user systems. Only the internal locks, described in Section 8.1.1, are of interest for the single-user system.

8.1 TYPES OF LOCKS

Locks are especially important in multi-user systems to insure that changes occur in proper sequence, and to avoid having changes occur in data while a user is viewing it. Concurrent use by multi-users invites the possibility that changes may occur in the wrong sequence, thus destroying the integrity of the database. The *ORACLE* locks are automatic, but in some cases it is possible for a user to override certain ones.

There are three main types of locks in *ORACLE,* and four modes of locking within the latter two types. The three types are:

- Internal
- Dictionary/Parse
- Table/Row

8.1.1 Internal Locks

Internal locks protect the *ORACLE* internal structures. The internal locks which appear in the *ORACLE* Display System (ODS) are shown in Table 8-1. (The ODS is discussed

Table 8-1. ORACLE Internal Locks.

Name	Description
asynchronous readahead (ARH)	Protects data structures used to communicate asynchronous read requests from foreground processes to the ARH process.
audit(AUD)	Protects the audit trail from simultaneous access by multiple users.
before image(BFI)	Protects disk blocks in the before image file from simultaneous reading and writing.
cache buffers(CBH)	Protects the data structures that track which database blocks are in buffers, and how they are being used.
control blocks(DCB)	Protects the special system blocks in the database that contain active transaction numbers, system constants (such as the next file number to allocate) and the table of database filenames.
dictionary cache(DCA)	Protects the SGA-resident caches of dictionary data (tables, columns, clusters, etc.)
enqueues(ENQ)	Protects the data structures that keep track of locked tables, rows and other resources; also is held during deadlock detection.
framing(FRM)	Protects the data structures that define recovery points for backout from process failures.
processes(PCB)	Protects the data structures that describe currently-logged-on users.
table access(TAC)	Protects the data structures that keep track of what tables are in use, by whom, and whether (and how) they have been updated.
temp tables(TMP)	Protects the cache of temporary tables, held while temporary tables are created or deleted.
transactions(ERT)	Protects the data structures that define the active data manipulation and data definition transactions.

in Section 8.4 in this chapter, and in Chapter 5, Section 5.4.3). Since they are inaccessible to users, no further description of the internal locks will be presented here.

8.1.2 Locking Modes for Dictionary/Parse and Table/Row Locks

Each Dictionary/Parse and Table/Row lock has four locking modes. These modes are:

SHARE
EXCLUSIVE
SHARE UPDATE
WAIT

SHARE Mode. Use the SHARE mode when you query the data. It will prevent others from putting exclusive locks on the data. It will not prevent others from executing a SHARE UPDATE lock on the data you are reading, but it will prevent anyone who does put on a SHARE UPDATE lock from actually doing the UPDATE.

SHARE mode is an explicit lock. You must obtain it with the following command:

```
LOCK TABLE tablename IN SHARE MODE;
```

You can release this lock by a COMMIT, a ROLLBACK, by logging off, or by any other termination.

EXCLUSIVE Mode. The EXCLUSIVE mode lock is the only way to guarantee that only one user is updating a table's data at any one time.

Use an EXCLUSIVE lock to change data and prevent anyone else from changing it at the same time. It will prevent others from updating data while you're reading it (although they can still read the same data you're reading). It will also prevent anyone else from putting SHARE, SHARE UPDATE or EXCLUSIVE locks on the table you're using. Other users can query data while you hold an EXCLUSIVE lock on those data. The replies to their queries however will not show the changes you are making while you have an EXCLUSIVE lock on the table.

You may obtain this lock explicitly with the following command:

```
LOCK TABLE tablename IN EXCLUSIVE MODE;
```

Or, it will be invoked automatically (implicitly) when you issue any of the following commands:

```
INSERT INTO tablename . . .
UPDATE tablename . . .
DELETE FROM tablename . . .
```

In other words, an EXCLUSIVE lock prevents any other user from obtaining a SHARE lock or from doing any of the DML transactions such as INSERT, UPDATE, or DELETE.

You can release this lock with a COMMIT, ROLLBACK, log off, or other termination. (But row-level locks are not released by Rollback. See Section 8.1.6 on row-level locks.)

SHARE UPDATE Mode. You can use the SHARE UPDATE mode lock to reserve the right to update single rows or sets of rows. It will allow others to query the table and/or to lock it in the SHARE UPDATE mode, but it will prevent them from changing the same rows you intend to work on, and it will prevent everyone else from putting EXCLUSIVE locks on the table. You may obtain it explicitly by the command:

```
LOCK TABLE tablename IN SHARE UPDATE MODE;
```

Or, you may obtain it implicitly by the command

```
SELECT row1, row2, row3 . . . FOR UPDATE;
```

You can release the SHARE UPDATE lock mode by COMMIT, ROLLBACK, log off, or other termination.

WAIT Locks. WAIT locks are issued to you by *ORACLE* when there is already an existing lock which prevents you from doing the locking you intend. To avoid receiving a WAIT, you should specify NOWAIT in your command, like this:

LOCK TABLE *tablename* IN EXCLUSIVE MODE [NOWAIT]

WAIT locks become actual locks when the user holding the lock releases it. When multiple users are waiting for an object (table, row, etc.), the object becomes available to each user on a first-in first-out (FIFO) basis. If multiple users are waiting for a shared lock, then all shared wait locks on that object become actual locks when the process holding the lock releases it.

Implicit and Explicit Locks. Some of the *ORACLE* locks are "implicit," that is, they occur automatically when certain commands are issued; others are "explicit"—they do not occur unless you request them explicitly by name. In each case, the text that follows will indicate whether the lock is implicit or explicit.

8.1.3 Dictionary/Parse (DDL) Locks

Dictionary/Parse (also called DDL) locks are enabled by the SQL Data Definition Statements. They lock the Data Dictionary so that changes to the data structures (for example, changes to definitions of tables, columns, and clusters, or changes in access privileges) do not interfere with ongoing work.

No user, including the DBA, can explicitly lock any ORACLE Data Dictionary table.

There are three types of dictionary/parse (DDL) locks, all of which are invoked automatically by *ORACLE,* and cannot be invoked explicitly by a user. These are:

- The Dictionary Operation Lock
- Dictionary Definition Locks
- Table Definition Locks

The Dictionary Operation Lock. The Dictionary Operation lock is always exclusive, thus insuring that only one dictionary operation can occur at any one time. It applies to operations affecting the Data Dictionary, such as CREATE TABLE, DROP TABLE, CREATE INDEX, DROP INDEX, CREATE VIEW, DROP VIEW, CREATE CLUS-TER, DROP CLUSTER, and when a table acquires another datum or index extent. (See Chapter 7 on space projections and allocations for the definition and discussion of extent.)

The dictionary tables are not locked for the entire duration of the operation; they are locked only while they are being directly updated by *ORACLE.* For example, the command CREATE INDEX locks the dictionary tables while new rows are added describing the index, not while the index itself is being built.

Since this lock is exclusive, the NOWAIT option does not apply, i.e., a user requesting a Dictionary Operation lock that is being used will wait until the lock is available.

Dictionary Definition Locks. There is only one EXCLUSIVE Dictionary Definition lock, but there are SHARED Dictionary Definition locks. If you are performing a user-originated DDL or DCL command, you own an exclusive Dictionary Definition lock. This will prevent parsing from occurring during your user-originated operation. It also prevents the structure of the table from being changed (and it prevents the table from being dropped) while the dictionary is being queried.

The NOWAIT option does not apply to this lock. A user requesting it while another user is applying it will have to wait until it becomes available.

Table Definition Locks. Table Definition locks are owned shared or owned exclusively. If you are modifying a table definition, then you own the table definition lock exclusively. If you are referencing a table(s) in a SQL statement, then you own the table definition lock shared.

Every active SQL statement will have the most common locks—shared locks. These locks prevent changes to the dictionary entries for a table while there is an active SQL statement against it. Processes attempting a Data Definition command (such as ALTER TABLE, CREATE or DROP TABLE, or INDEX) against a table referenced by an active SQL statement will receive an error message like:

```
data definition operation and resource being used
```

which means that you should try the operation again later.

8.1.4 Table/Row (DML) Locks

Table/Row (also called DML) locks are enabled by the SQL DML statements. In contrast to dictionary/parse locks, which lock the structure of the data, table/row locks provide for the consistency of the data itself. Since there are some differences in locking procedures and results, table locking will be treated separately from row locking here.

Table Locking. Table locking may be accomplished in either of two modes, Exclusive Mode or Share Mode. Exclusive table locking can be obtained implicitly by using any of the DML statements INSERT, UPDATE, DELETE. It can also be obtained explicitly by entering:

```
LOCK TABLE tablename IN EXCLUSIVE MODE [NOWAIT];
```

The EXCLUSIVE MODE lock prevents other users from obtaining a share lock or from accomplishing any DML statements which would inaugurate an EXCLUSIVE lock. This is the only method of guaranteeing that only one user will be changing a table's data at a time. However, other users may query the table during an EXCLUSIVE lock, although they may not obtain the updated data. In some situations, using an EXCLUSIVE table lock may reduce the likelihood of a deadlock.

The SHARE mode table lock is only obtained explicitly. The command is:

```
LOCK TABLE tablename in SHARE MODE [NOWAIT];
```

Using the SHARE MODE lock will prevent other users from updating a locked table, although they will be able to read it. The main purpose of using this lock is to keep data from changing between two queries.

The SHARE MODE table lock is released by COMMIT, ROLLBACK, log-off or other termination.

8.1.5 Row-Level Locking in SHARE UPDATE Mode

It is more efficient for the operation as a whole when row-level locks are used rather than table locks. The problem is that of insuring that changes do not occur in a heavily used system between the time a user fetches a row and the time that same user updates it.

Row locks are exclusive, but they only lock the table during the actual update. To perform a SHARE UPDATE mode row lock implicitly, use the command:

```
SELECT column1, column2, . . .
FROM tablename
WHERE . . .
FOR UPDATE OF . . . ;
```

or you can perform it explicitly by invoking the SHARE UPDATE mode, as follows:

```
LOCK tablename IN SHARE UPDATE MODE;
```

The NOWAIT option cannot be exercised in the SHARE UPDATE mode.

The SHARE UPDATE mode lock is released by COMMIT or ROLLBACK. Although it is never necessary to explicitly lock any table, you may wish to do so occasionally to avoid a potential deadlock, or to conduct experiments with ODS, or for some other reason. You can lock a table if you own that table, or if you have SELECT privileges on it, or if you have DBA authority. You cannot explicitly lock any *ORACLE* Data Dictionary table, regardless of the authority you hold.

8.2 LOCKING IN *SQL*Forms*

Special rules apply to locking procedures when you use *SQL*Forms*.

*SQL*Forms* works in SHARE UPDATE mode. This is due to the fact that row-level locks are useful in applications where a length of time may pass after a row has been fetched and updated, but before the COMMIT key is pressed. Using row-level locks guarantees that the row is not changed without warning while you're working with it. If the row requested is already locked, you will see a message like:

```
Attempting to reserve record for update (x to abort)
```

where x is your operating system's interrupt sequence. Then *SQL*Forms* will rerequest the lock for you and wait until it is available.

Any changes to base table data are not written until you fully specify all the changes to base table data and press COMMIT. If a ROLLBACK occurs, the locks are not released. Instead, *SQL*Forms* assumes that you will change some values and retry COMMIT.

*SQL*Forms* does not execute LOCK statements for triggers. If the trigger is against the base table for the current block, and if rows have been updated or deleted, then the table is already locked. However, if the trigger is against a non-base table, then your trigger should consist of at least two SQL statements, and the first statement should lock the non-base table in SHARE UPDATE mode. This will avoid long waits.

*SQL*Plus* users who want to update tables that are being used by *SQL*Forms* users should also use SHARE UPDATE mode.

To avoid deadlocks whenever two users try to access the same table at the same time:

- Lock tables only when necessary, and only to the extent necessary, i.e., don't use an exclusive lock where a SHARE UPDATE mode lock will do.
- Always lock tables in the same sequence: If one form or one trigger locks Table A, then Table B, and another does the reverse, this will increase the risk of deadlock. Coordinate the sequence of table locking with all designers of forms.
- Advise forms users to commit their work to the database frequently.

8.3 DEADLOCK DETECTION

Deadlock detection occurs when one user has locked a table, and each other user in the group is waiting to lock that same table. The result is that all work of the other users stops, and deadlock occurs. *ORACLE* detects the situation and rolls back the work with the fewest database blocks completed, so that work can continue.

Since deadlocks are disruptive and wasteful, applications should be designed to avoid this problem; one way is to provide whenever possible, that all users of a table access in the SHARE UPDATE mode. This also promotes maximum efficiency in multi-user systems.

8.4 THE LOCKS DISPLAY IN ODS

You can have the Locks Display option of ODS page through all of your locks and show you the number and type of locks in use by invoking the display with a zero argument, thus:

```
L 0
```

Each lock in the display represents one enqueue entry in the SGA. The display will show you:

- Any exclusive lock currently held by a process.
- Any process waiting for an exclusive lock.
- Any shared locks currently held by a process.
- Any process currently waiting for a shared lock.
- The number of CTL locks held.
- The number of dictionary/parse locks held.
- The number of table/row locks held.

8.5 GENERAL LOCKING RECOMMENDATIONS

The main purpose of locking is to reduce congestion and maximize output. To accomplish this, it is important to minimize the time between the first update and a COMMIT or ROLLBACK. The following suggestions are designed to accomplish that.

1. For UPDATE and DELETE operations where some time will elapse before you COMMIT, lock the records you are going to use so that they will not be changed until after you have made your changes.

2. For UPDATE and DELETE, defer changes until just before you COMMIT.

3. If other users are updating in SHARE UPDATE mode (as in *SQL*Forms*) use SHARE UPDATE mode instead of SHARE mode or implicit locking. This will maximize concurrency and will also allow other users to use row-level locking.

4. Whenever possible, design your applications so that all users of a table access it in the SHARE UPDATE mode. This will improve your system's ability to support many concurrent users.

5. Avoid modifying underlying structures such as tables, columns, indexes, clusters, views, and synonyms during periods when your applications are heavily used.

Chapter 9

Data Definition Statements: CREATE, ALTER, DROP

THERE ARE TWO BASIC TYPES OF SQL COMMANDS FOR SETTING UP AND MAINTAINING a database. Data Definition Statements (CREATE, ALTER, DROP) define and/or describe the database objects, while Data Manipulation Statements (SELECT, UPDATE, DELETE, INSERT) manipulate and/or process the contents of the database. This chapter explains and illustrates the use of the SQL Data Definition Statements for base tables, views, and indexes. Chapter 10 is devoted to the SQL Data Manipulation Statements.

Data Definition Statements can be executed at any time. This is one of the advantages of a relational database system. By contrast, in most non-relational systems, adding a new record type, index, or field is a major operation, often involving bringing the entire system to a halt, unloading the database, revising and recompiling the database definition, and reloading the database to conform with the revised definition. For this and similar reasons, relational databases are rapidly increasing in popularity.

9.1 CREATING A TABLE

To create a table in *ORACLE,* type in the words CREATE TABLE followed by the name you want applied to the table. The following rules apply. A table name can be up to 30 characters long, must begin with one of the letters from A through Z, and, after the initial letter, may contain: any letter from A through Z, any number from 0 through 9, and any of the four symbols __, #, $, @. (But see exception at the end of this list.) It is the same whether upper- or lowercase letters are used, e.g., EMPLOYEES, Employees, and employees are all the same table name as far as ORACLE is concerned. (But see exception at end of this list.)

Furthermore, a table name may not duplicate the name of another table or view (views are discussed in Sections 9.4 and 9.5 below), and may not duplicate an *ORACLE* or SQL reserved word. (Reserved words are listed in Appendix A.) If enclosed in apostrophes when created, it may contain any combination of characters, except that it cannot use an apostrophe in the name itself. In this case it will return the name exactly as entered with regard to upper- or lowercase, i.e., 'EMPLOYEES', 'Employees', and 'employees' are three different tables.

Your command to create a table will look like this:

CREATE TABLE *tablename*

You must then specify the name, width, and data type of each column of the table. (For coverage of types of data permitted in a column, see Chapter 3 on SQL commands.) Columns must be listed in parentheses following the table name. Information about consecutive columns must be separated by commas.

Column names may be up to 30 characters long. If you do not specify a column width, *ORACLE* will ask for a column width. (Check the documentation for the machine you are using to determine the maximum number of columns possible.) Each column name in a specified table must be unique. In other words, no table can contain more than one column with the same name. Column names follow the same rules as those shown above for table names.

You must specify the column widths by typing the name (e.g., Column 1 *name*), type (e.g., Char), and size (e.g., 10) of each column directly under your CREATE TABLE command. CHAR columns must specify a width; NUMBER columns may specify a width, but do not have to.

Specify NOT NULL if your operation requires that the data for a certain column is essential. Then if anyone tries to enter a record without filling in a value for that column, *ORACLE* will return an error message.

NUMBER values may consist of the digits 0 through 9, and may have a plus (+) or minus (−) sign. Number values may be up to 40 digits long. If the digits contain a decimal point, you should specify how many digits are to be on the right of the decimal point with the specification:

NUMBER(w,d)

where *w* is the total number of digits in the column, and *d* is the number of digits on the right of the decimal point.

Your CREATE TABLE command with columns specified will look like this:

CREATE TABLE *tablename*
(*column1_name* CHAR (5),
column2_name CHAR (30),
column3_name NUM (10), NOT NULL,
column4_name NUM (6,2));

This creates an empty base table with four columns, the first of which will be 5 characters wide, the second 30 characters wide. The third column will contain number values up to 10 digits long, and the fourth will contain number values up to 6 digits long, with 2 digits on the right of the decimal point. Note that the third column bears a NOT NULL specification; therefore when rows are inserted into the table, this column must be filled in with a value.

Example: In terms of the ABC Food Co., the above table might be used to list the employees in its 10 stores. It would look like this:

```
CREATE TABLE EMPLOYEES
( ETITLE     CHAR(5),
  ENAME      CHAR(30),
  ENUMBER    NUM(10) NOT NULL,
  ESALARY    NUM(6,2));
```

The above command will set up a table with four columns, the first of which will show the employee's title in a 5-character space. The second column will show the employee's name using up to 30 characters. The third column will list the employee's number with a total of 10 digits. This column must be filled in with a value whenever a row is entered in this table because of the NOT NULL specification. If the value is not filled in, *ORACLE* will display an error message. The fourth column lists the employee's salary, using a total of 6 digits, two of which are to the right of the decimal point.

Actually inserting rows of data values in this table requires one or more of the Data Manipulation Statements discussed in Chapter 10, or you will need to import data via the *ORACLE* Data Loader (ODL), which is discussed in Chapter 7.

While you cannot have two columns with the same name in the same table, two different tables may contain a column with the same name. For example, a table called "Suppliers," listing the suppliers you use, may list the parts those suppliers supply. At the same time, a table called "Orders," listing orders you have placed with certain suppliers, may list parts you have ordered. For this reason, you might want to distinguish the parts list in the Suppliers table from the parts list in the Orders table when selecting information. You can do so by prefixing the column name with the table name. Then you would have SUP.PARTS for the parts column in the Suppliers table, and ORD.PARTS for the parts column in the Orders table.

9.2 ALTERING TABLES

An existing base table may be altered at any time by adding a new column to the right of the existing columns. You may also modify the columns within a table by increasing a column width or changing the number of decimal places. You may decrease a column's width, or change its data type, only if all values in the column are NULL.

9.2.1 Adding a Column to an Existing Table

The SQL command for adding a column is ALTER TABLE followed by the name of the table you want to alter, and the command ADD followed by the column name where the change is to take place, and the desired change. It will look like this:

```
ALTER TABLE tablename
  ADD column__name data type;
```

For example, The ABC Food Co. might find it desirable to have the Employees table just created also contain the Store No. where each individual is stationed. This information can be added using the ALTER command as follows:

```
ALTER TABLE EMPLOYEES
   ADD STORE# NUM;
```

All existing records (i.e., rows) in the Employees table will now be expanded to include this additional column with the data type "NUMBER." The value of the new column at this point will be NULL for each row. You are not allowed to specify NOT NULL when using ALTER TABLE ADD.

When you add a column, this new column is placed to the right of the existing columns. All fields in the new column are initially NULL, but you cannot specify NOT NULL for a new column if your table already has some rows in it. (However, there is a way to add a NOT NULL specification to a table with existing rows. It is explained in the next section.)

9.2.2 Modifying a Column in an Existing Table

An existing base table may be altered at any time by increasing the column size, or by changing its number of decimal places. The SQL command is ALTER TABLE followed by the name of the table where the modification is to occur, followed by the SQL command MODIFY, then the column name to be modified and the desired modification. To increase a column size to 20 from any number below 20, the command will look like this:

```
ALTER TABLE tablename
   MODIFY column_name CHAR(20);
```

Suppose the ABC Food Co. intends to create new titles in some departments and needs more latitude in the size of the title names. Therefore it needs to increase the width of the ETITLE column in the Employees table. The change will look like this:

```
ALTER TABLE EMPLOYEES
   MODIFY ETITLE CHAR (20);
```

You can change a column from NOT NULL to NULL by adding the NULL clause to the column specification:

```
. . . MODIFY (ENUMBER (20) NULL);
```

You can change a column from NULL to NOT NULL in the same way as the change shown above, but only if there are no null values in the column.

You may want to add a NOT NULL column to a table which already contains data, but this cannot be done in one step. With the MODIFY clause, however, you can add a NOT NULL column to a table with existing rows by doing it in three steps as follows:

1. Add the column
2. Fill in a non-null value for every field in the column.
3. Use ALTER TABLE MODIFY to add the NOT NULL specification to the column.

To decrease a column's width or change the data type of a column, all values in the column must be NULL in all rows. The command to change the data type will look like this:

```
ALTER TABLE tablename
    MODIFY column_name (data type);
```

9.2.3 Copying Rows into a Table

You can create a table and copy rows into it from an existing table at the same time by using the CREATE TABLE command and the word AS. (Other uses of AS are explained in Chapter 12, Section 12.4.) You must specify the columns from the existing table that you want copied into your new table. All of the specifications listed after the AS must be in parentheses.

For example, suppose you wanted to create a table of company executives, defined as all personnel whose title is "manager" or whose salary is over $50,000. You could do this by drawing their names, jobs, and salaries from a table listing all personnel. Then you could create the table and fill it in with the appropriate rows in one command as follows:

```
CREATE TABLE EXECUTIVE (ENAME, JOB, SAL)
AS  (SELECT ENAME, JOB, SAL
    FROM  EMP
    WHERE  JOB = 'MANAGER'
    OR  SAL > 50,000);
```

Note that you do not specify column widths or data types when you use the AS command; these are determined by the widths and data types of the columns specified in the existing table.

9.3 THE DROP TABLE COMMAND

An existing base table can be removed from the database at any time. This is accomplished very simply by the SQL command DROP TABLE. It will look like this:

```
DROP TABLE tablename;
```

For example, at ABC Foods the Employees table created in this chapter replaces a similar table which was called STORE_PERSONNEL. Since the Employees table now contains everything in the old STORE_PERSONNEL table as well as other information, ABC can dispense with the old table. The command to do so looks like this:

```
DROP TABLE STORE_PERSONNEL;
```

Keep in mind that, when a base table is dropped, all views and indexes defined on that base table are automatically dropped as well.

9.4 THE CREATE VIEW AND DROP VIEW COMMANDS

The initial step in creating a view is the same as that in creating a table:

```
CREATE VIEW viewname;
```

Since the data in a view are drawn from base tables that are already created, however, the procedure involves manipulating data that are already in the database. Accordingly, Data Manipulation Statements must be used to specify the data in the VIEW. These are illustrated in Chapter 10. Therefore, you will find more details on creating views in Section 10.5 in Chapter 10.

Columns in a view will contain the same data type as the base table from which they were drawn.

As with a base table, views can be eliminated by the SQL command DROP VIEW. For example, the following command will remove a VIEW:

DROP VIEW *viewname*;

For example, ABC has no immediate use for a view of the employees at Store #5. The command to get rid of that view is as follows:

DROP VIEW EMPLOYEES__STORE#5;

Also dropped by this command will be any other views which may be defined on the view EMPLOYEES__STORE#5. However, the base table on which this view is defined will not be dropped when only the view defined on it is dropped.

9.5 Creating and Dropping Indexes

The purpose of an index is to speed up data retrieval. However, while an index speeds up retrieval, it may slow down updating.

There may be any number of indexes based on any one stored table. You could have an index for each column in the table, and in addition, you could have indexes for combinations of columns. For example, in a table containing names, department numbers, job titles, and salaries, you could have an index on each of the four columns named, as well as an index on the combination "job titles and salaries" (and/or any other combination of the four columns). The purpose of the combination would be to reduce the number of scans if "job titles and salaries" happened to be a frequent query. In other words, if only individual indexes existed on each of the four columns, the query "Find all the job titles with salaries below $50,000" would take two scans (because it involves two variables: "job titles" and "salaries"). But if the combined index existed, then that same query would require only one scan, thus saving scanning time.

The only operations that the user can perform directly on indexes are CREATE and DROP. SQL Data Manipulation Statements such as SELECT (see Chapter 10) cannot be implemented by the user for indexes because, in order to optimize retrieval, decisions about which index to use in answering a SQL query are made by the system. (However, see Chapter 13, for ways in which you can influence *ORACLE*'s use of indexes by strategic placement of expressions within the query.)

The SQL command for creating an index looks like this:

CREATE INDEX *indexname*
  ON *tablename*;

The types of indexes to be created is primarily an administrative decision. Therefore, details about the options available in creating indexes are in Chapter 5 on the functions of the database administrator.

To drop an index, use the SQL DROP INDEX command followed by the name of the index, like this:

```
DROP INDEX indexname
  ON tablename;
```

It is possible for two indexes for different tables to have the same name. If this is the case, you should indicate which index is being dropped by specifying the tablename after the ON, as shown in the example above. If you are sure there is no other index with that name on any other table, then the command:

```
DROP INDEX indexname;
```

is sufficient.

The above DROP INDEX command does not drop the tables or views on which the index is based.

Chapter 10

SQL Data
Manipulation Statements

THIS CHAPTER EXPLAINS AND ILLUSTRATES THE SQL DATA MANIPULATION LANGUAGE (DML) for base tables, views, and indexes. It also discusses creating and using views.

Chapter 9 illustrated the use of the SQL Data Definition Language (DDL) statements CREATE, ALTER, and DROP. Those commands alone merely set up, modify, and eliminate database objects. This chapter enables you to put data into tables, and to perform other manipulations on those data after they are entered. The SQL DML statements are INSERT, UPDATE, DELETE, and SELECT.

10.1 THE INSERT COMMAND

The INSERT command is used to add rows, or parts of rows, to tables.

Clearly, if a table has just been created, the INSERT command will be used to put in the initial row(s) of data. It follows then, that a table must be created before the INSERT command can be used. The general form of the INSERT command will look like this:

```
INSERT
INTO tablename [ (column1_name, column2_name, . . .)
VALUES ( 'value1', 'value2', . . . );
```

For example, ABC Foods has a new supplier whose name, location, and terms must be entered into the supplier table. The entry will look like this:

```
INSERT
INTO SUPPLIERS (name, location, terms)
VALUES ('Acme', 'Boston', 'Net30');
```

If the list of column names is omitted, then a value must be listed for every column in the table, and the list of values must be in the same sequence as the sequence of the columns in the table. In other words, you may state each column name as follows:

```
INSERT
INTO tablename (column1, column2, column3 . . . )
VALUES (value1, value2, value3 . . . );
```

Or, if the values are in exactly the same sequence as the columns, with no omitted values, you may omit the column names as follows:

```
INSERT
INTO tablename
VALUES (value1, value2, value3 . . . );
```

If you have no value for one or more of the columns, you may list "NULL" for the value of that column unless that column contains a NOT NULL specification. (If you attempt to enter a NULL value in a NOT NULL column, *SQL*Plus* will return an error message, and will not insert the row.)

For example, if you have no value for Column 2, and Column 2 does not contain a NOT NULL specification, you may insert the values in either of the following two ways:

```
INSERT
INTO tablename (column1, column3 . . . )
VALUES ('value1','value3' . . . );
```

or

```
INSERT
INTO tablename
VALUES ('value1', NULL, 'value3' . . . );
```

as long as the values are in exactly the same sequence as the columns in the table, or

```
INSERT
INTO tablename (column1, column2, column3 . . . )
VALUES ('value1', NULL, 'value3' . . . );
```

In general, there is no need to waste time and effort entering column names if (1) you are inserting values in all columns, and (2) you are inserting values in the same order as the sequence in which the columns appear in the table. The list of column names must be used when:

1. Inserting fewer column values than the number of columns existing in the table.

2. Entering column values in a sequence other than the sequence in which the columns appear in the table.

When you insert date values, they must be in the standard date format, DD-MON-YY, like 31-MAR-87. If your date data are in some other format, you must convert them to standard format by using the date formatting function TO_DATE. (See Section 11.2.3 in Chapter 11 for the use of date functions.)

In summary, values inserted must obey the following rules:

1. If a value is omitted, and column numbers are not specified, then *ORACLE* will assume that every column is to be filled with a value, and will insert NULL in place of the value it perceives as missing (unless that column has a NOT NULL specification).

2. Values inserted must match the data type of the column into which they are being inserted.

3. Values inserted must be separated by commas.

4. The INSERT command may be used to copy rows or parts of rows from one table into another.

5. Character values must be enclosed by single quotes.

10.2 THE UPDATE COMMAND

The UPDATE command is used to change the values in existing rows. The general form of the UPDATE command is:

```
UPDATE tablename
SET column1 = newvalue,
    column2 = newvalue,
    column3 = newvalue, . . .
WHERE condition;
```

The SET clause of the UPDATE command tells which columns to update, and what values to change them to.

The UPDATE command operates on all the rows that meet the WHERE clause condition(s). The WHERE clause is optional, but if it is omitted, all rows will be updated.

You may use the UPDATE command to set a column to NULL if the column does not contain a NOT NULL specification. You may update a column using the *ORACLE* functions that operate on a single row in the SET clause. You may use the same expressions to update fields in a column that you would use to select those values.

Multiple columns in each row may be updated with a single UPDATE command by listing multiple columns after the SET keyword, and you may update several rows at once by selecting those rows with the WHERE clause. All rows satisfying the WHERE condition will be updated.

Suppose you want to give a 5% raise to all Salesmen listed in the Employees table. Then enter:

```
UPDATE EMP
```

```
    SET   SAL  =  SAL * 1.05
  WHERE   (JOB  =  SALESMAN);
```

This would result in each salesman's salary being multiplied by 105%. The resulting salary would replace each existing salesman's salary in the Employees table. If you omit the WHERE clause in the above example, all employees, regardless of job title will receive a 5% raise.

The WHERE clause in an UPDATE command may contain a subquery. (Subqueries are discussed in detail in Chapter 12, Section 12.4.) For example, suppose each employee who is listed in the table of managers is to receive a 10% raise. Then, you would enter:

```
UPDATE   EMP
   SET   SAL  =  SAL * 1.10
 WHERE   ENAME IN
         (SELECT ENAME
         FROM   MANAGERS);
```

Note that the subquery must be enclosed in parentheses.

A subquery may also be used in the SET clause of the UPDATE command.

10.3 THE DELETE COMMAND

The DELETE command is used to remove rows from a table. The general form of the DELETE command is:

```
DELETE FROM  tablename
WHERE   condition;
```

You cannot DELETE partial rows, so it is not necessary to specify column names.

The WHERE clause determines which rows will be removed. If the WHERE clause is not specified, all rows will be removed. The WHERE clause may be complex and may include multiple conditions, operators, and/or subqueries (also called *nested SELECTS*).

If you want to delete just one row from a table, use the DELETE command with a WHERE clause specifying the identifying characteristic of that row. For example, to delete the supplier named Jones from your table of suppliers, enter:

```
DELETE FROM  tablename
WHERE   SNAME  =  'JONES';
```

If you want to delete several rows from a table all with one command, select the rows with the desired condition in the WHERE clause. For example, to delete all suppliers from Dallas from your table of suppliers, enter:

```
DELETE  FROM SUPPLIERS
WHERE   CITY  =  'Dallas';
```

To delete all the rows from a table, enter only the command

```
DELETE FROM tablename;
```

and omit the WHERE clause. This will remove all rows from the table, leaving only the column specifications and tablename.

10.4 THE SELECT COMMAND

The SELECT command is used to retrieve data from a table. The general form of the SELECT command is as follows:

```
SELECT column1, column2, column3 . . .
FROM tablename;
```

If you want to retrieve all columns in a specified table, use the asterisk (*) to indicate all columns instead of listing the columns. For example, suppose ABC Foods wants to retrieve all information contained in the SUPPLIERS table regarding the suppliers. You would do it like this:

```
SELECT  *
FROM    SUPPLIERS;
```

The SELECT command and the FROM clause are required for every SQL query, and the items specified after SELECT must be separated by commas.

Also remember that constants may be selected and will have the same value in every row; that the rows returned in response to a SELECT command are returned and displayed in an arbitrary order; that expressions as well as column names may be selected; and that default column headings will be the column name or the expression unless other headings are specified.

The SELECT command and the FROM clause must appear before any other clauses in a query.

10.5 CREATE VIEW

Instead of formulating a complicated query to get specific information out of a table, you may want to create a view of the table showing only the information you want. You may then obtain selected information with a simpler query than if you queried the entire table. To do this in one step, use the CREATE VIEW command and specify your query after the word AS. The syntax is:

```
CREATE VIEW viewname
AS          query;
```

The query part of the command selects specific columns and rows from a specific table.

For example, suppose you wanted to separate out salesmen from other employees for purposes of computing commissions. You would create a view out of the table of employees thus:

```
CREATE VIEW  SALESMEN
AS  (SELECT ENAME, ESAL
     FROM  EMP
     WHERE  JOB = SALESMAN);
```

After you have created the view, you may query it just as you would query any table.

You may use any valid query in a CREATE VIEW command, except that you cannot use an ORDER BY clause. If you want to order the above salesmen in the view in some way other than the way they are ordered in the Employees table, you must do it in a separate query directed to the view. To display the contents of the view created above, enter:

```
SELECT  *
FROM    SALESMEN;
```

And when you query a view, you may use a WHERE clause, just as you do with a table:

```
SELECT  ENAME,
FROM    SALESMEN
WHERE   SAL = 50000;
```

When you change the information in the table underlying the view, that is, the table from which the view was created, the information in the view will also change. If you update the table EMPLOYEES, these updated values will also appear in the view you now have called SALESMEN. If you INSERT or DELETE rows in the underlying table, these rows will be added to or deleted from the view.

Updating and Deleting Rows in a View. You may update a view rather than the underlying table, but only if the view refers to only one table, and does not contain a GROUP BY clause, a DISTINCT clause, a group function, or a reference to the pseudo-column ROWNUM.

You may delete a row from a view with the same restrictions that apply to updating, plus the added restriction that the view may contain no columns defined by expressions. (See Chapter 11 for a discussion of expressions.)

Views on More Than One Table. To create a view from more than one table, you must define the view with a query containing a join. (See Chapter 12 for further details on joins.) You may join any number of tables in a view.

Using Expressions and Functions in Views. In creating a view, you may want to combine columns or perform other operations on column values in the table from which the view is drawn. The resulting columns in the view will appear like any other columns, but they are not the same because of the following:

Since the values in these columns are not stored in the underlying tables, they are calculated anew each time the view is displayed. For this reason, they are called *virtual columns*.

You must specify all column names if you use expressions or functions in a view.

You may use GROUP BY clauses and group (Aggregate) functions such as Average, Maximum, Minimum, and Total in view definitions. (These Aggregate functions are discussed in detail in Chapters 11 and 12.)

Chapter 11

Clauses, Functions, Expressions, and Operators

TO MAKE USE OF THE DATA DEFINITION LANGUAGE AND DATA MANIPULATION LANGUAGE of Chapters 9 and 10, the commands explained in those chapters must usually be accompanied by other short terms. Of necessity, some of these appear in those two chapters in conjunction with the DDL and DML terms. All such connecting terms are defined and explained in detail in this chapter. They are:

Clauses:	FROM, WHERE, ORDER BY, GROUP BY, HAVING
Functions:	Character, Numeric, Date, Aggregate, Miscellaneous
Expressions:	Logical, Arithmetic, CHAR.
Operators:	Quantitative, Qualitative, Boolean

11.1 CLAUSES

Certain terms, usually consisting of one word, are defined as *clauses*. (While this usage may seem inconsistent with the grammatical meaning of the word "clause," you will find that when you fill in your instructions, the entire statement will be a clause in the usual grammatical sense.) They are described in subsequent sections.

11.1.1 The FROM Clause

The FROM clause is used with the SELECT command to retrieve data from a table in the database. The general form of the query will look like this:

```
SELECT column1, column2, column3 . . .
FROM tablename;
```

The FROM clause must follow a SELECT command, the combination is required for every SQL query, and the SELECT command and the FROM clause must precede all other clauses in a query.

You may place the SELECT command and the FROM clause on the same line, or (as above) on two separate lines.

11.1.2 The WHERE Clause

The WHERE clause is used to identify a specific subset of rows to be retrieved from a table. The general form will look like this:

```
SELECT column1, column2, column3 . . .
FROM tablename
WHERE condition;
```

The WHERE clause must follow the FROM clause. Columns used in the WHERE clause do not have to be among those selected.

ORACLE will return every row in the table that belongs to the subset specified by the WHERE clause. A SELECT command with a WHERE clause will retrieve only those rows that meet your search conditions.

You can use NUMBER, CHAR, or DATE values in a WHERE clause, but when you use a CHAR or DATE value you must enclose it in single quotes. You do not need to enclose NUMBER values in quotes.

By using the WHERE clause, you may compare a column value to a numeric constant or a character constant. To find a match between the constant specified and the value(s) in the database, the constant must be enclosed in single quotes (unless it is a number), and the case (upper/lower) must be the same as the value stored. You also may use WHERE to compare a column value to an arithmetic expression involving column values and/or constants, and to compare a column value to another column value.

For the functions, expressions, and operators that combine with WHERE clauses to accomplish these results, see Sections 11.2 through 11.5 in this chapter.

11.1.3 The ORDER BY Clause

Since *ORACLE* stores rows in random order, use of the ORDER BY clause is the only way to ensure that rows will be retrieved in a specified sequence. If this clause is omitted, rows will be returned in random order.

Default is ascending order (smallest value first) for numerical values, and alphabetical for CHAR values. Descending sequence may be specified by entering DESC after the column name in the ORDER BY clause. If you order by columns that include NULL values, the NULL entries will always be displayed first, regardless of whether you choose ascending or descending order.

The ORDER BY must be the last clause to appear in the SQL statement, the general form of which is:

```
SELECT column1, column2, column3 . . .
FROM tablename
WHERE specified conditions are true
ORDER BY column_name[DESC];
```

If you use ORDER BY with date values, and use the default setting (ascending), the oldest dates would appear first, followed by the more recent dates.

11.1.4 The GROUP BY Clause

The GROUP BY clause is used to group data on which calculations are to be performed. The general form will look like this:

```
SELECT columns or functions
FROM tablename
WHERE specified conditions are true
GROUP BY column_name;
```

For example:

```
SELECT storeno
FROM stores
WHERE profit > 1000000
GROUP BY size;
```

As always, the WHERE clause will restrict which rows will be selected to form the group. It is not necessary to have a WHERE clause, however; if you wanted to group all stores, not just the million-dollar profit centers, you would omit the WHERE clause in the above example. Then all stores would be grouped by size regardless of the amount of profit.

If your query has a WHERE clause, the GROUP BY clause must come after the WHERE clause. If it does not have a WHERE clause, then the GROUP BY clause should be placed after the FROM clause.(For a discussion of using GROUP BY in subqueries, see Section 11.2.3.)

11.1.5 The HAVING Clause

The HAVING clause must involve only GROUP BY items (see Section 11.1.4) or aggregate functions (see Section 11.2.4). It can only be applied to group data, specifying the conditions the group must satisfy. The general form is:

```
SELECT columns or functions
FROM tablename
GROUP BY column1 . . .
HAVING specified group characteristics;
```

The HAVING clause must be placed after the GROUP BY clause. For example:

```
SELECT      STORENO, TITLE, COUNT(*)
FROM        EMPLOYEES
GROUP BY    STORENO
HAVING      COUNT(*) > 10;
```

will list the employees by store number and title for all stores with more than 10 employees.

If you include both a WHERE clause and a HAVING clause in the same query, *SQL*Plus* handles the query as follows:

1. The WHERE clause is used to select rows.
2. The groups are formed and any group functions are calculated.
3. The HAVING clause is applied to select the groups.

In this example;

```
SELECT          STORENO
FROM            EMPLOYEES
WHERE           TITLE = 'CASHIER'
GROUP BY        STORENO
HAVING          COUNT(*) > 2;
```

all the stores with more than two cashiers will be listed, and they will be grouped by store number.

You may use the HAVING clause to compare a property of the group with a constant value, or you may use the HAVING clause to select a group based on a comparison with another group. If you want to SELECT groups and compare them with another group (which is the same idea as comparing a group with a constant), do this by including the characteristics of the comparison (i.e., the constant) group in a subquery. (Subqueries are discussed in Chapter 12.)

11.2 FUNCTIONS

The functions discussed in this section are Character string, Numeric string, Date, Aggregate (or Group), and Miscellaneous.

11.2.1 Character String Functions

Character string functions may be used in the SELECT command, the WHERE clause, and the ORDER BY clause. These functions will not change the internal data. Table 11-1 contains the SQL character string functions.

The DECODE function translates coded entries into the meanings of the code. For example, suppose that all stores are coded as (1) large, (3) medium, and (5) small. If you wanted a meaningful listing of the stores according to size, you would want the decoded values shown. You would do this by entering the following command:

```
SELECT STORENO, SIZE
    DECODE(SIZE, 'LARGE' ,1, 'MEDIUM', 3,'SMALL' 5, 2)
    STORE__SIZE
FROM  STORES;
```

If there are stores in your list which do not have the listed classifications, but have some other classification (such as "very small" or "medium to large"), the numeral 2

Table 11-1. CHAR Functions.

Function	Purpose
CHARTOROWID(*char*)	Converts a CHAR value to a row ID.
column || *column*	Concatenates columns with no intervening blanks.
DECODE(*from, val, code, val, code, . . . default*)	If *from* equals any *val*, returns the code following; if not, returns *default*. The *from* may be any data type; *val* must be the same type. Value returned is forced to the same data type as the first *code*.
HEXTORAW(*char*)	Converts a CHAR value containing hexadecimal digits to a binary value (suitable for inclusion in a RAW column.)
INITCAP	Capitalizes first letter of each word.
LENGTH(*char*)	Outputs the length of the string.
LOWER(*char*)	All letters forced to lowercase.
RAWTOHEX(*raw*)	Converts a raw value to a CHAR value containing a hexadecimal number.
ROWIDTOCHAR(*rowid*)	Converts a row ID to a CHAR value.
SOUNDEX(*char*)	A CHAR value representing the sound of the word(s) in CHAR.
String1 || String2	Concatenates strings of characters with no intervening blanks.
TO__CHAR(*n*[, *fmt*])	Converts *n* to a CHAR value in the format specified. If *fmt* is omitted, *n* is converted to a CHAR value exactly long enough to hold the significant digits.
TO__NUMBER(*char*)	Converts a CHAR value containing a number to a number.
TRANSLATE(*oldstr,newstr*)	Substitutes the character in *newstr* for the corresponding character in *oldstr*.
UPPER(*char*)	Changes lowercase characters to uppercase.
USERENV(*char*)	Returns information about the user that is useful in writing an application-specific audit trail table. If char is 'ENTRYID,' returns an available auditing entry identifier; if 'SESSIONID,' returns user's auditing session identifier; if 'TERMINAL,' returns user's terminal operating system identifier.

in the DECODE statement determines that all of these stores would be included under the default code number 2.

You can use the DECODE function for any type of decoding: grade point numbers into arithmetic expressions, job codes into job titles, part numbers into part names, etc.

The arguments of DECODE determine the column to be decoded (STORENO); the original and translated values in the column ('LARGE', 1,) etc.; and any default value into which original values that are not specified in your DECODE statement are to be decoded (2).

11.2.2 Numeric String Functions

Numeric string functions may be used in the SELECT command, the WHERE clause, and the ORDER BY clause. Table 11-2 lists and explains the numeric string functions.

The ROUND function rounds off a number to a specified number of decimal places. For example, if you wanted to calculate the average daily profit for each store during a 30-day month, with the results rounded to the nearest penny, you would set it up this way:

```
SELECT SNAME, PROFIT, PROFIT/30, ROUND(PROFIT/30,2)
FROM   STORES;
```

ROUND(PROFIT/30,2) means that you want the result rounded to two decimal places. If the query had asked for

```
ROUND(PROFIT/30,0)
```

that would mean you wanted the amount rounded to the nearest dollar (or the nearest whole integer).

The TRUNC function cuts off (truncates) numbers to a specified number of decimal places without rounding them. For example, if you truncate 56.99 to an integer, the result is 56, whereas if you ROUND 56.99 to an integer, the result is 57. Set up the query using TRUNC just as you set up the query using ROUND. TRUNC(PROFIT/30,0) would mean to cut off all numbers after the decimal point. But keep in mind that the results can be very different from results that are rounded.

Table 11-2. Numeric Functions.

Function	Description
ABS(n)	Absolute value of n.
CEIL(n)	Smallest integer greater than or equal to n.
FLOOR(n)	Largest integer equal to or less than n.
MOD(m,n)	Remainder of m divided by n.
POWER(m,n)	Value of m raised to the nth power.
ROUND($n[,m]$)	Value of n rounded to m decimal places; m may be positive or negative. If m is omitted, round to 0 places. If m is negative, round to the left of the decimal point; if m is positive, round to the right of the decimal point.
SIGN(n)	If $n<0$, -1; if $n=0$, 0; if $n>0$, 1.
SQRT(n)	Returns the positive square root of n. If $n < 0$, result is NULL.
TRUNC($n[,m]$)	Value of n truncated to m decimal places; if m is omitted, to 0 places. If m is negative, leave 0 left of the decimal point.

Table 11-3. Date Functions.

Function	Purpose
date + number	Adds a number of days.
date + hours/(24)	Adds a number of hours.
date + minutes/(24*60)	Adds a number of minutes.
date + seconds/(24*60*60)	Adds a number of seconds.
date − number	Subtracts a number of days.
*date − hours/*24	Subtracts a number of hours.
date − minutes/(24*60)	Subtracts a number of minutes.
date − seconds/(24*60*60)	Subtracts a number of seconds.
date − date	Determines number of days between.
*(date − date)*24*	Determines number of hours between.

11.2.3 Date Functions

The default date format is "DD-MON-YY" for both input and output. The date data type contains Century, Year, Month, Day, Hour, Minutes, and Seconds, as shown in Table 11-3.

In order to display time, the TO_CHAR function must be used. Notice that "MI" stands for "minutes" and "MM" is "months."

SYSDATE is a reserved word that can be used to represent today's date in any type of SQL statement (SELECT, INSERT, UPDATE . . .).

You must always add/subtract a number of days and/or fractional days to a date field. You can perform arithmetic on date fields, as follows:

date + number	Adds a number of days to a date and produces the resulting date.
date − number	Subtracts a number of days from a date and produces the resulting date.
date − date	Subtracts one date from another and produces the resulting number of days.

11.2.4 Aggregate Functions

Aggregate functions (also called *group functions*) apply to groups of records. They summarize a column of values and return a single value. All aggregate functions may be applied to numeric values, but only the aggregate functions MIN, MAX, and COUNT can be applied to character and date values. The aggregate functions supported by *ORACLE* are shown in Table 11-4.

To find the average of a column of values, use the function AVG. For example, to find the average salary of cashiers, enter:

```
SELECT AVG(SAL)
FROM EMPLOYEES
```

117

Table 11-4. Aggregate Functions.

Function	Description
AVG([DISTINCT|ALL] *n*)	Average value of *n*, ignoring null values.
COUNT([DISTINCT|ALL] {*|*expr*})	Number of times *expr* evaluates to something other than NULL. The asterisk makes COUNT count all selected rows.
MAX([DISTINCT|ALL] *expr*)	Maximum value of *expr*.
MIN([DISTINCT|ALL] *expr*)	Minimum value of *expr*.
STDDEV([DISTINCT|ALL] *expr*)	Standard deviation of *expr*, ignoring null values.
SUM([DISTINCT|ALL] *expr*)	Sum of values of *expr*.
VARIANCE([DISTINCT|ALL] *expr*)	Variance of *expr*, ignoring null values.

These functions can be used only in SELECT commands and subqueries.

```
WHERE TITLE = 'CASHIER';
```

All the rows that satisfy the condition WHERE TITLE = 'CASHIER' will be used to calculate the average. This query will return a single value, AVG(SAL).

You can use more than one group function in a SELECT command. For example:

```
SELECT AVG(SAL), AVG(COMM)
FROM EMPLOYEES
WHERE TITLE = 'SALESMAN';
```

This would return the average salary and the average commission of all employees with the job title "Salesman."

The COUNT function counts the number of non-null values, distinct values, or rows selected by the query. If you want to count the number of unique items in a list, (i.e., disregarding duplicates), then use the term DISTINCT. For example, if you wanted to count the number of different job titles held by a large group of employees, many of whom have the same title, you would set up the query this way:

```
SELECT    COUNT (DISTINCT TITLE)
FROM      EMPLOYEES
WHERE     CITY = 'CHICAGO';
```

This command will eliminate duplicate values before the values are counted. When DISTINCT is used, only the unique values in the column will be returned.

There is a special form of count, COUNT(*) which will count the number of rows satisfying the conditions in the WHERE clause. For example, to count the number of employees in a specific department, the query would be:

```
SELECT      COUNT(*)
FROM        EMPLOYEES
WHERE       DEPT = 'SALES';
```

It is important to be aware of null values when you use aggregate functions, since the effects of the null values will be hidden in the results. You will get different results depending on how *ORACLE* treats the null values. The *Null Value Function* (NVL) is useful for guaranteeing that you get the type of result you want; it is discussed in detail in Section 11.2.5 below.

Group Functions versus Individual Functions. When you put a group function in a SELECT command, you cannot also put an individual function in that same command. For example, if your command begins with SELECT EMPLOYEE_NAME, then you cannot follow this with AVG(SAL). EMPLOYEE_NAME has a value for each row selected, while AVG(SAL) has a single value for the whole query. If you combine a group function with an individual function, *ORACLE* will return an error message.

There are two exceptions to the above rule, however. You can request individual results based on a group function in a subquery, or group results based on individual selections in a subquery. (Subqueries are discussed in Chapter 12). You also can select individual columns to form subgroups. This is explained below.

Summarizing Several Groups of Rows. If you wanted to know the average salary of the employees in each of several stores, you could enter separate AVG(SAL) queries for each store. However, you could get the same information with one query by using the GROUP BY clause discussed in Section 11.1.4 above.

The GROUP BY clause divides a table into groups of rows, where the rows in each group have the same value in a specified column. For example, to obtain the average salary in each of several stores, you would enter:

```
SELECT      STORENO, AVG(SAL)
FROM        EMPLOYEES
GROUP BY    STORENO;
```

This would return a listing of each store number and the average salary at each store.

The example above does not contain a WHERE clause; therefore the GROUP BY clause is placed after the FROM clause. If your query contains a WHERE clause, the GROUP BY clause would come after the WHERE clause.

You also can divide the rows of a table into groups based on values in more than one column. You might want to group all employees by store number and title. Do this by specifying both store number and title in the SELECT list and the GROUP BY clause.

Putting a Group Function in a Subquery. Suppose you want to find out which of several stores in the group made the greatest profit. You cannot enter SELECT SNAME, MAX(PROFIT) because SNAME has a value for each row selected, while MAX(PROFIT) has a single value for the whole query. But you can get this information with a subquery.

It will look like this:

```
SELECT SNAME, CITY, PROFIT
FROM   STORES
WHERE  PROFIT =
       (SELECT MAX(PROFIT)
       FROM STORES);
```

11.2.5 Miscellaneous Functions

The miscellaneous functions are GREATEST, LEAST, and NVL. Their uses are explained below.

GREATEST. You can perform certain calculations with functions. GREATEST is a function with two or more arguments, which are value names separated by commas. When GREATEST is evaluated by *ORACLE*, its value is the largest of its argument values. All expressions after the first are converted to the type of the first before the comparison is done. The syntax is:

```
SELECT column__name, GREATEST (argument1, argument2)
FROM   tablename;
```

For example, you might want to know which job title commands the highest income regardless of whether that income is from salary or commissions. To find out, you could enter the following query:

```
SELECT JOB__TITLE, GREATEST (SALARY, COMMISSION)
FROM   EMPLOYEES;
```

GREATEST can return any type of value. The type of value returned is the same as the type of the value of the first argument. When GREATEST is applied to date values, a later date is considered greater than an earlier one. When applied to CHAR values, the greater value is the one that comes later in alphabetic order.

LEAST. The function LEAST works in exactly the same way as GREATEST except that it returns the smallest value of its argument values. Like GREATEST, it can return any type of CHAR, Date, or Numeric value, depending on the type of value of its first argument.

NULL VALUE Function (NVL). The NULL VALUE function (NVL) substitutes a value for NULLS. Sometimes you might want to treat null values as zero (or some other number). For example, if your company employs people who receive commissions, then a null commission should perhaps be treated the same as a zero commission. On the other hand, if you find a null value in a column listing Social Security numbers, it would not be appropriate to convert this to a zero.

You can use the null value function NVL to convert a null value to a specified non-null value for the purpose of evaluating an expression. NVL requires two arguments, an expression and, a non-null value. The syntax is:

NVL (*x, expr*)

Whenever NVL is evaluated, it will return the value of the expression if that value is non-null. If the value of the expression is null, then it will return the value of the second argument—the non-null value.

NVL is especially important for use with group functions such as AVG, SUM, where *ORACLE* will automatically ignore, or count as zero, any null values in the data unless you specify otherwise by means of NVL.

NVL can return a CHAR or DATE value as well as a number value, and the same two arguments as above apply.

11.3 EXPRESSIONS

An *expression* is a group of values and operators which may be evaluated to a single value. There are three types: Logical, CHAR, and Arithmetic expressions.

11.3.1 Logical Expressions

A Logical expression is an expression containing a WHERE clause with more than one condition, such as the collection of three conditions in the following expression:

```
WHERE CITY = 'CHICAGO' AND STORE__NO = 10 AND PROFIT < 500000
```

11.3.2 Arithmetic Expressions

An Arithmetic expression contains two or more column names and column values connected by quantitative operators such as $+, -, *, /$, or between ... and .... An arithmetic expression can be included in a SELECT command, just as you would include a single column.

For example, this query will return the names of all bread suppliers, the cost of their product, the shipping charge for that product, and a column showing the sum of cost plus shipping charge:

```
SELECT  SNAME, COST, SHIPPING__CHARGE, COST + SHIPPING__CHARGE
FROM    SUPPLIERS
WHERE   PRODUCT = BREAD;
```

An arithmetic expression can also be used in a WHERE clause:

```
SELECT SNAME, COST, SHIPPING__CHARGE
FROM SUPPLIERS
WHERE SHIPPING__CHARGE < 0.05 * COST;
```

This query will return the names of all suppliers whose shipping charges are less than 5 percent of the cost of their product.

11.3.3 CHAR Expressions

A CHAR expression is the result of appending one CHAR value (a column or a constant) to another with the *concatenation operator* (||). For example, you might want to join the Store Number with the city in which it is located, and put these into a single column, separating the two values with a blank space, a dash, and another blank space. The command to do so is:

```
SELECT STORENO || ' — ' || CITY LOCATIONS
FROM STORES;
```

The query gives the alias "LOCATIONS" for the new (concatenated) column's heading. The resulting column would look like this:

LOCATIONS
---

10 — DALLAS
12 — BOSTON
15 — DENVER
20 — ATLANTA

Keep in mind that you cannot do arithmetic with CHAR expressions, even if they happen to contain numbers.

A CHAR constant is always surrounded by single quotes. Therefore, you cannot use a single quote within a CHAR constant because then *SQL*Plus* would interpret the position where the quote occurs as the end of the CHAR constant. For example, the following could be misleading:

```
'BROKER'S INTERESTS'
```

would be interpreted by *ORACLE* as two constants: 'BROKER' and 'S INTERESTS'. Instead, to handle this type of constant, use double quotes. The following is valid:

```
'BROKER''S INTERESTS'
```

11.4 OPERATORS

A WHERE clause in a query specifies a condition that must be tested in order to answer your query. The SELECT part of the query depends on the result of that testing. The condition specified in the WHERE clause consists of three parts:

1. A column name
2. A comparison operator
3. Another column name, constant value, or list of values.

For example, consider the following simple query:

```
SELECT *
FROM STORENO
WHERE PROFIT > 500000;
```

The three parts of the WHERE clause listed above are:

1. The column name (PROFIT)
2. The comparison operator (the greater-than sign, >)
3. The other column name, constant value, or list of values ($500,000).

Thus, when your query is entered, the SELECT must test for this combination of three items to make its selection of which rows to process. The *operator* then forms the link between what you already know (the Store Numbers) and what you want to know (which store numbers are making a profit over $500,000).

Operators are used to compare a column value to a numeric or to a CHAR constant. To make such comparisons, a CHAR or DATE constant must be enclosed in single quotes (a numeric constant does not need to be), and the case (upper or lower) of the constant must be the same as the case of the column value.

Operators also are used to compare a column value to an arithmetic expression such as INCOME/COST, or to compare a column value to another column value.

The general form of a statement using an operator is:

```
SELECT column_name, column_name, . . .
FROM tablename
WHERE (value = constant) operator (value != constant);
```

For example:

```
WHERE PRICE = 1.25*COST
```

11.4.1 Quantitative and Qualitative Operators

A *quantitative operator* directs *SQL*Plus* to perform a quantitative operation. Table 11-5 lists the quantitative operators.

The qualitative operators are shown in Table 11-6. You may search for a CHAR value where you don't know all the characters in the value. For example, if you are searching for a supplier's name beginning with the letters DET, but don't know the exact spelling of the rest of the name. In this case, you can use the character matching symbol % in the WHERE clause, like this:

```
SELECT SNAME, CITY
FROM SUPPLIERS
WHERE SNAME LIKE 'DET%';
```

SQL*Plus will return all suppliers whose names start with DET, and the city where each is located, no matter how many characters come after the DET.

The character matching symbol, %, may be used at any point in the character string, and it may appear more than once. If for example, you know that the supplier's name ends with the letters ''Neal,'' but you don't know whether the full name is MacNeal, McNeal, or O'Neal, you would set up the WHERE clause like this:

```
WHERE SNAME LIKE '%NEAL';
```

Table 11-5. Quantitative Operators.

Operator	Meaning
=	equal to
!=	not equal to
>	greater than
>=	greater than or equal to
<	less than
<=	less than or equal to
BETWEEN . . . AND . . .	between two values
IN (*list*)	any of a list of values
LIKE	match a character pattern
IS NULL	is a null value

To negate the last four operators, use the operator NOT, e.g., NOT BETWEEN, NOT IN, NOT LIKE, and IS NOT NULL.

In a large list, using the character matching symbol might return a great many rows. You can cut down the number returned if you happen to be missing only one letter in the name (or other item) you are looking for. For example, if you know the name is Johnson, but don't know whether it is spelled "Johnson," or "Johnsen," you can use the underscore, __ , (called a wild card) to represent the missing letter. To find the Johnson you are looking for, set up the WHERE clause like this:

WHERE SNAME LIKE 'JOHNS__N';

Table 11-6. Logical Operators.

Operator	Function
%	Represents a string of zero or more characters that may appear anywhere in the quoted string and may appear more than once.
underscore	Wildcard. Each underscore inside single quotes represents one wildcard CHAR position.
IN	Equivalent to a series of OR's, e.g., "WHERE employee in Dept 30, 42, 52" is the same as saying "WHERE employee is in Dept. 30 OR 42 OR 52."
LIKE	"Matches following pattern." The % wildcard matches any string of characters, while the underscore (__) matches any single character.
NOT	Reverses a condition's result.
NOT IN	Equivalent to a series of negated AND's.
NULL	Signifies the absence of data, is not necessarily the same as zero, takes no storage space in the row, and is not necessarily equal to another NULL value.

Like the percent sign, the underscore can be used more than once in a character string. Therefore, if you are unsure of more than one letter in a name (or other item), such as "houwegian," which could also be spelled "houwejian" or "hauwegean" (or several other possibilities), set up the WHERE clause with an underscore in place of every doubtful letter, like this:

```
WHERE SNAME LIKE 'H__uwe____an';
```

Each underscore represents only a single character. Therefore, if you are not sure how many syllables are in the latter part of the name (or other item), then you might want to combine use of the underscore with the percent sign, as follows:

```
WHERE SNAME LIKE 'H__uwe%an';
```

This will insure that the name will be found no matter how many letters are missing in the spot where you have placed the percent sign.

The word NOT may be used to negate the LIKE. This would SELECT all rows that do not match the pattern you specify with the operator(s).

11.4.2 Boolean Operators

The two operators AND and OR are called *Boolean connectors* in mathematics. They are used in *ORACLE* when it is necessary to specify more than one qualification of an item being selected. Both ANDs and ORs may be used in WHERE clauses.

Connecting Conditions with AND. AND is used to retrieve rows meeting more than one condition. The number of conditions to be met is the number of ANDs plus one. Both the condition before the AND, and the condition after the AND must be true in order for a row to be retrieved. (If you are familiar with Boolean algebra, you will recognize the AND condition as the intersection of two or more sets.):

```
WHERE CITY = 'CHICAGO' AND PROFIT > 500000;
```

Connecting Conditions with OR. OR is used to retrieve rows that meet any one of two or more given conditions. Only one condition specified in the OR statement needs to be true for a row to be retrieved, but more than one condition may be met. (In Boolean algebra, OR constitutes the union of two or more sets.)

```
WHERE CITY = 'CHICAGO' OR PROFIT > 500000;
```

11.4.5 OPERATOR PRECEDENCE

Both AND's and OR's may be used in a single WHERE clause. When both AND and OR appear in the same WHERE clause, all the AND's are performed first, then all the OR's are performed. This is because the AND operator has a higher precedence than the OR operator.

Operators are all arranged in a hierarchy in *ORACLE* that determines which are performed first. In any expression, operators are performed in the order of their assigned

Table 11-7. Hierarchy of Value Operators.

Operator	Function	Example
( )	Overrides normal operator precedence rules.	SELECT (X+Y)/(X−Y)
+ −	Sign prefixed to a number expression.	QTYSOLD = −1 WHERE A< −(5∗B);
∗ /	Multiplication and division	SELECT 2∗X+1 WHERE X>Y/2;
+ −	Addition and subtraction	SELECT 2∗S+1 WHERE X>Y−Z;
‖	CHAR value concatenation	CODE := CODE ‖ SUBCODE
:=	Assigns a value to a user variable.	X := 15;

Operators are shown in descending order of precedence. Operators with equal precedence are grouped together with broken lines.

precedence from highest to lowest. If operators in a query have equal precedence, then they are performed in the order you placed them in the query, reading from left to right.

Table 11-7 lists some logical operators in their order of precedence.

If you want to change this established hierarchy of precedence, you can do so by using parentheses. The part of the expression inside the parentheses will be evaluated before the rest of the expression. For example, the following two WHERE clauses will be evaluated differently:

```
WHERE SAL>50000 AND TITLE= 'MANAGER' OR TITLE= 'SUPERVISOR'
WHERE SAL>50000 and (TITLE= 'MANAGER' OR TITLE= 'SUPERVISOR')
```

The first WHERE clause will return all managers with salary over $50,000, and all supervisors regardless of their salary. This is because the values on either side of the AND will be evaluated first. The second WHERE clause will return all managers and all supervisors with salaries over $50,000. This is due to the fact that the expression inside the parentheses will be evaluated first.

It is important to consider operator precedence in making up a query, but it may sometimes be difficult to determine or to remember the exact hierarchy. In that case, it is always simpler to override the hierarchy by using parentheses to make certain that the query returns what you are looking for. Keep in mind that parentheses always take precedence over everything else in the hierarchy.

Chapter 12

Using *ORACLE*

THIS CHAPTER PRESENTS WAYS OF HANDLING YOUR DATA TO FIT YOUR OWN NEEDS. Depending upon the size of your database, and the special requirements of your own installation, you may find it helpful to make use of some or all of the methods described. COMMIT and ROLLBACK must be used by all systems. Whether or not aliases, joins, equijoins, and subqueries will be useful to you will depend on the needs of your own installation.

12.1 TRANSACTION PROCESSING: COMMIT AND ROLLBACK

Work should be processed into the database in logical groupings rather than in individual units. A *logical grouping* may be seen as a grouping that leaves the database consistent, whereas any one command in the group would not. For example, if an increase in "Number of items sold" has been entered, the database might not be consistent until "Inventory" has been decreased by that amount.

A *transaction* then, is that group of changes that constitutes a logical grouping of entries, and your database should be designed around transactions as the basic units of your installation, rather than around individual entries. In general, a transaction can be defined as the changes made in the database between COMMIT statements that enter the group of changes into the database.

The size of the transactions, and the frequency with which they are permanently entered into the database, will have an effect on requests for locks on tables and rows, the amount of data lost in a system failure, and the probability of deadlocks occurring in a multi-user system. Therefore, the concepts of committing data and ROLLBACK of data entered but not committed, should be tied in with the concept of logical units of work.

12.1.1 The COMMIT Statement

Changes such as INSERT, DELETE, or UPDATE should be made in groups as logical transactions, and then committed to the database. This ensures consistency and integrity of the data.

Before a COMMIT statement is issued, the changes made are visible only to the user performing them. After the COMMIT statement is issued, the changes are visible to all users. Before a COMMIT statement is issued, the changes may be corrected, revised, or eliminated (see ROLLBACK in Section 12.1.2 below) without ever going into the database. After the COMMIT statement is issued, the changes can only be corrected, revised, or eliminated by using another INSERT, UPDATE, or DELETE command on them.

The general form of the COMMIT statement is:

COMMIT WORK

After a system failure, only committed changes will be saved.

Turning on the AUTOCOMMIT option will cause every change to be committed as soon as it is entered. While this would appear to be an advantage to be used whenever making changes, this is not the case. The AUTOCOMMIT option should be used when the changes being made are not logically related. If it is used when logically related changes are being made, in a properly designed system the database may refuse to accept part of the change because of possible inconsistency, as illustrated above.

Since one INSERT, UPDATE, or DELETE command can cause many different rows to change, care should be taken not to make too many changes before issuing a COMMIT statement. A great many changes committed all at once will put a drain on the system. And, should a system failure occur before a large number of changes are committed, all such changes would have to be reprocessed when the system comes up again. Therefore, frequent—but judicious—use of the COMMIT statement is desirable.

Some commands cause an automatic COMMIT. These are:

ALTER	EXIT
AUDIT	GRANT
CREATE	NOAUDIT
DISCONNECT	QUIT
DROP	REVOKE

If you have just entered other transactions, and have not yet committed them, and you enter one of the commands shown above, then all of the prior uncommitted work will get committed. In effect, this ends the unit of work you were performing.

12.1.2 The ROLLBACK Statement

ROLLBACK cancels out changes completed but not committed to the database, thus leaving the database as though the changes were never made. The general form is as follows:

ROLLBACK WORK

ROLLBACK is automatically performed for all users when *ORACLE* recovers from a system failure. The commands that COMMIT automatically (see list in Section 12.1.1

above) execute immediately, and cannot be rolled back.

Certain errors, such as attempting to insert a bad record, a duplicate record, or an invalid number into a column, will cause rollbacks. Syntax errors discovered during parsing however, will not cause rollbacks.

12.2 USING ALIASES FOR TABLE NAMES

If repeated use makes it advisable to shorten table names, you can use an alias for the table name. You can do this by defining the alias in your FROM clause. For example, we can abbreviate "Bakeries" to the letter B, and "Canneries" to the letter C, by defining the alias in the FROM clause. Separate each alias from the table name by a space.

```
SELECT  BNAME, BLOC, CNAME, CLOC
FROM   Bakeries B, Canneries C
WHERE  . . .
AND  . . .
```

On the other hand, it may be that the abbreviated column names already in your database may not be what you want to have printed out. A column name such as AVG(PRC) might not be as easily understood as Average Price in a printed report. Therefore you may want *ORACLE* to print out an "alias" in returning the answer to your query. Do this by using the spelled out meaning of your database column title as the alias, like this:

```
SELECT  AVG(PRC) 'AVERAGE PRICE'
FROM   SUPPLIERS
WHERE  . . . . . . .
```

The single quotes around AVERAGE PRICE are necessary to indicate that even though AVERAGE and PRICE are two words, they must appear in the response as the single alias where *SQL*Plus* would normally print out the column name AVG(PRC). If the alias is a single word, no quotes are necessary.

12.3 JOINS

A join occurs when a query requires information from two or more tables which have one variable in common. The syntax for a simple join is:

```
SELECT  column_name
FROM   table1name, table2name
WHERE  table1_column_name = table2_column_name;
```

The complete name of the above join is actually *equijoin*, since the column names in the WHERE clause have an equal sign between them. Since this is the most common kind of join, it is usually referred to simply as a "join." In Section 12.3.4 below, however, "non-equijoins" are discussed where the columns in the WHERE clause are not equal to each other, but have some other relationship.

An example of a join would be if ABC Foods needed a list of all those baked goods distributors and canned vegetable distributors where both kinds of distributors are in the same city. The data would come from the table containing baked goods distributors, and the table containing canned vegetable distributors, with the common element being City. The command to retrieve this information would be:

```
SELECT  B. *, C. *
FROM    BAKERIES B, CANNERIES C
WHERE   B.CITY = C.CITY;
```

This is a "join" of the tables Bakeries and Canneries over the common column City.

12.3.1 Joining Views

If you want to create a view based on columns from more than one table, define the view with a query containing a join. An example of this for selecting from two tables is as follows:

```
CREATE VIEW viewname (view_column_name1, view_column_name2) AS
    SELECT table1_column_name, table2_column_name
    FROM table1_name, table2_name
WHERE table1_column_name = table2_column_name;
```

The *view_column_name* arguments are enclosed in parentheses to indicate to *ORACLE* that these will be the column names in the view being created. The order of these must correspond to the order of the column names in the SELECT command. If the column names in the view are to be the same as the column names in the two tables from which the columns are to be selected, then you don't need to name the columns in the CREATE statement.

You cannot UPDATE, INSERT, or DELETE a view made up of more than one table.

12.3.2 Joining More Than Two Tables in a View

You can join any number of tables in a view. If you wanted to look at a view of suppliers of several different types of products all at once, you could join the relevant columns from the separate tables for each type of supplier in just the same way as joining two tables.

12.3.3 Joining Tables to Views

You can also join views to tables or to other views in the same way that you join tables to each other. Use the column names you created in the view just as though they were column names in a table. If you want to combine all the columns in the view you have created with a column in a table, use the notation *view_name. *, like this:

```
SELECT view_name.*, table_column_name
FROM view, table
    . . .
```

12.3.4 Non-Equijoins

There are several types of joins. The above type of join, where you join two tables by means of an equal sign (=), is called an *equijoin*. All other joins are *non-equijoins* because the relationship between the objects joined is not an equal sign. The syntax is the same as that shown in Section 12.3.1 for joins, except that the WHERE clause should show an inequality (!=) instead of the equal sign, as in the following:

WHERE *table1_column_name* != *table2_column_name;*

or

WHERE *table1_column_name* > *table2_column_name;*

or where you use any of the other arithmetic expressions except the equal (=) sign between the two column names, as in the following examples:

```
WHERE X.SALARY > Y.SALARY
WHERE X.EMPLOYEE_NO != Y.EMPLOYEE_NO
WHERE X.SALARY < Y.SALARY
```

In both equijoins and non-equijoins, a column in one table may be joined to many columns in another table.

12.3.5 Outer Joins

An *outer join* is a row that does not satisfy the join condition. Suppose you want to display the rows in the first table listed in your join condition that do not meet that condition in the second table. Do this by using the outer join symbol (+) at the end of your WHERE clause. Then the non-matching rows will be displayed along with the matching ones, and will show a NULL value in every column that corresponds to a column of the second table.

12.3.6 Joining a Table to Itself

You can join one row in a table to another row in the same table by specifying the join columns in the WHERE clause. For example, suppose you have a table listing cashiers and managers, along with their salaries and employee numbers. You want to link each cashier with her/his manager in every case where the cashier earns more than the manager. You would join the appropriate cashier and manager rows from that table with the following:

```
SELECT  CASHIER.ENAME, CASHIER.SALARY, MANAGER.ENAME, MANAGER.SALARY
FROM  EMPLOYEESCASHIER, EMPLOYEES.MANAGER
WHERE  CASHIER.MANAGER = MANAGER.EMPLOYEE_NO
AND    CASHIER.SALARY > MANAGER.SALARY;
```

12.4 SUBQUERIES

A nested SELECT is a *subquery;* in other words, it is a query within a query, or an additional condition placed in the query. Looked at another way, a subquery is a query contained in the WHERE clause of another query.

Subqueries provide you with results you need to complete the main query. They are useful when you want to select rows from a table with a condition that depends on what data are found in the table.

You may use subqueries wherever you can use a WHERE clause, specifically in the SELECT, INSERT, UPDATE, and DELETE commands. A subquery is usually a SELECT-FROM-WHERE expression that is nested inside another such expression. (You should always enclose subqueries in parentheses.) The subquery also may include GROUP BY and HAVING clauses, but it *cannot* include ORDER BY or UNION. You may put subqueries within subqueries, with up to 16 subqueries linked to the higher-level query.

Here is an example of the simplest type of subquery. Suppose you want to know the name of all those suppliers who supply the same products as X Company. You would need two queries to accomplish this, one to find what product X Company supplies, and one to find the other suppliers who can furnish that product. Instead, you can do this in one operation by using a subquery.

The system handles this by looking at the subquery first. That is, it looks first for the product supplied by X Company. After that is done, the rest of the query is answered. It is clear that this is more efficient than looking first at the larger group of suppliers, then hunting through that to pick out members of the smaller group of those who supply the same product as X Company. The query can be handled by using the following subquery (nested SELECT).

```
SELECT SNAME, PRODUCT
FROM  SUPPLIERS
WHERE  PRODUCT IN
     (SELECT PRODUCT
     FROM  SUPPLIERS
     WHERE  SNAME = 'X');
```

The command will always be evaluated by working from the last (or innermost) SELECT back to the first, except in the case of correlated subqueries discussed in Section 12.4.7.

All such subqueries may also be written as a series of joins. The result will be the same. Whether to use nested SELECTs or a series of joins will depend upon which suits your purpose better, or which seems to you to be a more reasonable way to express the query.

12.4.1 ANY and ALL: Subqueries that Return a Set of Values

Since use of the operators ANY and ALL can be confusing and error-prone, we suggest that you use instead the EXISTS operator. EXISTS covers cases where you might use ANY and ALL, and using EXISTS is more likely to give you the answer you are looking for.

12.4.2 Subqueries that Test for Existence

The conditional subquery EXISTS searches for data that may or may not be included in the table being searched. If the data are there, the subquery is said to be "true"; if not, it is said to be "false." (In formal logic, EXISTS in this context is the Existential Quantifier.)

For example, suppose you wanted a list of all Supplier Names (from a table of suppliers) for suppliers (if any) who supply Product P1 (from a table of products). You would set up the query and subquery this way:

```
SELECT  SNAME,
FROM    SUPPLIERS
WHERE   EXISTS
    (SELECT *
    FROM  PRODUCTS
    WHERE P# = 'P1');
```

Note that the predicate is represented by the expression (SELECT * FROM . . .) in a subquery using EXISTS.

Using EXISTS is another way of setting up a query where you could use IN or a join. Actually, any query that you can express using IN you can express using EXISTS. But the converse is not true (i.e., for every query using EXISTS you cannot necessarily use IN).

12.4.3 IN and NOT IN: Subqueries that Return a List of Values

You can substitute IN for = ANY and NOT IN for != ALL. For example, to list suppliers in Chicago who supply the same product as anyone in Dallas, enter

```
SELECT SNAME, PRODUCT
FROM    SUPPLIERS
WHERE    CITY = 'CHICAGO'
AND      PRODUCT IN
            (SELECT  PRODUCT
            FROM  SUPPLIERS
            WHERE   CITY = 'DALLAS');
```

In this example, the subquery returns a list of products provided by suppliers in Dallas. The main query selects suppliers in Chicago whose product is among those returned by the subquery.

12.4.4 Subqueries that Return More Than One Column

The subqueries discussed up to this point selected only one column from a table, but you may also select more than one column. If a subquery is set up to select more than one column, you must put parentheses around the columns on the right side of the comparison operator.

Suppose you want a list of suppliers who supply the same product at the same price as Jones, a cannery that charges $10 per carton. To do so, enter:

```
SELECT  SNAME, PRODUCT, PRICE
```

```
FROM     SUPPLIERS
WHERE    PRODUCT, PRICE =
         (SELECT PRODUCT, PRICE
         FROM   SUPPLIERS
         WHERE  SNAME = 'JONES');
```

12.4.5 Multiple Subqueries

The WHERE clause of a query may contain any number of conditions with subqueries connected by AND and OR. You may also put subqueries within subqueries, up to a maximum of 16 subqueries linked to the next higher-level query.

To list the suppliers with either the same product as Jones or a price greater than or equal to Smith, in order by product and price, enter:

```
SELECT   SNAME, PRODUCT, CITY, PRICE
FROM     SUPPLIERS
WHERE    PRODUCT IN
         (SELECT PRODUCT
         FROM   SUPPLIERS
         WHERE  SNAME = 'JONES')
OR       PRICE > =
         (SELECT PRICE
         FROM   SUPPLIERS
        WHERE  SNAME = 'SMITH')
ORDER BY PRODUCT, PRICE;
```

12.4.6 Subqueries that Refer to More than One Table

The operators UNION, INTERSECT, and MINUS are useful for constructing subqueries that refer to more than one table. However, these three operators apply certain restrictions to the queries on which they operate. Queries (or subqueries) containing UNION, INTERSECT, and MINUS must select the same number of columns, and the columns selected must be of the same type. They do not have to be the same length, but these queries cannot refer to any column with type LONG.

The ORDER BY clause in a query employing UNION, INTERSECT, or MINUS must be used only once, and it must be at the end of the entire query, not at the end of each SELECT. You cannot specify the ordering of columns by name, since their names could be different in each table queried. Instead, you must specify them by their positions in each SELECT list.

For example, suppose ABC Foods had several tables similar in structure, containing records on suppliers of different types of products. To make a query on two of those tables, ordered by supplier number, you could enter:

```
SELECT SNAME, PRODUCT__NO
FROM   SUPPLIERSA
UNION
SELECT SNAME, PRODUCT__NO
FROM   SUPPLIERSB
ORDER BY SUPPLIERSA;
```

134

12.4.7 Correlated Subqueries

In the subqueries considered so far, each subquery was executed once; then the resulting value was used by the WHERE clause of the main query. You can also set up a subquery that is executed repeatedly. For this process, we need to introduce the concept of *candidate row*, which is a row that may, after certain operations are performed, fit the conditions in the query.

For example, suppose you want to find the suppliers whose price for a given product is higher than the average price for other suppliers of that product. We cannot pick out the suppliers simply by looking at the table of suppliers. The candidate rows are the suppliers whose prices will be compared to the average price for the product they supply. The evaluation proceeds as follows:

First, set up a main query to select the suppliers from the SUPPLIERS table:

```
SELECT   PRODUCT, SNAME, PRICE
FROM     SUPPLIERS
WHERE    SPRICE > (average price of candidate supplier's product);
```

Then set up a subquery to calculate the average price of each candidate supplier's product:

```
SELECT AVG(PRICE)
FROM  SUPPLIERS
WHERE  PRODUCT = (candidate supplier's product);
```

The main query will consider each candidate row. As it does so, it must invoke the subquery and tell it the supplier's product. Then the subquery must compute the average price for that supplier's product. Finally, the main query must compare the supplier's price to the average price for the product.

The above procedure is called a *correlated subquery*, because each execution of the subquery is correlated with the value of a field in one of the main query's candidate rows.

To set up the subquery, it is necessary to use the letter X (or some other alias name) as a table alias. The X appears in the main query shown below (FROM SUPPLIERS X) and in the subquery (WHERE X.PRODUCT = PRODUCT). In the subquery, the table alias X refers to a candidate row's value of PRODUCT, i.e., a candidate supplier's product.

When the subquery is executed for each of the main query's candidate rows, it compares the value of the PRODUCT in the candidate row (X.PRODUCT) to the value of PRODUCT in each row of the table (. . . = PRODUCT). It returns the value of AVG(PRICE) computed over the selected rows. The complete correlated subquery is set up as follows:

```
SELECT   PRODUCT, SNAME, PRICE
FROM     SUPPLIERS X
WHERE    PRICE >
         (SELECT  AVG(PRICE)
         FROM  SUPPLIERS
         WHERE  X.PRODUCT = PRODUCT);
```

The main point of the preceeding discussion can be summarized thus: A correlated subquery is signaled by a reference to a table alias. The table alias refers to the value of a column in each candidate row.

12.4.8 Subqueries Using INSERT

You can use INSERT to copy rows from one table into another by replacing the usual VALUES clause in the INSERT command with the subquery. For example, suppose you have just hired several new salesmen who were formerly listed in a table of job applicants. You now want to add these new personnel to your personnel table. Do this as follows:

```
INSERT INTO PERSONNEL (ENAME, JOB, SAL)
(SELECT ENAME, JOB, SAL
        FROM   APPLICANTS
        WHERE  JOB = 'SALESMAN');
```

12.4.9 Subqueries Using AS

The AS clause is useful when you want to copy rows from one table into a new table you are creating. Creating the table, and copying the rows into it can be done with one command. The procedure for doing this is explained in Section 9.2.3 of Chapter 9.

12.4.10 Using Subqueries to Update Rows or Values

You can use a subquery to update a specified group of rows in a table. The subquery is placed after the WHERE clause. You also can use a subquery in the UPDATE command's SET clause, but it must return exactly one row, and it must return the same number and type of columns as the columns being updated. Both these procedures are illustrated and explained in Section 10.2.1 of Chapter 10.

Chapter 13

Optimizing
System Performance

THE PERFORMANCE OF A SYSTEM WILL DEPEND FIRST UPON THE SYSTEM DESIGNER'S knowledge of relational theory and its practical application (see Chapter 4 for a discussion of database design). While there may be an unlimited number of ways to set up the tables in a database, the tables actually used can either take maximum advantage of relational theory—and thereby be maximally efficient—or not.

In addition to appropriate table design, the indexing and clustering features of *ORACLE* will enhance performance. Also, since there are usually at least two ways to formulate any SQL query, continued use of the system will exhibit to the alert user that one SQL statement is often more efficient than another. Similarly, the use of ORDER BY, GROUP BY, and JOIN can contribute to efficiency.

There are many steps the single user can take to improve his or her own transactions by judicious use of indexes and clusters. The DBA and the applications designer can improve the efficiency of other users by adjusting INIT.ORA parameters and setting database defaults. There also are operating system considerations that will improve performance in the *Installation and User's Guide* for your system.

13.1 OPTIMIZATION IN SINGLE-USER SYSTEMS

Most gains to be achieved in a single-user system lie in the area of database design. How data are stored, and the setup of tables defining it, are prime considerations. If the single user does not have, and does not have the time to acquire, the appropriate background for a thorough understanding of relational theory and its practical application, it might be well to obtain professional advice at the outset on the design of a database. There are also many ways, however, that the single user can improve the performance of his operation by efficient use of indexes, clauses, and the other operators discussed in this chapter.

13.2 INDEXES

Indexes have two primary purposes: The first is *speed of execution*; indexes are the primary means of reducing disk I/O. Second, they offer a *guarantee of uniqueness;* an index can ensure that data in one column, or combination of columns, are unique for every record in a table.

Let's first distinguish between indexes and keys. Indexes actually exist in the database, implemented by SQL to perform the two purposes stated above. They are mandatory in *ORACLE*. One of the first uses in *ORACLE* of an index is the index on the column(s) that forms the key.

Keys, on the other hand, are logical entities. A key is a column, or a combination of columns, that can be used to uniquely identify a row. It does not have to be present in *ORACLE* as such. (For a precise definition of key, see Chapter 4.)

Foreign keys are also logical entities. A foreign key is a column (or columns) in one table which is not a key in that table, but is a key somewhere else, usually in another table (see Chapter 4). Foreign keys are useful in combining data from several tables, using joins. They do not have to be present in *ORACLE* as such.

There are several different types of indexes, including concatenated, compressed, noncompressed, unique, and nonunique, as well as various ways to use indexes. These types and special uses will be discussed below.

13.2.1 Creating Indexes Efficiently

The owner of a table, as well as any user who has been granted INDEX access on that table, can create indexes on it. The syntax for creating indexes has already been shown and its clauses defined in Chapter 9, Section 9.6.

When the CREATE INDEX command is entered, the column(s) to be indexed are ordered, and for each row the ROWID is saved. In other words, a sort is done on the column and ROWID for all existing rows.

Once created, an index is automatically maintained and used by *ORACLE* with no further effort by the user no matter how many additions, updates or deletions are made to the data.

Any number of indexes may be made on any one table. However, the more indexes that are made, the more overhead that is used up as the table is updated. Thus, it may be a trade-off between speed of updating versus speed of lookup. For example, if a table is only read, then more indexes may be desirable. But if a table will be frequently updated, then fewer indexes would be better.

It is more efficient to load a table using ODL before any indexes are created on it. For that and other reasons, an index usually is created after the data are in it. If the index is created before loading the data, then the index must be updated every time a row is inserted. You can make an exception to this at the expense of performance if you want to assure that a specific value is unique for every row loaded. In that case, a unique index can be created on the column(s) you want to be unique.

13.2.2 Concatenated Indexes

A *concatenated index* is one created on more than one column of a table. Concatenated indexes are the only way to ensure uniqueness across several columns (as, for example, in the combination of area code and phone number). If it takes more than one column to ensure uniqueness, then the required number of columns should be used in the concatenation.

Concatenated indexes speed the retrieval of data returned by SQL statements when those statements contain several different criteria in the WHERE clause. You may include up to 16 columns in the concatenated index, subject to the number of characters that can be indexed. The maximum number of characters in any index is 240, including 1-byte separators used to distinguish the columns. You can determine the width of your concatenated index by summing the width of each column to be indexed and adding the number of columns to be indexed minus 1 (to take account of the separators).

An example of a concatenated index would be one where you want to combine the names of vendors, and their location, as follows:

```
CREAT UNIQUE INDEX IND VEND__ID
ON VENDORS (VEND__ID, CITY);
```

This would be a reasonable index to construct if queries like the following one were issued often:

```
SELECT *
FROM VENDORS
WHERE VENDOR__ID = '502'
AND CITY = 'DENVER';
```

The order in which you name the columns in the CREATE INDEX command does not have to correspond to the order in which they appear in the table definition. But you can favorably influence performance by putting the most-used column first.

A concatenated index will speed performance on any query using the leading portion of the index. Queries with WHERE clauses using only the first column of a concatenated index will also benefit. If the WHERE clause does not name the first column in the index, the concatenated index cannot be used, and no gain in performance will result.

In general, using concatenated, noncompressed indexes will speed performance when the query can be satisfied by reading only index blocks instead of data blocks.

13.2.3 Compressed and Noncompressed Indexes

Indexes are created compressed by default. Index data are stored using forward and rear compression. Less storage is needed for compressed data, and this reduces I/O. However, the initial compression and the decoding necessary at retrieval result in a processing cost. To retrieve the actual values, *ORACLE* must go to the table's data blocks. In so doing, it may fetch records that satisfy the compressed key but not the query. The resulting loss in processing time must be weighed against the storage advantage of compression.

By specifying the NOCOMPRESS option in the CREATE INDEX command, you can create an index without compression. Since noncompressed indexes store the entire data value, results are sometimes returned sooner than for compressed values. This is especially true where the query can be processed entirely within the index blocks, without going to the table; it is the case when every column referenced in the SQL statement is in the noncompressed index and a WHERE clause is used. For example, given a noncompressed index on SNAME, both the following queries can be processed using only the index:

SELECT SNAME   SELECT COUNT (SNAME)
FROM SUPPLIERS   FROM SUPPLIERS
WHERE SNAME LIKE 'S%H';   WHERE SNAME = 'SMITH';

Compressed indexes require about 10 bytes per entry, while noncompressed indexes require about 17 bytes per entry. In planning space allocation, these factors should be taken into consideration. Chapter 6, Section 6.5.5, gives a formula for computing the number of index segments to be allocated.

13.3 CLUSTERS

The purpose of clustering is to store close together data that are accessed together, and to reduce storage space by storing the common element in sets of data only once. For example, if a cluster's key were AREA__CODE and there were several hundred telephone numbers with the same area code, then the area code would be stored just once instead of for each of the several hundred phone numbers.

Clustering is an alternative method of storing the data. It has no effect on the SQL statements used to retrieve those data. To identify data which might better be stored in clustered form than not, look for tables which have one or more columns in common (usually key columns), and look for tables that are frequently accessed together, as in joins.

Once clusters are created and the data stored, users can query clustered data just as they would query nonclustered data. In fact, the users will not even know whether the data are clustered or not.

13.3.1 Logical Format of Clustered Data Blocks

The overhead for a clustered block is 44 bytes for each physical block and 32 bytes for each logical block. There may be several logical blocks for each physical block. Further details of the format of clustered data blocks is in Chapter 6, Section 6.6.

13.3.2 The Cluster Key

The CREATE CLUSTER statement names the columns which form the cluster key. This key is stored once per logical cluster block. It also appears in every chained cluster block. *ORACLE* automatically builds and maintains an index on the cluster key. Therefore, you do not have to use CREATE INDEX to build an index on the columns forming the cluster key. However, you may build an index using the cluster key if you make it part of a concatenated key, or if you want to make it a unique index for one of the tables in the cluster.

You can update the data in columns of a table corresponding to the cluster key. Since the placement of data depends on the cluster key, changing the cluster key for a record causes the physical relocation of the record.

13.3.3 Creating Clusters

The syntax for creating a cluster is:

```
CREATE CLUSTER cluster_name
( cluster_key1 data type, cluster_key2 data type, . . . )
[ SPACE space_name]
[ SIZE logical_block_size ]
[ COMPRESS | NOCOMPRESS ];
```

where SPACE references a space definition, just as for CREATE TABLE, and
COMPRESS/NOCOMPRESS indicates whether or not the cluster key is to be compressed.
SIZE refers to the requested logical block size, which is adjusted by *ORACLE* to the actual
logical block size. If SIZE is not specified, the operating system's *ORACLE* block size
minus physical block overhead is the default. See Section 13.3.4 below on determining
the logical block size.

The following rules apply to creating clusters:

1. No more than 16 columns may be clustered together.
2. The data type and size of the cluster key in the table must match those in
   the cluster key in the cluster.
3. At least one clustered column in each table must be NOT NULL.
4. The cluster key may be multiple column.

13.3.4 Determining the Logical Block Size

While your choice of the logical block size for the cluster will affect performance,
there is no hard and fast rule for making your choice. At the same time, choosing a good
logical block size will mean that space will be better utilized, and fewer read operations
will be required during physical scans. Therefore, some limiting conditions follow.

The logical block size should be less than the *ORACLE* block size, which is dependent
on your operating system. The size you request will be adjusted by *ORACLE*. Usually
it will end up somewhat larger to conform to the next integral division of the physical
block. The algorithm used and the number of logical blocks per *ORACLE* block varies
according to the cluster key size, and also according to operating systems. But generally
one logical *ORACLE* block can equal up to six or seven logical cluster blocks. In most
cases, logical blocks can be no smaller than 300 bytes. To see the requested and actual
sizes, use the query:

```
SELECT REQBLK, LOGBLK
FROM CATALOG
WHERE TNAME = tablename;
```

Try to use smaller logical block sizes without creating many chained blocks. If few
records are clustered on the same key, smaller logical block sizes are preferable to avoid
wasting storage space. You should choose a size between the average and the maximum
logical block size. This will strike a balance between wasted space in the blocks and the
need to create chained blocks.

13.3.5 Clusters and Space Definitions

The size of a cluster is determined by the space definition in use when the cluster is created. (For more information on space definitions, see Chapter 6.) That space definition defines the space available for all tables in that cluster. The parameter PCTFREE does not apply for clusters.

13.3.6 Setting Up Clusters

If more than one column is common to the clustered tables, make the cluster key a concatenated key. Too few rows per cluster key will waste space and result in little performance gain.

If you have two or more tables that are often joined, this is a good situation for clustering. If clusters are later considered not useful, the tables can be unclustered. When one or more columns of a single table have several values in common that are frequently used in queries, this situation warrants clustering that table only.

Bulk loading a table into a cluster from an existing table can place heavy demand on the BI file if the cluster already contains one or more tables.

13.3.7 Loading Clusters

After you create a cluster, you can specify which tables it will contain. At least one column in the table (corresponding to one of the cluster key columns) must be defined as NOT NULL in the CREATE TABLE statement. Add tables to the cluster using the CREATE TABLE statement. To cluster a new table, enter:

```
CREATE TABLE new_table
(column1 data type, column2 data type, . . . )
CLUSTER cluster_name (table_column);
```

To copy an existing table into a cluster, first create, cluster, and load a new table in one statement as follows:

```
CREATE TABLE <new tablename>
CLUSTER <clustername> (<table_column>)
AS SELECT * FROM <existing_table>;
```

Then drop the old table which was not clustered:

```
DROP TABLE (existing_tablename);
```

Then rename the table you created in a cluster with the previous table's name if you wish:

```
RENAME <new_tablename> TO <old_tablename>;
```

While tables may be clustered with or without data, less overhead is entailed if empty tables are added. This only requires some updates in the Data Dictionary and changing the initial blocks assigned to the table. More overhead in the form of performance or execution time is required to copy tables with data. This is because all existing data must be read and moved from the table's blocks to the cluster's blocks.

Before a cluster can be dropped, each table in the cluster must be dropped from the cluster. Then, the syntax for dropping a cluster is:

DROP CLUSTER *clustername*;

13.4 OPTIMIZING SQL STATEMENTS

Some SQL statements are automatically optimized by *ORACLE*, and others are not. This section will discuss only those where you have some control over efficiency by your choice of syntax.

13.4.1 Optimizing Queries (SELECT)

On a small table, *ORACLE* will perform reasonably fast scans, therefore making indexes unnecessary. When you retrieve from multiple tables such as joins, however, or large tables with many rows, using indexes and clusters can noticeably improve performance. This is especially true if columns named in the WHERE clause are indexed or clustered.

When many columns are named in the WHERE clause, *ORACLE* follows a set of rules to decide which WHERE conditions to test first. *ORACLE's* choice of where to start with all the testing against WHERE clauses is called the *driving column*. In other words, this column's criteria will "drive" the query. For example, evaluating one WHERE clause first may immediately eliminate 75 percent of the rows from a large table, whereas evaluating some other clause first might only eliminate 15 percent.

Oracle Corporation is constantly doing research and development on optimization. Therefore, the rules underlying the query optimizer may change from time to time. At present, Oracle Corporation offers the rules of thumb regarding query optimization shown in Table 13-1.

13.4.2 Optimizing NOTs

Indexes are not used in *ORACLE* for predicates containing NOT EQUAL clauses. Usually in queries with "NOT =" the number of rows retrieved is greater than the number of rows skipped. For *ORACLE* to read the index and then the table requires an extra I/O. Therefore it is usually faster for it to do a full table scan than to use an index.

Table 13-1. Query Optimization Guidelines.

These:	are faster than	These:
indexed columns		unindexed columns
unique indexes		nonunique indexes
ROWID (= *constant*)		any other search
bounded range		unbounded range
noncompressed indexes	$< - \; ?? \; - >$	compressed indexes
pattern match like 'x %'		pattern match like '% x '

It may, however, use an index on another part of an expression containing a not-equal-to operator. For example, in the clause:

```
WHERE X !=7 AND Y = 8
```

although no index is used for column X, an index might be used for Y.

When the predicate contains NOT along with other operators, *ORACLE* transforms the expression into one with which indexes can be used. For example:

```
NOT  >   becomes  <=
NOT  >=  becomes  <
NOT  <   becomes  >=
NOT  <=  becomes  >
```

13.4.3 Optimizing ORs

When using ORs, it is best to put the most specific predicate first in the predicate list, and the predicate that passes the most records last. This is true because when you enter a query like:

```
SELECT *
FROM SUPPLIERS
WHERE CITY = 'DALLAS' OR SHIP__BY = 'AIR';
```

and indexes exist on both the columns CITY and SHIP__BY, *ORACLE* will go through a procedure similar to the union of these two queries:

```
SELECT *                    SELECT *
FROM SUPPLIERS              FROM SUPPLIERS
WHERE CITY = 'DALLAS';      WHERE SHIP__BY = 'AIR' AND CITY =
                            'DALLAS';
```

Putting the most specific predicate first in queries like the above will minimize the number of checks for "not equal to."

Indexes are used for statements containing OR clauses under some circumstances. The optimization also applies to IN clauses which translate to ORs. For example:

```
SUPPLIER IN (X, Y, Z)
```

means the same as:

```
SUPPLIER = X
OR SUPPLIER = Y
OR SUPPLIER = Z
```

OR predicates are not used for optimization in the following cases, however:

• When the SQL statement contains a CONNECT BY.

144

- When the SQL statement contains an outer join (see Chapter 12 for details on outer joins.)
- When the rules built into *ORACLE* indicate that use of indexes will not optimize the query.

13.4.4 Optimizing ORDER BY

The only way to guarantee ordering is to put the ORDER BY clause at the end of your SQL statement. Orderings obtained any other way may not be returned in that same ordering in future queries. Therefore you should explicitly request the ordering with OR-DER BY.

When ORDER BY is used, *ORACLE* first obtains the data requested, then sorts it using the Sort/Merge routine (for details of the Sort/Merge routine, see Chapter 2).

13.4.5 Optimizing GROUP BY

Eliminate the rows that do not meet the selection criteria as early as possible in a WHERE clause. For example, the query:

```
SELECT JOB__TITLE, AVG(SAL)
FROM EMPLOYEES
WHERE JOB__TITLE != 'PRESIDENT' AND JOB__TITLE != 'MANAGER'
GROUP BY JOB;
```

will be processed faster than:

```
SELECT JOB__TITLE, AVG(SA)
FROM EMPLOYEES
GROUP BY JOB__TITLE
HAVING JOB__TITLE != 'PRESIDENT' AND 'JOB__TITLE' != 'MANAGER';
```

This is true because, in the second query, there is no WHERE clause. All rows will incur processing. A WHERE clause would have discarded some rows earlier. Furthermore, HAVING clauses are for eliminating grouped data (such as those less than a minimum or greater than average). HAVING clauses should not always be used interchangeably with WHERE clauses.

13.4.6 Optimizing Joins

There are two general rules for optimizing performance by using joins. Columns used in join clauses should be indexed, and SQL statements should be worded to make use of the indexes, rather than to suppress them.

If there are no indexes on the joined columns, *ORACLE* performs a sort/merge if there is no other query path that *ORACLE* can use, and if the join clause is in the form

table__a expression = table__b expression

This means that the join expression cannot be in the form greater-than, less-than, greater-than-or-equal-to, etc.

In the sort/merge join, each table is processed separately. Records that pass a table are sorted, then the sorted lists are merged based on the column forming the join.

If only one of the tables in a join has a usable index, the other table (the unindexed table) is usually the driving table. The exception to this is when a query path is a single-row query path, in which case the optimization is automatic.

If there are indexes on both of the joined columns (or on subsequent selection predicates), then *ORACLE* chooses the optimal path based on which is more selective. In general, it will make this choice based on which predicates can use indexes, which indexes are unique, and whether indexes are on NOT NULL columns. Therefore, in constructing the query, you should consider the number of records in the tables being queried and the distribution of data that is indexed by a nonunique index in order to have the utmost impact on performance.

The query path *ORACLE* will take is the result of weighing all paths against each other according to a ranking scheme. Table 13-2 shows the relative rankings *ORACLE*

Table 13-2. ORACLE Query Path Optimal Speed.

Rank	Path
1	ROWID = constant
2	Unique indexed column = constant
3	Entire unique concatenated index = constant
4	Entire cluster = corresponding cluster key in another table in same cluster
5	Entire cluster key = constant
6	Entire nonunique concatenated index = constant
7	Nonunique index = constant
8	Entire noncompressed concatenated index > = lower bound
9	Entire compressed concatenated index > = lower bound
10	Most leading noncompressed concatenated index specified
11	Most leading compressed concatenated index specified
12	Unique indexed column BETWEEN low value AND high value, or unique indexed column LIKE 'C%' (bounded range)
13	Nonunique indexed column BETWEEN low value and high value, or nonunique indexed column LIKE 'C%' (bounded range)
14	Unique indexed column < or > constant (unbounded range)
15	Nonunique indexed column < or > constant (unbounded range)
16	Sort/merge (joins only)
17	MAX or MIN of single indexed column
18	ORDER BY entire index
19	Full table scans

(Lowest ranks are fastest paths)

uses for different types of queries. Each WHERE clause joined by an AND is ranked, as is each join or outer-join. Joins are scored according to the number of tables to be joined without an index, and the number of Cartesian products.

If the scoring indicated in Table 13-2 results in an equal ranking of two paths, then *ORACLE* uses the last table in the FROM clause as the driving table. Therefore, you should list large tables with the smallest number of qualified rows last in the FROM clause. Also, when you write a multi-table join, you should list the join clause for the pair of tables with the smallest result last in the list of join clauses.

If a table has a low score (and therefore a fast path) for a search, but can only be joined to other tables without using indexes, then another table that can join with index will be chosen as the driver. The join score always dominates the cumulative score.

13.5 ARRAY PROCESSING

ORACLE Version 5 includes a new feature, array processing, which allows multiple-row processing. This can result in improving performance by a factor of 10 over single-row operations. The utilities ODL and Export/Import can use arrays to speed execution time. Also, you will see performance gains when using INSERTs and SELECTs if you use arrays in the *Pro** products *(Pro*FORTRAN, Pro*COBOL, Pro*C, Pro*PL/I, Pro*Pascal,* etc.)

For descriptions of data type and call syntax for array processing, see the guide for the programming language you are interested in, either the *Pro*C User's Guide,* the *Pro*FORTRAN User's Guide, the Pro*COBOL User's Guide,* etc.

13.6 TAKING ADVANTAGE OF INDEXES WITH SQL

There are two basic ways of accessing data in a database, using a full table scan, or using indexes. Using an index is usually preferable to using a full table scan because most of your SQL statements will extract only selected rows, rather than all rows, from tables.

A full table scan is preferable when you know ahead of time that about 25 percent or more of the records in the queried tables should be selected. Using the index to find all of these records would only add overhead.

Here are some rules of thumb for when to maximize performance by using the index. An index may be used if it is referenced in a predicate clause. (A *predicate* is each portion of selection criteria that you use to include or exclude rows from a result.) For example, the following WHERE clause contains two predicates:

```
WHERE DEPTNAME = 'Suppliers'
AND CITY = 'Dallas';
```

It also may be used if the indexed column is not modified by a function or arithmetic operation.

An index will be used by *ORACLE* if the *ORACLE* optimizer decides it is appropriate. You can influence this choice by considering the rules to which the optimizer will respond. An index will not be used if:

- There is no WHERE clause.

- The predicate modifies the indexed column in any way, for example, via a function or arithmetic expression. If the column must be modified to meet the selection criteria as in the following example, an index cannot be used:

```
SELECT * FROM EMPLOYEES
   WHERE SAL * 12 = 36000;
```

The exception to this is if the query includes an expression containing the following, and no other columns:

$$\{MIN \mid MAX \} (< col >\{ + \mid - \} < constant >)$$

- The search is explicitly for records with NULL or NOT NULL values in the indexed column, i.e., the predicate contains either IS NULL or IS NOT NULL.

The same query can be worded in different ways that will need or avoid the use of an index. For example, assume that the column BIRTHDATE is defined as DATE and has a nonunique index. Then the query:

```
SELECT *
FROM EMPLOYEES
WHERE TO__CHAR(BIRTHDATE, 'Month dd, yyyy') = 'April 4, 1986';
```

modifies the BIRTHDATE column with the TO__CHAR function. The index on BIRTHDATE is not used. In this query, however:

```
SELECT *
FROM EMPLOYEES
WHERE BIRTHDATE = TO__DATE '(April 4, 1986', 'Month dd, yyyy')
```

the constant (April 4, 1986) is converted to a date, and therefore *ORACLE* will use the index to do the search. In general, it is better to make constants that are used as selection criteria match the data types defined for the table.

The four sections that follow discuss how to write SQL statements to use or avoid the use of indexes, and how to determine which indexes should be used.

13.6.1 Single Indexes

In a simple query on one table where a predicate refers to an indexed column, once *ORACLE* has identified the index and decided it will use it, it searches rather than scans the index for the value(s) of interest. (A *scan* is a sequential lookup through a table; a *search* uses an index.) Thus, both a full table scan and an index scan are avoided. For the following query, once *ORACLE* finds that the TITLE column has an index (either unique or nonunique), it will search for the desired value in the index 'SALESMAN, ' and return all records with the value 'SALESMAN. '

```
SELECT EMPLOYEE__NUMBER, EMPLOYEE__NAME
FROM EMPLOYEES
WHERE TITLE = 'SALESMAN';
```

13.6.2 Indexes and Null Values

Whenever possible, define columns of tables as NOT NULL. This will allow index use on a greater number of queries.

Indexes will not be used by *ORACLE* if the predicate contains either IS NULL or IS NOT NULL. However, if you are interested in obtaining the NOT NULL values, you can usually write the SQL statement so that it will use an index. This can return rows where the column has a value, not columns where the value is NULL. For example, suppose you want to see all employees who make a commission, i.e., whose commission is NOT NULL. You could use either of the following queries:

Query 1:
```
SELECT * FROM EMPLOYEES
WHERE COMM IS NOT NULL;
```

Query 2:
```
SELECT * FROM EMPLOYEES
WHERE COMM > 0;
```

If an index exists on the COMM column, it is not used for Query 1, but it would be used by Query 2 to get the results without performing a full table scan. However, if most records in the EMPLOYEES table have a value for COMM, then Query 1 is preferred. Query 2 is preferred only if most records have a null value for COMM.

13.6.3 Multiple Indexes on One Table

A query with two or more predicates can use multiple indexes to speed retrieval if the indexes are nonunique column indexes, if the predicates are equalities, and if the predicates are on the same table. Data retrieved from each index's search is "merged" with previous results to obtain the final result.

Multiple indexes are not used for *bounded range and equality predicates*, such as:

```
SELECT *
FROM EMPLOYEES
WHERE TITLE = 'MANAGER'
AND STORENO > 8;
```

Instead, the index for the equality will drive the query.

13.6.4 Choosing Among Multiple Indexes

When there is no clear preference between multiple indexes, *ORACLE* will choose the driving index based on the types of indexes (compressed/noncompressed, unique/nonunique) and the column characteristics.

When both a unique and a nonunique index are available, *ORACLE* uses the unique index and ignores the nonunique index, thus avoiding the "merge." For example, assume there is a unique index on EMPLOYEE__NO and a nonunique index on SALARY in the following query:

```
SELECT EMPLOYEE_NAME
FROM EMPLOYEES
WHERE SALARY = 4000
AND EMPLOYEE_NO = 4703;
```

Then *ORACLE* will use only the index on EMPLOYEE_NO. If a row is found with EMPLOYEE_NO 4703, the actual SALARY field will be examined, instead of using the index on SALARY, to see if it is 4000.

13.6.5 Suppressing the Use of Indexes

Since all appropriate indexes are merged, it is sometimes possible that using an index can decrease performance. Another possibility: Since up to five indexes are used in a query, if you are writing a SQL statement with predicates referencing more than five indexed columns, then you might wish to suppress the use of the least selective indexes.

To suppress the use of indexes, use a "dummy" function or expression with the column of the index you don't want to invoke. To do this, you will usually either add a zero to a numeric column or concatenate a null string to a character column, like this:

```
SELECT EMPLOYEE_NAME, STORE_NO, SALARY
FROM EMPLOYEES
WHERE STORE_NO + 0 = 30
AND EMPLOYEE_NAME = 'JONES';
```

Keep in mind the points made in Section 13.6 above about how to avoid indexes.

13.6.6 The VALIDATE INDEX Command

You can use the VALIDATE INDEX command to check a specific index for consistency. You can also validate an index created by another user. The syntax is:

```
VALIDATE INDEX indexname [ON tablename] [WITH LIST]
```

where the WITH LIST option is used to create a trace file. It should be used only at the request of *ORACLE* support personnel.

If the response to the above command is anything other than "Index validated," then the index is not valid. This is an abnormal condition which should be reported. After reporting the problem, you can drop and recreate the index.

Index validation can detect invalid index formats, bad index structure, and index entries that do not match row data. However, it does not detect data rows that have no corresponding index entries.

Chapter 14

The *ORACLE* Report Writer

THE *ORACLE REPORT WRITER* IS USED TO GENERATE REPORTS. IT COMBINES TEXT FOR-
matting features with SQL's query capabilities. It can be used for a wide variety of
documents, from simple letters to budget reports, and information from the database can
be embedded in all of them. It can also be used to fill out preprinted forms.

The *Report Writer* consists of two utilities: Report Generator (RPT), which enables
you to use information from your *ORACLE* database in your letters and reports, derives
database information through SQL statements; and Report Text Formatter (RPF) enables
you to control the final form of your report formats containing the information from the
database, based on commands included in the text. Each of the two utilities will be explained
separately in Sections 14.1 and 14.2. Their combined use will be illustrated in Sections
14.3 through 14.8.

Note: The terms *table* and *column* do not have exactly the same definitions in the
Report Writer as in the other chapters of this book. They will be defined specifically for
the *Report Writer* as they are encountered below.

14.1 THE TEXT FORMATTER (RPF)

It is necessary to become familiar with RPF before attempting to use the Report
Generator (RPT). RPF is a text formatter for word processing applications. RPF commands
must be included in the text of your document to control the formatting of the information.
RPF commands specify:

- Horizontal and vertical margins
- Centering and underlining
- Tabulation
- Page numbering
- Spacing and placement of text
- Output directed to a line printer, typewriter terminal, or CRT.

RPF can be used independently of RPT, but the reverse is not true—RPT cannot be used without RPF or some other text formatting language.

You must put your RPF formatting commands directly into the file to be formatted. This can be done manually or by using a text editor. If the file is constructed by a program, RPF commands can be inserted into the program.

14.1.1 RPF Commands

All RPF commands start with either a period (.) or a "pound sign" (#). Words that begin with a pound sign or period but are not valid commands will be treated as text. If you want a valid command to appear as text, then you must precede it with a backslash (\ ); otherwise, it will execute as a command and will not be printed in the text. For example, #B is a valid command to insert a blank line, but \ #B is treated as text and will print out as #B.

You can write commands in either upper- or lowercase characters. Each command must be followed by one or more parameters. The command and the parameters should be separated from each other by at least one blank, tab, or form feed character. Use a single period or pound sign to terminate commands with several parameters, or commands that operate on a group of words (as may be the case with centering or underlining).

RPF views text as a series of words, which it defines as a series of characters terminated by at least one space or an end-of-line character. RPF inserts an end-of-line character into the text whenever you enter a carriage return. Regardless of how many spaces you put between words, RPF will separate words by one space on output. Blanks, tabs, carriage returns, form feeds, and new line characters have no effect on word placement in RPF output.

By default, text is right-justified. In other words, ends of words will be lined up by RPF at the right margin just as they are at the left margin. It does this by respacing the words on the line so that the right margin is straight, not ragged. If you do not want the uneven line spacing that this produces, then you can turn off the right justification, so that the right margin will be ragged and the words will be evenly spaced on the line. (Words should never be split between one line and the next.) RPF will continue processing until it reaches the end of the input file.

The area on a line where text is placed is called a *column*. If you fail to specify the limits of the column, RPF will place text in a default column with the left margin at 1 and the right margin at 132. The maximum width of a report line is 254 characters.

14.1.2 Using RPF

To use the RPF formatter, you must enter text in *tables* of one or more columns. Note that an RPF table is not the same as an *ORACLE* database table. An RPF table is simply a rectangular space. For example, a single business letter would be a table to RPF, with the width determined by your DT command (see below) and the length determined by the amount of information and text you put into the letter.

14.1.3 The Default Table

A table consists of from 1 to 20 columns and defines the boundaries for word placement in the current line. The default table consists of 1 column and serves as the initial table definition. Its margins extend from position 1 to position 132. All lines in the default table are right-justified with the exception of the last line. Other tables are defined within these limits, with the margins and the number of columns specified.

14.1.4 Formatting a Table

Four steps are necessary to format a table:

1. Define the table.
2. Invoke the table.
3. Enter the text and the formatting commands.
4. Terminate the table.

Each of the steps will be examined in detail below.

A table definition begins with a period or a pound sign at the beginning, followed by the define table command DT and a number from 1 to 19 identifying the table. Next come numbers indicating where the left and right margins are located. Finally, the table definition ends as it started, with a period or pound sign. There must be at least one space between the DT command and each of the numbers that follow: For example,

#DT 4 10 70 #

defines Table No. 4 with margins of 10 and 70.

The second step, invoking the table, is accomplished simply by using the invoking command T and the table identifier. For example, #T4 invokes the table defined above.

At the third step, you can enter your text and, if the default values are appropriate for it, you need not do any further formatting. This will probably not be the case, however; default is a single-spaced column extending from position 1 through 132 with no paragraph indentation, and no double spacing. Therefore you may want to use some of the formatting possibilities described below.

Length. The PAGE command defines the top and bottom margins of a page. RPF will begin placing the text on the 6th line down from the top of every page, and automatically go to the next page after completing line 58. It assumes that all pages are 66 lines long. With 6 lines of print to an inch, this covers a standard 11-inch page. The PAGE command is:

#PAGE 6 58

which will start the text 6 lines down from the top, and extend it through line 58.

Spacing between Lines. Default is single spacing. To change this, use the SP command and a number representing how many lines you want RPF to space down for each line. Keep in mind that the convention is that text with no blank lines between lines of text is called "single" spacing, text with one blank between text lines is "double" spacing, etc. If you want one blank line between each line of text, the command is:

#SP 2

Controlling New Lines. Since the spacing in your commands has no effect on the spacing in the output, you must tell RPF when to start a new line. Do this with the letter N where you want the end of the line to be in the finished product.

Defining Paragraphs. The paragraph command P will cause the text which follows it to be printed on the next line and indented five spaces. The body of the text will then be printed within the column boundaries.

The last step is to terminate the table by issuing the table end command TE. At that point RPF will revert back to default values. If you do not terminate the table, you will get an error message saying "unexpected end of column" when RPF is run.

14.1.5 Running RPF

After you have set up the table, you can run it by entering a command with the format shown below:

RPF *filename* [*output_filename*] [*device_name*] [*-switches*]

Figure 14-1 is an example of RPF input showing the use of the commands explained in Section 14.1.4 above in setting up a business letter. (The line numbers are added only for purposes of this text; you would not put line numbers in the setup of an actual letter.) These formatting commands produce the letter shown in the bottom half of the figure.

To set up a report with several columns, you will also need the following commands:

1. Defining columns
2. Centering and underlining
3. Nesting tables
4. Entering data into columns
5. Justifying text within a column
6. Moving to a new line
7. Automatic adjustment of column text
8. Defining a two-column table

14.1.6 Tabular Reports

The *Report Writer* is especially useful in preparing tabular reports. This is best illustrated by an example with a line-by-line explanation. Figure 14-2 shows a listing of the commands for setting up a five-column table, and the tabular report itself with nested tables. (As with Fig. 14-1, the line numbers are added only for purposes of illustration.) The general principles for setting up this report follow.

1. Define the Overall Margins. Overall horizontal margins are defined by "Table 1," which is the total extension of the report on the page. These margins are 13 and 73. This entire area is called a *column*. Any tables within the report will be *nested* within these boundaries.

2. Define Columns. Another table, Table 2, is defined on line 2. This divides the overall column into 5 columns. The column boundaries are: 1 to 5, 9 to 28, 32 to 39, etc. The last column is defined by the numbers 58 and 0. The 0 means that the column ends on the right-hand margin of the overall column within which this table exists. In other words, the right-hand margin was defined as 73 in the overall column set up in the DT command on line 1.

```
1.  #DT 1 13 73 #
2.  #Page 6 58
3.  #SP 1
4.  #T 1
5.  #S 3
6.  April 7, 1987
7.  #S3
8.  Mr. George    B.    Jones #N
9.  483 Norwood St.#N  Seabreeze CT  33234
10. #S 4
11. Dear Mr. Jones:
12. #S 4 #P
13. We received your shipment today.
14. #S 1
15. #P Under separate cover we are returning the entire shipment
16. because it arrived too late for our sales promotion.  Since
17. our order stated that we must have the product by March 15 at
18. the latest, we are also returning your invoice.
19. #B #P
20. Perhaps we can do business sometime in the future.
21. #S 2
22. Sincerely,
23. #S 4
24. John Green
25. #TE
```

April 7, 1987

Mr. George B. Jones
483 Norwood St.
Seabreeze, CT 33234

Dear Mr. Jones:

We received your shipment today.

Under separate cover we are returning the entire shipment
because it arrived too late for our sales promotion. Since
our order stated that we must have the product by March 15 at
the latest, we are also returning your invoice.

Perhaps we can do business sometime in the future.

Sincerely,

John Green

Fig. 14-1. Example of a Report Formatter input file with embedded commands, and the business letter it produces.

```
1.    #DT 1 13 73 #
2.    #DT 2 1 5 9 28 32 39 42 52 0 #
3.    #page 6 58
4.    #T 1
5.    #S 4
6.    #CUL "PRODUCE DEPARTMENT " #
7.    #S 2
8.    #CUL MONTHLY SALES REPORT #
9.    #S 4
10.   #T 2
11.   ITEM #n AMT. #NC
12.   #CEN PRODUCT # #N #CEN DESCRIPTION # #NC
13.   #R LAST #N MONTH #NC
14.   #R THIS #N MONTH #NC
15.   #R Y-T-D #NC
16.   #S 2
17.   500 B Apples #NC $329.26 #NC $438.50 #NC $1836.30 #NC
18.   #S 1
19.   40 T Lemons #NC $100.39 #NC 308.22 #NC $803.20 #NC
20.   #S 1
21.   48 C Oranges $839.22 #NC $798.33 #NC $2305.98 #NC
22.   #S 1
23.   #NC #NC -------- #N  $1258.87 #NC -------- $1545.05 #
24.   $2945.48
25.   #TE #S 3
26.   #CUL SEE \ NEXT \ PAGE #
27.   #TE
```

<u>" PRODUCE DEPARTMENT "</u>

<u>MONTHLY SALES REPORT</u>

ITEM AMT.	PRODUCT DESCRIPTION	LAST MONTH	THIS MONTH	Y-T-D
500 B	Apples	$329.26	$438.50	$1836.30
40 T	Lemons	$100.39	$308.22	$803.20
48 C	Oranges	$839.22	$798.33	$2305.98
		-------	-------	--------
		$1258.87	$1545.05	$2945.48

<u>SEE   NEXT   PAGE</u>

Fig. 14-2. Commands for setting up a five-column tabular report, and the report these commands produce.

3. Define Vertical Margins. Line 3 defines the top and bottom margins of the output page, and line 4 invokes Table 1. Since Table 1 has only one column, its text will be formatted within the column boundaries.

4. Center and Underline (CUL). The CUL command on line 6 states that the text between the command and the terminating period should be centered within the current column and underlined. Since the current column extends from 13 through 73, this text is centered on the page. The CUL command on line 8 produces a second line of centered and underlined text.

5. Nesting Tables. The command on line 10 invokes Table 2, which was set up in item 2 above, and places it within Table 1. This is the same as setting tabs on a typewriter for dividing the overall column into five separate columns.

When a table is invoked while another table is still active, the new table becomes the "current" column. The new table's boundaries must, of course, fit within the boundaries of the "parent" column.

The boundaries of the second table are interpreted relative to the boundaries of the first table. That is, the first table actually starts at position 13. But Table 2 starts at the first position of Table 1; therefore Table 2's left boundary is shown at relative position 1, and it extends through relative position 5. The point here is that Table 1 contains 61 printable spaces. In stating positions for the five columns of Table 2, you must work in terms of those 61 spaces. Thus, the column specifications for Table 2 name the first printable space as position 1, and the last as position 61. This allows you to keep track of the limits of the space.

6. Enter Data into Columns. The text on line 11 is placed within the first column. The N command causes the text "No." to be placed on a new line within this column. The NC command causes the placement of text within the current column to stop. Any text that follows will be placed on the first line of the next column in Table 2.

7. Justify Text within a Column. The CEN command on line 12 stipulates that the words ITEM and DESCRIPTION must be centered on the first two lines of the second column. The R (right justify) command on lines 13, 14, and 15 specifies that all subsequent text lines for columns 3, 4, and 5 must be right-justified. Note that the dollar values in the last 3 columns are right-justified.

8. Move to a New Line. When the last column is filled for each row, a command is needed to move back to the first column again. NC on line 15 does this. The S2 command on line 16 would have the same effect, and would also give the instruction to skip two lines. Line 17 places the first line of data into each column of the report. Lines 19 and 21 define the output for the second and third lines of the report.

9. Adjust Column Text Automatically. RPF will place as many words as possible on a line of a column. When that line is full, the last word is right-justified, and the remaining text is placed on the next line of the column. Since PRODUCT DESCRIPTION required 2 lines, RPF spaced down after that line so that all columns for the next item appear on the same line.

10. Summarize Information. Summary information is specified on lines 23 and 24. Since there is no information in the first two columns, two NC commands are required to position the first information for that row in the third column. The output for the last 3 columns will contain a line of dashes; the column totals will appear on the next line.

11. End the Table. The TE on line 25 terminates the current table. At this point, the previously invoked table (Table 1) becomes current again. The text on line 26 will be centered and underlined within Table 1's column boundaries. The backslash (\ ) asks RPF to insert a second blank character between each of the words instead of the usual single blank between words. The TE on line 27 terminates Table 1, causing the default table to become current.

14.1.7 Other Formatting Commands and Procedures

Table 14-1 lists the syntax of all of the RPF commands and gives a brief explanation of each.

14.1.8 Executing RPT

RPF can be invoked from the user's terminal. Output can be directed to a file or to any terminal or line printer device, including the system printer. The command to execute RPF is:

RPF <*input__file*> <*output__dev*> [−*switches*]

where *input-file* is the name of the input text file, *output-dev* is the name of the output device, and *switch* specifies one or more switches to control the execution of RPF (see description of switches below).

14.1.9 Switches

You may specify one or more switches to control the execution of RPF, including forcing the output directly to a device (by using the device switch), or by naming the output device of the system desired. These switches are described below.

A=All Bold. The A switch causes the entire output to be printed in boldface; this is supported only for Diablo-type printers. For other printers, the switch is ignored. The B (Boldface) switch does not need to be specified when this switch is used.

B=Boldface. The B switch causes all underlined text to be printed in boldface. This is supported only for Diablo-type printers; for other printers, this switch is ignored.

D:D = Device: Diablo-type Printer. The D:D switch specifies that the output device is a Diablo-type printer and will support boldface and bidirectional printing.

D:V = Device: VT100. The D:V switch specifies that the output device is a VT100 terminal. This switch causes all underlined text to be output in reverse video. An output file will be created, but it will be empty. If not specified for a video display terminal, underlined text will be displayed and then overwritten with underline characters.

F = Form Feed. The F switch sends a form feed character to the terminal before printing a page. If not used, the appropriate number of blank lines is printed to position the printer at the top of the next page. RPF assumes a 66-line page when inserting blank lines. Forms of other lengths require the use of the F switch for positioning. This switch is ignored for terminals that do not support a form feed character.

I = Initial Page Eject. The I switch ejects a page before the output device starts to print.

P:N:M = Page. The P:N:M switch prints a range of pages, from *n* to *m*. For example:

P:5   Print the fifth through the last page.
P:5:7   Print pages 5, 6, and 7.
P:5:5   Print only page 5.

R = Reverse Underlining Order. Not all devices allow overstriking. By default RPF

158

Table 14-1. Description and Syntax of RPF Commands.

Command	Syntax	Description
APN	#APN *<position>*	Alternate page number: placement for even numbered pages.
B	#B	Blank: Insert one blank line in output text.
CEN	#CEN *<text>* #	Center: Center following text in the current column. CLOSED*
CL	#CL . . . . . . *<text_lines>* . . . #	Column Literal: Suspend formatting for the following lines in the current column. CLOSED*
CS	#CS *<n>*.	Column Skip: Skip *n* lines in the current column.
CUL	#CUL *<text>* #	Center With Underline: Center and under-line the following text within the current column. CLOSED*
DT	#DT *<table_id>* *<sp1>* *<epl>* *<sp2>* *<ep2>* . . . *<spn>* *<epn>* #	Define Table: Define the column boundaries for the specified table. CLOSED*
F	#F *<page_no1>* *<page_no2>* . . . #	Figures: Reserve specified page numbers in output document for figures or charts; *<page_no1>* is the page number to be skipped in output document. CLOSED*
FR	#FR	Flush Right: Justify both the left and right margins. This is the default setting.
HS	#HS *<spacing>*	Horizontal Spacing: for characters on Di-ablo printers. Default is 6, or 10 characters per inch.
I	#I *<number_of_spaces>*	Indent: Indent the following text in current column.
L	#L . . . . . . *<text_lines>* . . . #	Literal: Suspend formatting for the follow-ing text lines; column definitions are ig-nored. CLOSED*
N	#N	New line: Move to the next line in the cur-rent column.

Command	Syntax	Description
NC	#NC	New Column: Advance to next column.
NP	#NP	New Page: End the current page and start a new page.
PAGE	#PAGE <top__line> <bottom__line>	Page: Define top and bottom page boundaries.
P	#P	Paragraph: Start a new line within the current column. Indent the beginning of the line 5 spaces.
PAUSE	#PAUSE	Pause: Stop printing until there is a signal from operator.
R	#R	Right justify: Set/reset switch to right-justify all text placed in the current column.
RR	#RR	Ragged Right: Give an unjustified (ragged) right margin.
S	#S <no__of__lines>	Skip: Skip specified number of lines.
SP	#SP <no>	Spacing: Define spacing for current column.
SPN	#SPN <type> <pos> <skip__lines> <start__number> <sect__number> #	Start Page Numbering: Specify page numbering. CLOSED*
T	#T <table id>	Table: Invoke the specified table within the current column.
TE	#TE	Table End: Terminate table and revert to the previous column definition.
TTL	#TTL <w> <title1> [| <title2>] #	Title: Specify title to be centered at top of each page. CLOSED*
TTLU	#TTLU <w> <title1> [| <title2>] #	Title With Underline: Specify title to be centered and underlined at top of each page. CLOSED*
UL	#UL <text> #	Underline: Underline the following text. CLOSED*
VS	#VS <spacing>	Vertical Spacing: Define vertical spacing for Diablo printers.

* The comment ''CLOSED'' means that the command must be terminated by a period (.) or a pound sign (#).

prints characters first, so that on devices where overstruck characters are not allowed, an underline character will not replace a character. To reverse this default, use the R switch.

S = Spool to Line Printer. The S switch automatically directs the output file to the line printer, to be queued for printing.

U = Upper Case. The U switch prints all alphabetic characters in upper case.

W = Wait. The W switch (pause) will cause RPF to suspend printing at the end of each page and whenever a PAUSE command is encountered. Printing is resumed after any single character is entered. The entered character is not printed. The W switch is used with a device specification D:V or D:D.

14.2 THE *ORACLE* REPORT GENERATOR (RPT)

This section assumes that you are familiar with the *ORACLE* Text Formatter (RPF) described in Section 14.1 earlier in this chapter.

While both RPT and RPF statements may be preceded by either a period (.) or a pound sign (#), the pound sign will continue to be used for RPF statements in this section and the period will be used for RPT statements to make it easier for you to distinguish RPF from RPT statements in the examples.

The purpose of RPT is to enable you to extract information from the database and use it in the construction of reports, documents, computer-generated letters, or any other data use. With RPT you can:

1. Use SQL queries to retrieve *ORACLE* database information.
2. Use other SQL statements to manipulate these data.
3. Use specific data output formats.
4. Include report heading and footing information.
5. Use RPF commands to combine your data with your text when you produce reports.

The RPT interprets and executes a report "script" or program consisting of any combination of report writer statements, RPF commands, and text. The general form of an RPT statement is:

    <command> <argument1> <argument2> . . .

Either upper- or lowercase entries may be used.

An RPT command may begin anywhere on the input line, and it occupies the entire line. You may include report text or other commands on this line. All the arguments associated with a command must be specified on the same line.

A command may have one or more arguments. Arguments are specified by their position in the defined order. Each argument can be either an alphabetic or numeric character string, and must be separated from the next by at least one blank space. The argument itself may contain blank spaces; if it does, the entire argument must be enclosed in double quotation marks.

14.2.1 The Process of Generating a Report

The sequence of operations in generating a report is: SQL enables the desired data to be obtained from the database; then the RPF commands and RPT statements permit the data to be inserted into the report format. This section explains and illustrates the statements necessary to construct the report program.

The purpose of the report program is to conduct the retrieval of data from the database, and place those data into an interim file. Each datum that RPT places in the interim file is treated by RPF as a word when it processes the interim file.

The program file may contain RPF (or other) formatting commands, as well as text in addition to the RPT program statements. RPT copies the text and formatting commands as it encounters them, directly into the interim file. The report program statements (i.e., the RPT statements), on the other hand, are interpreted and executed. In this way, the database information is merged with text to form the finished report.

RPT may be executed from a terminal or included in a batch procedure. It is executed with the following command:

RPT *<input_file>* *<output_file>*[*userid/password*] [−cN]

where *input_file* is the name of the file containing the RPT report program, and *output_file* is the name to be assigned to the interim file created by RPT and subsequently processed by RPF. The *userid* and *password* arguments are your user ID and password. This is required because *userid* must have been granted SELECT privileges to the desired data. Finally, cN specifies the size of the SQL work area to be requested for each SQL query defined in the report. If this is omitted, the default value specified in the INIT.ORA file will be used.

14.2.2 Structure of the Report

The RPT program may be seen as having three sections. These sections are not defined by any statements; they are merely logical groupings. While there are few restrictions on the positioning of RPT statements within a program, variables must be defined before they are used. RPT commands and report text may be included anywhere within a program, and will be copied to the interim file as it is encountered during the program's execution.

1. **Data Declaration Section.** The Data Declaration Section contains the definition of your local variables which will be used to store temporarily retrieved database information. Variables may also be defined for counters, for storing totals, and for temporary storage.

2. **Macro Definition Section.** Two types of macros may be defined in the Macro Definition Section. A SELECT macro is used to define a SQL SELECT statement, and a procedural macro, similar to a programming subroutine, is a collection of executable RPT statements.

3. **Procedure Section.** The Procedure Section contains the executable RPT statements making up the main body of the report program. Within this section, SELECT and procedural macros can be executed either explicitly or implicitly.

14.2.3 Nested Reports

A nested report is one that contains a list or some other kind of formal information within the body of the main report. The nested report can be thought of as an "inner report" contained within the "outer," or main, report.

14.3 REPORT WRITER STATEMENTS

There are six types of RPT statements:

- Declarative
- Macro Definition
- Macro Execution
- Program Control
- Arithmetic
- Miscellaneous

The format of these six statements is shown in Table 14-2 and the statements are explained in the sections that follow.

Table 14-2. Summary of RPT Statements.

Statement	Format
Declarative	.DATABASE <string> .DECLARE <program variable name> <format> .SET <program variable name> <literal value> .EQUAL <destination variable> <source variable>

Macro Definition	.DEFINE |<SELECT *macro name*> |
	            |<*procedural_macro_name*> |
	
	           .
	        macro text lines
	           .
	           .
	
	 ..

Macro Execution	.<*procedural_macro_name*> .EXECUTE <SELECT *macro_name*> .REPORT <SELECT *macros* > <*body macro*> [<*head_macro* [<*foot macro*>]]
Program Control	.&<*label_name*> .GOTO <*label_name*> .IF ['] <*expression*> ['] THEN <*label1*> [ELSE <*label2*>] .IFNULL <*variable_name*> <*label_name*> .STOP

Arithmetic	| ADD |
	 .| SUB | |<*dest_var*> |<*source_var1*> ||<*source_var2*> |
	   | MUL | | <*literal*> || <*literal*> |
	   | DIV |
	   | dsub |

Miscellaneous	.PRINT <*program_variable_name*> [*variable_name*] ... .FPRINT [*spacing*] <*variable_name*> [[*spacing*] [*variable_name*]] ... .ASK '<*message*>' <*program_variable_name*> .REM <*comment_text*>

14.3.1 Declarative Statements

DATABASE. The DATABASE statement is required in early versions of *ORACLE*, but is not required from Version 4 on. It specifies the *ORACLE* database to be processed within the report.

DECLARE. The DECLARE statement defines a program variable and the format of the printed variable. All program variables must be set to specific values. The syntax for the DECLARE statement is:

.DECLARE <*var_name*> <*format*>

where *var_name* is the name assigned to this program variable, which can be from 1 to 8 characters, starting with an alphabetic character; *format* is the edit format used when placing this variable in the interim file. This format will also control rounding and overflow when used in arithmetic statements. The data type of the variable is indicated by its format specification.

Data Types. The data types supported in the format of the DECLARE statement are *date, alphanumeric,* and *numeric.* These are discussed below.

There are three types of date variables in RPT, date, edate, and YYMMDD. The value of any of these variables is stored internally in terms of the Julian date. This allows date calculations to be performed, and one type of date can be set to the value of another. For example, to find the Julian date, set a numeric variable equal to a date variable using the RPT .EQUAL command.

For a date-type variable, the input (.ASK or .SET) and output (.PRINT or .FPRINT) format is MM/DD/YY. For an edate-type variable, the format is DD/MM/YY ("European format"). For a YYMMDD variable, the format is YYMMDD.

Internally, each date variable is a numeric variable containing the associated date in an absolute Julian day number. This allows one date to be subtracted from another. It also allows numeric values to be added or subtracted from a date, as in printing invoices in which the due date may be computed as the current date plus 30 days.

If you are not performing computations on dates within the report itself, Oracle Corporation recommends that you treat dates as alphanumeric strings within RPT. The TO_CHAR function can be used to convert a date column to the desired format. For example:

TO_CHAR (<*column*>, 'MM/DD/YY')

If you select a date directly without the TO_CHAR function, this will result in the default format of DD-MON-YY.

A date variable may have its value initialized in one of several ways. It may be assigned a literal value (*date* is set in the format MM/DD/YY), or it may be set equal to the value of another date variable. If its value is assigned from a column or expression returned in a SQL SELECT, the database value must be in internal Julian date format. You can SELECT an *ORACLE* date column by using the conversion function:

TO_CHAR (<*column*>, 'J')

To create a date-compatible column, the column must be defined as a number in the SQL CREATE TABLE statement. The column's value must be entered initially and always updated using an IAF application (See Chapter 2 for an explanation of IAF) where the field type is defined as *date*.

Keyword Constants. RPT contains two keyword constants which relate to dates, $$DATE$$ and $$TIME$$. These evaluate to strings. Therefore, if you enter:

.SET *txtvar* $$DATE$$

you will get the Julian day in the text variable. If you enter:

.SET *numvar* $$DATE$$

you will get the Julian day in the number variable.

The $$TIME$$ constant returns the 24-hour format of HH:MI:SS, as in 15:28:53 for 15 hours, 28 minutes, and 53 seconds.

Both of these constants ($$DATE$$ and $$TIME$$) are set once when RPT starts running, so time and date are computed with relation to that time.

Alphanumeric. An alphanumeric variable may contain any printable character. It is defined by specifying a format of:

An

where *n* is the number of characters. When a report is executed, all alphanumeric variables are assigned the NULL value.

Numeric. Use the following symbols to specify numeric values:

9   Defines each digit of a numeric variable. Leading zeros are not displayed.

.   Defines the position of the decimal point within a numeric variable. The position is used for arithmetic alignment and is displayed on output.

,   Inserts a comma on output. It is omitted on output if there are no digits to the left of this position.

$ Puts a dollar sign before the number on output.

MI   Displays the minus sign to the right of a negative number. The default is to display the minus sign to the left.

PR   Causes the variable to be displayed within "< >" brackets when negative.

0   May be used instead of 9 to designate a digit. Normally leading zeros are suppressed, but a zero in the format will cause every digit position to be filled.

V   Defines the position of the decimal point within a numeric variable. The position is used for alignment in arithmetic statements, but the decimal point is not displayed on output.

B   Causes the variable to be output as blanks if its value is zero.

Table 14-3 shows examples of numeric formats:

Table 14-3. Examples of Numeric Formats.

Format	Value	Display
999.99	56.478	56.48
999V99	56.478	5648
9,999	8410	8,410
9,999	639	639
99999	607	607
09999	607	00607
9999	-5609	-5609
9999MI	-5609	5609-
9999PR	-5609	<5609>
B999	564	564
B999	0	blanks
99.99	124.98[1]	##.##
		24.98
$99.99	45.23	$45.23
DATE	2441453[2]	12/23/80
A5	Customer	Custo
A20	Customer	Customer

[1] If the value retrieved from the database for this variable is greater than can be displayed by the format, pound signs (#) will be displayed. If the variable overflows because of an arithmetic operation, a truncated value will be displayed.

[2] Julian day number for 12/23/80.

SET. The SET statement sets the value of the variable equal to the specified literal value. The syntax is:

.SET <variable_name> <literal_value>

where *variable_name* is any previously defined program variable, and *literal_value* is a numeric or character literal. The literal type must match the variable type. The special literal $$DATE$$ may be used to assign the system date to a date variable. Here are some examples:

.SET name SMITH	Sets the current value of the variable "name" equal to SMITH.
.SET storeno 13	Sets the current value of the numeric variable "storeno" equal to 13.
.SET today $$DATE$$	Sets the value of the date variable "today" equal to the current date.

EQUAL. The EQUAL statement will set the value of one variable equal to the value of another variable, both of which are the same datatype. For example:

.EQUAL *<dest__var> <source__var>*

For character variables, the value of *source__var* will be truncated if longer than *dest__var,* and filled with blanks if shorter. For numeric variables, if the format of *dest__var* contains fewer decimal places, the value of *source__var* will be rounded. No provision is made for overflow.

If the value of *source__var* cannot be stored within the format of the *dest__var,* the value will be truncated in the destination.

14.3.2 Macro Definition Statements

There are two types of macro statements in RPT, SELECT macros and procedural macros. SELECT and procedural macros are defined in the same way. RPT will recognize them by the way they are invoked, and the type of statements they contain.

DEFINE. The DEFINE statement is used for both procedural and SELECT macros, as shown below. When this statement is executed, the macro will be stored away for future use, with nothing output to the interim file. Two periods (. .) on a line by themselves complete the macro definition.

```
.DEFINE   |   <SELECT__macro__name>   |
          |   <Procedural__macro__name>   |
              .

  macro text lines

              .
              .
              .

  . .
```

where *SELECT__macro__name* is the name of the SELECT macro being defined, *Procedural__macro__name* is the name of the procedural macro being defined, and . . is used to indicate the end of the macro definition.

SELECT Macro. A SELECT macro contains only one SQL query. It may include any SELECT clause or parameter that is valid within a SELECT statement.

The maximum size of a SQL statement in RPT is 2048 bytes. Since RPT strips off leading, trailing, and embedded-multiple blanks from each line of the SQL statement, reformatting the SELECT statement will not change the required space.

An INTO clauses must be included in the SELECT statement (in addition to the standard SQL clauses). This INTO clause will specify the program variable that will receive the column values returned in the SELECT clause. For example, say that a report program has three variables defined, A, B, and C. If the SELECT macro named SAMPLE were executed, the values returned for STORENO, SNAME, and CITY would be stored in the program variables A, B, and C, respectively:

```
.DEFINE sample
   SELECT storeno, sname, city
   INTO   a, b, c
   FROM   stores, suppliers
   WHERE  store.supplierno = suppliers.supplierno
          and profit = 500000
```

The program variable must be the same data type as the column or expression in the SE-LECT clause. An INTO clause, and any SQL clause, may be defined in a free format.

The value of a program variable can be substituted for any literal defined in the WHERE or SELECT clause of a SQL query. When used this way, however, the variable name must be preceded with an ampersand (&). For example:

```
.DEFINE AcctDept
   SELECT deptname, location
   INTO   dname, loc
   FROM   dept
   WHERE  deptno = &dno
```

If the above were executed with dno = 15, the value 15 would be substituted into the WHERE clause. (Note that the variable name cannot include an underscore wildcard character.)

To summarize: The results of one query can be stored into a program variable and used as a substitution variable within another query. This technique can be used to construct queries that produce nested reports.

14.3.3 Macro Execution Statements

The procedural and SELECT macros are executed as described below.

Procedural Macro Execution. A procedural macro may be explicitly executed anywhere within an RPT program, including from within another procedural macro. The named macro must have been defined in the program before you attempt to execute it. The named macro is executed by specifying:

```
.<procedural_macro_name>
```

For example, the statement:

```
.review
```

will cause the procedural macro named "review" to be executed. Then, after the macro is executed, the next statement in the sequence is executed.

There are three procedural macros. These correspond to the head, body, and foot of a report.

SELECT Macro Execution. A SELECT macro may be explicitly executed with the following RPT statement:

    .EXECUTE *<SELECT_macro_name>*

Following the execution of this query, the first row will be returned. Values of the selected columns will be placed into the corresponding program variables as defined by the INTO clause.

    Note that executing a query this way will return only the first row. If the macro is executed again, the entire query will be reprocessed, but again only one row will be returned. Thus, explicit execution of SELECT macros is useful when you need only one row.

    For automatic execution of SELECT macros, see the next section on REPORT statements.

    REPORT Statements. The REPORT statement causes the automatic execution of the SELECT and procedural macros that generate most reports. Unlike the EXECUTE statement described above, the REPORT statement will cause every row to be returned from the SELECT being processed. The procedural macros are executed for each row. The head, body, and foot are standard procedural macros and may contain any valid RPT statement. Other macros can be executed within them.

    The procedural head macro is executed once within a REPORT statement when the first row is returned. Included in this macro would be column headings, descriptive text, and report titles. Since the procedural body macro is not executed for the first row returned (if the heading argument is included), you should either execute the body macro as part of the heading or make other arrangements to print the first row.

    The procedural body macro is executed for the second-through-last rows. If you have not specified a foot macro, the body macro will be executed for the last row. Its function is to output each row of data within the desired format. Other functions for this macro can be to accumulate totals, maintain counters, or control page breaks.

    The foot macro is executed after the last row of the query has been processed. Summary calculations and footnotes can be included in this macro.

    One or more REPORT statements can be executed within the head, body, or foot macro of another REPORT. Two or more SELECT macros may be specified in a REPORT statement; a row from each will be returned when they are executed. Furthermore, data retrieved from multiple SELECTs may be independent, coming from different tables.

    Multiple SELECT macros may be specified with an AND or an OR between them. The AND specifies that the report should be executed only if the SELECTs on both sides of the AND return at least one row. The OR specifies that the report should be executed if at least the SELECT on one side of the OR returns at least one row. (If only one SELECT is specified in a report and no rows are returned, the report will not be executed. If two or more SELECTs are specified, the SELECT argument must be enclosed in double quotes, e.g., "supplier1 AND supplier2".

    The format of the REPORT statement is:

    .REPORT *<SELECT_macros> <body_macro>* [*<head_macro>*
<foot_macro>]

where *SELECT_macros* is the name of SELECT macros executed for this report (if two are specified, they must be joined by an AND or OR and enclosed within double quotes; *body_macro* is the name of the body macro which will be executed for the second through the last returned rows; *head_macro* is the name of the head macro which is executed for the first row returned (this parameter is optional); and *foot_macro* is the name of the foot macro which is executed after the last row is returned. The *foot_macro* parameter is optional, and can be specified only if a head macro is also specified.

14.3.4 Program Control Statements

RPT includes statements to control the program execution within a procedural macro. These program control statements are the label definition statement, the GOTO statement, the IF statement, the IFNULL statement, and the STOP statement. Only the STOP statement can be used outside of a procedural macro.

Label Definition Statement. The syntax of the label definition statement is:

.& < *label_name* >

where *label_name* is a name containing from 1 to 8 characters, the first of which is alphabetic, and the ampersand is used to indicate a program variable. (See below for use of the ampersand.) A label may be referred to only within the macro in which it was defined. Since label definitions do not span macros, however, the same label name may be used in more than one macro.

GOTO Statement. The GOTO statement is an unconditional branch to the specified label. The format is:

.GOTO < *label_name* >

where *label_name* is the name of a label defined within the current procedural macro.

IF Statement. The IF statement causes a branch to the specified macro depending on the result of an expression. The IF statement is only valid within a procedural macro. The format is:

.IF < *expression* > THEN < *label1* > [ELSE < *label2* >]

where *label1* means that if *expression* evaluates to True, processing control will be transferred to *label1*, and *label2* means that if *expression* evaluates to False, then processing control will be transferred to *label2*. If ELSE < *label2* > is omitted and the expression is False, the next sequential statement is executed.

An *expression* may compare the value of a program variable with other program variables or literal constants. Program variable names must be preceded by an ampersand (&). If the ampersand is omitted, an "Invalid Column Name" message will be displayed.

The IF statement supports the complete set of relational operators, logical operators, and arithmetic expressions permitted within the WHERE clause of a SQL statement.

Character constants must be enclosed in single quotation marks. All literal values and program variables within an expression must be of the same data type. If the literals, program variables, and relational operators are separated by one or more blank characters, the entire expression must be enclosed within double quotation marks (").

A NULL value is not allowed in a program variable used in an expression. If the value is NULL, the report program will terminate. To prevent this, all variables should be initialized to either zeros or blanks. If the variable is assigned a value from a database column that allows NULLs, the Null Value Function (NVL) should be used to assign a non-NULL value. For example, if the variable salary is used in the following IF statement:

```
.IF " &salary > 10000 " THEN . . .
```

then the SELECT macro should define the NVL function in the SELECT list:

```
SELECT NVL(sal,0)
INTO    salary
FROM   . . .
```

which means that any NULL values will be set to zero. If any value in the expression has a *NULL* value, the ORACLE "unexpected end of SQL statement" error message will appear.

Guidelines for IF statements. Since IF statement processing is time-consuming, it should be used cautiously within a report, and some uses of the IF statement are not recommended by Oracle Corporation for use with long reports. Executing an IF statement for each row processed could severely lengthen the report execution time if many rows are being processed.

SQL functions can be substituted efficiently for some uses of IF statements. For example, computing the maximum and minimum values of a variable over a range of rows could be done by comparing each new value with the previous maximum and minimum values. This requires two IF statements for each row. It would be more efficient to execute a SELECT in the report foot which used the SQL MIN and MAX functions.

IFNULL Statement. The IFNULL statement is an efficient way of testing for NULL program variables, and can sometimes eliminate the need for an IF statement. The format is:

```
.IFNULL <variable_name> <label_name>
```

where *variable_name* is the name of the variable to be checked for a null value, and *label_name* is where RPT will branch if the given variable is null. There is no ELSE clause.

STOP Statement. The STOP statement will terminate the execution of the report program. STOP may be included in the procedure section or in a procedural macro. The format is:

```
.STOP
```

If a STOP statement is not included, the program will terminate following the execution of the last program statement.

14.3.5 Arithmetic Statements

RPT supports addition, subtraction, multiplication, and division between two program variables. The formats are:

```
  | ADD  |
  | SUB  |
. | MUL  |  <dest_var>  <source_var1>  <source_var2>
  | DIV  |
  | DSUB |
```

where *dest_var* is the result of the arithmetic operation, *source_var1* and *source_var2* are previously defined variables, and DSUB stands for the subtraction of one date variable from another. For all arithmetic statements except DSUB, a numeric literal may be substituted for the input arguments *source_var1* and *source_var2*.

The numeric values have been defined in Table 14-3. The maximum number which can be stored in a variable is determined by the format specified in the DECLARE statement. If the result of the arithmetic operation overflows the *dest_var*, the high-order digits (the ones starting on the left) will be lost, and no error will be indicated. These digits are lost both on output and in subsequent arithmetic operations. For example, if the result of an arithmetic operation is 456 and the format of *dest_var* is 99, then the 56 will be stored in *dest_var* and the high-order digit 4 will be lost.

If the decimal portion of the result contains more digits than defined in the *dest_var* format, the low-order digits (the ones on the right) will be rounded off. For example, if the result of the arithmetic operation is 46.576 and the format of the *dest_var* is 99.99, the number 46.58 will be stored.

For DIV, if a number is divided by zero (i.e., *source_var2*=0), a "** DIVIDE BY ZERO X/Y **" error message will appear and the report program will terminate.

The DSUB statement subtracts one date variable from another, storing the result in a numeric variable. The number of days between two dates is computed. For example, if DATE1=01/24/81 and DATE2=12/25/80, then:

```
.DSUB RESULT DATE1 DATE2
```

sets the value of RESULT=30. Neither DATE1 nor DATE2 can be literals.

14.3.6 Miscellaneous Statements

Several miscellaneous statements are described below. These include the PRINT and FPRINT statements, the ASK statement, and the REM (Remark) statement.

The PRINT Statement. The PRINT statement inserts the contents of the specified program variable into the output interim file. This is the only mechanism for inserting database information into the output report. Formatting of the contents of the variable will be done according to the format defined in the DECLARE statement. The format of the PRINT statement is:

```
.PRINT <variable_name>
```

PRINT statements may be interspersed with RPF commands to PRINT the data in the various columns of a tabular report.

The FPRINT Statement. Like the PRINT statement, FPRINT outputs values of program variables into the intermediate file. However, it formats the intermediate file differently. Each variable output is padded with blanks according to its declared format. In addition, the number of blanks between each padded variable may be set by including a spacing constant in the argument list. This spacing constant will affect the intervariable spacing for all items in the list to the right. If the spacing constant is zero (0), the variables output will be concatenated. This statement is only useful when used inside the scope of an RPF literal since RPF will normally ignore any spacing.

The format of the statement is:

.FPRINT [*spacing*] <*variable_name*> [[*spacing*] [*variable_name*]] . . .

where [*spacing*] is the number of blanks you want in front of the variable. The default is zero. No blank spaces will be included if the spacing clause is omitted. The *variable_name* argument, of course, is the name of the variable to be printed.

The ASK Statement. The ASK statement puts a message on your terminal, and allows you to enter a value to be assigned to the specified program variable. ASK provides a means for you to dynamically control the flow and the output of your report. The format is:

.ASK "<*message*>" <*variable*>

where *message* is a 1- to *x*-character message which will be displayed on your terminal. If the message contains blank characters, the message text must be enclosed in double quotes (″).

The *variable* argument is the name of the program variable whose value will be set equal to the data value you entered. The entered data value must be of the same type as the program variable. If a numeric variable is specified, and the entered data are alphanumeric, the variable is set equal to zero and no error is indicated. If a date variable is specified, the format of the input is MM/DD/YY. The date routine will verify that the entered date is valid. If invalid, you will be asked to reenter the data.

The Remark Statement (REM). The REM statement (remark) allows you to include comment lines within the program source file. The entire line of text following the REM statement is treated as a comment and ignored by RPT. The remark statement will not be output to the interim file. The format of this statement is:

.REM <*comment_text*>

Chapter 15

*SQL*Forms:* Blocks, Fields, and Windows

S*QL*FORMS* IS AN INTERACTIVE PROGRAM FOR CREATING CUSTOM FORMS, MODIFYING existing forms, dropping form definitions from the database, and running forms. *SQL*Forms* guides the forms designer by a series of windows (less than full-screen displays) that pop up over part of the contents of the screen, defining the form, the blocks within the form, and the fields within the block.

SQL*Forms has two major features. The first is a facility for creating and modifying forms, called the *screen painter*. This is used exclusively by *SQL*Forms* designers in developing forms. It allows the designer to "paint" a form on the screen and specify certain of the form's functions by means of windows. The second main feature is a facility for running forms to be used by end users. It is designed to be as close as possible to the experience of filling out paper forms.

SQL*Forms Version 2.0 replaces the previous Interactive Application Facility (IAF) components IAG, IAP, CRT, and *Fastform*, and adds two new components: The Interactive Application Designer (IAD) and The Interactive Application Converter (IAC). It is not necessary to know which component of *SQL*Forms* performs which function. However, the following brief descriptions of the components may be of interest.

The Interactive Application Generator (IAG) reads an INP file and generates a FRM file. It is executed by *SQL*Forms,* after IAC, when control is returned to the main menu by the CREATE or MODIFY function. It may also be used to convert a FRM file to an .INP file. The Interactive Application Processor (IAP) reads a form from a FRM file and runs it. It is executed by the RUN option of the *SQL*Forms* main menu. The FSF creates an INP file for a default form. It is executed by the DEFAULT part of the CREATE option.

IAD allows a form designer to paint a form directly on the screen. It creates or modifies a form in the database. It is executed by the CREATE or MODIFY options of the *SQL*Forms* main menu. IAC loads existing forms into the forms definition dictionary so that the forms can be modified by IAD, and it creates an .INP file for forms for input to IAG. IAC reads a form from the database and creates an .INP file or vice versa. It is executed by *SQL*Forms* when control is returned to the main menu by the CREATE or MODIFY function.

15.1 DEFINITIONS

For purposes of this chapter, the following definitions will apply:

form—A fill-in-the-blanks arrangement allowing easy data entry, update, and query.

page—A division of the space on a form. Only one page is visible on your screen at a time.

block—Information from a single table in the database containing one or more records from that table. Many blocks can appear on a single page of the form, or a single block may spread over many pages.

record—A single row from a database table. (Same as defined in other chapters of this book.)

field—A specific part of a form used for entering and/or displaying a single item. Fields sometimes represent columns from database tables, but not always.

window—A box appearing on your screen, covering part of the screen's contents. The window contains a number of items from which you can select and manipulate by means of function keys.

trigger—a sequence of SQL commands and *SQL*Forms* commands that are executed when a certain event occurs.

With *SQL*Forms,* you "paint" a form on the screen with the screen painter. As you enter commands, their effects on the current page of the form are immediately shown on the screen. In this way you specify the appearance of a form, what fields and constant text will be on the form, and where they will be.

From the screen painter, you can invoke pop-ups which specify the function of the windows form, for example, what table column will correspond to each field, what each field's characteristics are, and what triggers are associated with each field and block.

15.2 STARTING *SQL*FORMS*

The command for starting *SQL*Forms* is:

```
SQLFORMS
```

ORACLE will then prompt you for your user name and password. After this is validated, *SQL*Forms* will display its main menu.

15.3 HOW TO CREATE A FORM

There are two types of forms you can create with *SQL*Forms*, a default form already existing in the database which you modify with the main menu's MODIFY option, or a custom form starting from scratch. Creating and modifying a default form is usually easier than creating a custom form.

Note: When *SQL*Forms* is installed, certain keys are assigned specific functions. This differs with each system. A "keypad diagram" will tell you the key assignments for your system. Obtain one from your database administrator before starting to work with *SQL*Forms*. In the text that follows, only the *function* is named (e.g., [Select]), not the specific key you must press in your operating system to activate that function.

15.3.1 How to Create a Default Form

When you request a default form, *SQL*Forms* asks for information about the form you want, then creates the default form. It then returns control to the main menu. The steps are:

1. At the CHOOSE FORM window, enter the name you intend to give the form. The maximum number of letters it can contain ranges from 8 to 30, depending on the operating system.

2. Position the cursor on CREATE in the CHOOSE FORM window and press [Select].

3. The CHOOSE BLOCK window will appear. Position the cursor on DEFAULT and press [Select].

4. *SQL*Forms* will display the DEFAULT BLOCK window. The block name you specified in Step 1 above will appear in the TABLE NAME space on this window if it is a valid table name. If it is not an existing table name, then you will have to specify a valid table name on this DEFAULT BLOCK window. This valid table name then becomes the "base table."

5. The DEFAULT BLOCK window will show a 1 beside the number of rows to be displayed. You can change this to any number you want. It will also show a 1 beside Base Line; this indicates that the first row of this block will begin at the top of the screen. *SQL*Forms* will automatically place the next block you create below this one, with an empty space between blocks, unless you specify otherwise.

6. By default, all columns from the base table will be on the form you are creating. If you want to keep all columns on the form:

   a. Press [Accept] and the CHOOSE BLOCK window will be redisplayed.
   b. Press [Accept] again to return to the CHOOSE FORM window.
   - c. Go to Step 7 below. (The form must be GENERATED before it can be RUN.)

   If you don't want all columns to be on the form, you must specify which columns should be excluded. To do this:

   a. Position the cursor on COLUMNS in the DEFAULT BLOCK window, and press [Select]. *SQL*Forms* will display the SELECT COLUMNS window with all the columns in the base table listed and highlighted for inclusion in the form.
   b. Press [Next Field] until the cursor is on a column name you want to exclude. Then press [Select] to remove the highlight from that column name.
   c. Continue removing highlighting from column names you want to exclude from the form. When you finish excluding column names, press [Accept]. Press [Accept] again to return to the CHOOSE FORM window.

7. Select the GENERATE item from the CHOOSE FORM window and press [Accept]. You can now run this form by specifying its name on the CHOOSE FORM window and selecting the RUN option.

Block Content. The first block begins at the top of page 1. Each successive block is placed below the preceding one; if a block will not fit entirely on the current page, it is started on the next page. Each block consists of three lines containing some constant text and the name of the block, followed by a variable number of lines containing fields. You may give a block any name you like; it can be different from the base table name.

If a block displays just one record, its fields are arranged in English reading order, two fields per line, beginning in columns 20 and 60. Any field more than 20 characters long will be in column 20 on a line by itself. The title for each field appears at the left of the field. Fields are placed on alternate lines with blank lines in between them.

If a block displays two or more records, the fields of each record are arranged from left to right on a single line, with two empty positions between fields. Consecutive records appear on consecutive lines. The title for each field, which is the name of the corresponding column in the table, appears above the field. If the fields cannot fit on a single line, *SQL*Forms* will only display one record in the block.

Fields. Information from database tables appears in fields on the form. Each field is a window on one column of the database, or on other information such as a calculation from other fields.

There are three types of fields you can use in a block. A *base-table field* corresponds to a column in the base table for the block; through this field you can update, insert, and delete data in the table column. A *table lookup field* corresponds to a column in a table that is not the base table for this block. You can use a trigger to read the data from the table into a table lookup field. But you cannot query, update, insert, or delete data in the table column from this block. Table lookup fields are usually used to display related information on the form. Finally, a *temporary-data field* doesn't correspond to any single table column. You can use a trigger to calculate and display information in a temporary-data field, based on table values, other fields in the form, or operator input. Temporary-data fields are usually used for calculations, messages, and menu choices.

The width of a CHAR field is the same as the width of the corresponding table column. The field display width is 60. If your CHAR field data width is greater than 60, the field must be scrolled horizontally to view the entire value.

The data width and the display width of a DATE field are both nine. The width of a JDATE or an EDATE is eight.

The data width of a numeric field is two positions greater than the width of the corresponding table column. This allows room for a decimal point and a minus sign. If the width of the column is not explicit, the data width of the field is 14 positions. The display width of a data field is 10. If the data width of your numeric field is greater than 10, the field must be scrolled to view the entire value.

To CREATE and DEFINE a field, see Section 15.13.1.

15.3.2 How to Create a Custom Form

To create a custom form, the steps (after you have typed in *SQL*Forms*, given your user ID and password, and pressed [Accept]) are as follows:

1. The CHOOSE FORM menu will appear. Move the cursor to CREATE, and press [Select].

2. The CHOOSE BLOCK window will appear. Enter the name you want the

new block to have. You may now have *SQL*Forms* generate one or more DEFAULT blocks that you can modify later (see Section 15.3.1); develop a new CUSTOM form by building each block from scratch, putting the cursor on CREATE and pressing [Select]; or you may combine both methods and create a form containing both default and custom blocks.

3. If you selected CREATE from the CHOOSE BLOCK window, control will pass to the screen painter. It will display the first page of the form. You may now use the screen painter's function keys to "paint" constant text on the screen, define the properties of blocks, change the current block, create fields and define their properties, change the current display page, and specify properties of blocks and fields, such as triggers and field characteristics.

4. After you complete this block of the form, press [Accept]. *SQL*Forms* will return to the CHOOSE BLOCK window. To create another block, fill in the name you want the block to have, select the CREATE option, and return to Step 3.

5. To save the completed form, you must press [Accept] to return to the CHOOSE FORM window, select file and press [Accept], and then, on the FILE window, select SAVE and press [Accept].

6. You must now GENERATE the form before it can be RUN. To do so, return to the CHOOSE FORM window and select GENERATE. (You must GENERATE the form each time you make changes to it.) The name of the file being generated will be in the File Name Box. Press [Accept]. When the File Name disappears, the form has been generated.

7. You may now RUN the new form from the CHOOSE FORM menu.

*SQL*Forms* will store your new form in the database. Then it will compile the form, create the INP and FRM files, and return you to the main menu.

15.4 HOW TO MODIFY A FORM

Modifying a form or block is similar to creating a custom form. These are the steps:

1. Specify the form or block name in the Name space on the CHOOSE FORM window. (Or select the LIST option which lists the form names. Then move the cursor to the desired form name and select that form by pressing [Select].)

2. *SQL*Forms* will display the CHOOSE BLOCK window.

3. Move the cursor to MODIFY and press [Select]. This will place you in the screen painter where you can redesign your form or block.

15.5 COPYING, RENAMING, OR DROPPING A FORM

You can copy, rename, or drop a form by using the FILE option on the CHOOSE

FORM window as follows:

1. Fill in the name of the form or block you want to copy, rename, or drop on the CHOOSE FORM menu.

2. Select FILE to display the FILE window.

3. Select the appropriate action on the FILE window. *To copy the form,* select SAVE AS. Then type a name for the copy in the fill-in field that appears, and press [Accept]. *To rename the form,* select RENAME. Type the new name for the copy in the fill-in field that appears and press [Accept]. *To drop the form,* select DROP.

4. To return to the CHOOSE FORM window, press [Exit/Cancel].

The above FILE actions apply only to the form as it is defined in the database. None of them has any effect on the run files for the form. Therefore, if you are copying or renaming a form, you must generate run files for the new form. If you are renaming, you must use operating system commands to delete the run files for the old form.

Renaming a form renames the form in the database only. *SQL*Forms* does not generate new INP and FRM files for the renamed form, nor does it delete the INP and FRM files associated with the old name of the form. To delete the renamed form's old INP and FRM files, use your host operating system's DELETE command.

15.6 DELETING A FORM

In addition to the procedure described in Section 15.5 above, it is also possible to delete a form with the EXIT BLOCK window, but the DROP option method is preferred. This procedure deletes a form from the database only. It does not delete the associated INP and FRM files. To delete the form's INP and FRM files, use your host operating system's DELETE command.

15.7 RECOVERING FROM AN ERROR

Whenever an error message is displayed, you must acknowledge the message by pressing [Accept]. *SQL*Forms* will not accept any further input until you do this.

15.8 LEAVING THE SCREEN PAINTER

To leave the screen painter, press [Accept] or [Exit/Cancel], and you will be returned to the CHOOSE BLOCK window. Pressing [Exit/Cancel] will not cause *SQL*Forms* to discard the changes you have made with the screen painter as it does on windows. To discard a single change, use [Undo]. To discard all of the changes you have made to the form, leave the screen painter, leave the CHOOSE BLOCK window, and select the QUIT option from the EXIT FORM window.

15.9 UNDOING A FUNCTION

To undo the most recent screen painter function, press [Undo]. As you continue to press [Undo], it will remove successively earlier operations. The [Undo] key has no effect on options set in windows or on constant text that has been entered on the screen. However, it can affect text indirectly by undoing a function that modified text, such as MOVE or DELETE.

15.10 MOVING THE CURSOR

Immediately after you enter the screen painter, the NEXT FIELD function moves the cursor to the first field on the screen in English reading order. As you continue to move the cursor, it will go on to succeeding fields in that same order, finally looping back from the last field to the first field again.

In the same way, the PREVIOUS FIELD function moves the cursor to the first previous field, then to the one before that, finally looping from the first field to the last. The cursor will move only among fields in the current block that are on the current page.

15.11 CHANGING THE CURRENT BLOCK

Most screen painter functions operate on the current block. You choose the current block in the CHOOSE BLOCK window when you enter the screen painter. You can change the current block by leaving the screen painter, changing to another block in the CHOOSE BLOCK window, and reentering the painter.

15.12 CREATING A BLOCK

The terms *create* and *define* do not mean the same thing in *SQL*Forms*. To *create* an object means to bring it into existence. For example, you create a block with the CHOOSE BLOCK window, by selecting the CREATE option. Creating a block will be described in this Section. To *define* an object, however, means to specify its properties. For example, you define a block by making it the current block, then pressing SELECT BLOCK followed by DEFINE. Defining a block will be described in Section 15.12.1.

To create a new block and make it the current block, leave the screen painter, and enter the name of the block in the "Name" field of the CHOOSE BLOCK window. When the screen painter displays a page, enter a page number in its "Page #" field. Then select the CREATE option. *SQL*Forms* will create the new block, make it the current block, and reenter the screen painter.

15.12.1 Defining a Block

To define a block, enter the screen painter by specifying the block name and page number, then press [Select Block], then press [Define]. This invokes the DEFINE BLOCK window. You can now define or change:

- The sequence number of the block. This is the order in which it appears when you press [Next Block] or [Previous Block] while running the form.

- The name of the block. However, if you change the name of the block, this does not change any triggers that refer to the name of the block. You must find these triggers and change their references yourself.

- The description of the block, which is a brief statement of its contents; it is displayed when you press [Menu]. If the first character of the description is an asterisk, the block will not appear in the menu.

- The name of the table or view associated with the block. If you leave this entry blank, this will make the block a control block.

- The block's triggers. Select the TRIGGER option, which will invoke the DEFINE TRIGGER window.

- The order in which *SQL*Forms* will display records selected by a query. Select ORDERING to invoke the SPECIFY DEFAULT ORDERING window.

- Record display and validation. Select OPTIONS to invoke the SPECIFY BLOCK OPTIONS window.

Press [Accept] to save your changes and return to the screen painter. Or, to discard your changes, press [Exit/Cancel].

15.12.2 Block-Level Triggers

A trigger is executed in a sequence of steps, one command per step. *SQL*Forms* has several types of block-level triggers. (It also has field-level triggers, described in Section 15.3.2. Triggers that perform both block- and field-level functions are discussed in Chapter 16.)

Block-level triggers can set default values in a field, perform consistency checking, do validity checking requiring the comparison of values in different fields (called *validation*), and perform computations and store the results in the current record, in other blocks, or in tables. This last ability is called *propagation*.

There are eight types of independent block-level triggers, which are described in Table 15-1. You may define any or all of them in any block. The two "query" triggers, *pre-query* and *post-query*, are executed when you press [Execute Query]. The other six types of triggers are executed when you (or a trigger) commit changes to the database.

15.12.3 Using Triggers

Pre-query triggers are used to restrict table access to certain users, certain times, certain days, and/or certain types of queries. (To be effective, such restrictions should be implemented in the pre-insert and pre-update triggers as well.)

Post-query triggers are used for updating statistics about the records retrieved by a query, such as average price paid for a certain type of product. (Such statistics are normally displayed in a control block, and must be initialized by a pre-query trigger.)

Pre-insert, pre-update, and pre-delete triggers are used to validate data before it is inserting it in a table, for example, by ensuring that a yield value exists in some other table (e.g., checking that a Social Security number in a list of bonus recipients actually exists in an employees table), or by ensuring that the values in two different fields are consistent (e.g., checking that a percent-of-salary increase is not larger than the salary).

These three triggers also are used for making changes to inserted or updated rows (that should be invisible to the user); such changes include assigning a unique, sequential order to a row inserted in a table; updating a "last date modified" column in a table; and changing the format of a date when inserted in a table.

Post-insert, post-update, and post-delete triggers can be used to ensure consistency within or among tables by making appropriate changes. For example, updating employee's salary in a list of managers when that salary is updated in the table of employees.

Table 15-1. Types of Block-Level Triggers.

Trigger Type	Description
Pre-Query	Executed once when EXECUTE QUERY or COUNT QUERY HITS is pressed, before query is performed. Commands have access to field values entered by operator, but not to field values fetched by query.
Post-Query	Executed once for each record selected by the query, just after the record has been fetched and displayed on the screen for the first time. Commands have access to all field values in the fetched record. (Field-level triggers are also executed at this time.)
Pre-Delete	Executed once for each deleted record, just before the corresponding row is deleted from the table. Commands have access to all field values in the row and the record.
Post-Delete	Executed once for each deleted record, just after the corresponding row is deleted from the table. Commands do not have access to field values in the row.
Pre-Insert	Executed once for each inserted record, just before the corresponding row is inserted in the table. Commands have access to all field values in the record.
Post-Insert	Executed once for each inserted record, just after the corresponding row is inserted in the table. Commands have access to all field values in the record and row.
Pre-Update	Executed once for each updated record, just before the corresponding row is updated in the table. Commands have access to all field values in the record (which is updated) and the row (which is not yet updated).
Post-Update	Executed once for each updated record, just after the corresponding row is updated in the table. Commands have access to all field values in the updated row and the record (both of which are updated).

15.12.4 Defining Block-Level Triggers

To define a block-level trigger, you invoke the DEFINE BLOCK window and select the TRIGGERS option. *SQL*Forms* will then display the CHOOSE TRIGGER window. Use this window to select the type of trigger you want to define.

Select a type either by entering it in or by using the LIST TYPES option. Then select CREATE to display the trigger step window. (See Section 15.15 for SQL statements in triggers.)

15.12.5 The SPECIFY DEFAULT ORDERING Window

When you select the ORDERING option of the DEFINE BLOCK window, the SPECIFY DEFAULT ORDERING window will be displayed. Use this window to define a default WHERE clause and/or ORDER BY clause that you want to incorporate into the SELECT statement to be constructed for each query in the block.

The WHERE and/or the ORDER BY clauses begin on the second line of the window.

Follow these rules in entering the clauses:

1. If both WHERE and ORDER BY are present, the WHERE clause must be first.

2. If the WHERE clause is present, it must begin with the word WHERE; the ORDER BY clause (if present) must begin with the words ORDER BY. If only the ORDER BY clause is present, the clause must begin without the words ORDER BY. That is, only the expression(s) defining the order should be entered.

3. If the WHERE clause is present, with or without the ORDER BY clause, the clause(s) may be entered on any number of lines. If the clauses are too long to fit in the window, they may be scrolled. If only the ORDER BY clause is present, it must be entered on a single line.

The SPECIFY DEFAULT ORDERING window has three options. FORWARD and BACKWARD will scroll the WHERE and ORDER BY clauses up and down. You can use these to view different parts of the clauses if they are too long to fit in the window. The DELETE option will delete the WHERE and ORDER BY clauses.

To leave the SPECIFY DEFAULT ORDERING window, press [Accept] to preserve the changes you have made in the window, or [Exit/Cancel] to discard them.

15.12.6 The SPECIFY BLOCK OPTIONS Window

When you select the OPTIONS from the DEFINE BLOCK window, *SQL*Forms* will display the SPECIFY BLOCK OPTIONS window. Use this window to define other properties of the block.

If CHECK FOR UNIQUE KEY is enabled, *SQL*Forms* will ensure that any record inserted in the block has a unique set of values in its primary key fields. This check is performed when you perform a commit if (a) the record is being inserted, or (b) the record is being updated and the value of a primary key field has been changed.

This option offers a convenient way of ensuring that each record inserted in the associated table is unique in those fields. However, giving the table an index with the UNIQUE property is a much more efficient way of ensuring uniqueness. Also, defining several unique indexes will allow you to check for uniqueness in several separate fields, while primary key fields only allow you to check for uniqueness across the entire primary key.

DISPLAY IN BLOCK MENU will display the block description on the DEFINE BLOCk window when the operator presses [Menu]. This is the default. You can hide the block by deselecting this.

NUMBER OF ROWS DISPLAYED determines how many records will be displayed in the block at one time, and NUMBER OF ROWS BUFFERED determines how many records will be held in the computer's main memory at once. *SQL*Forms* reserves enough space to buffer at least 300 rows for the form. The blocks in the form compete for this buffer space. NUMBER OF ROWS BUFFERED guarantees that an individual block will get space to buffer at least the specified number of records. This may result in reserved space for more than 300 records.

NUMBER OF LINES PER ROW determines how many display lines will be occupied by each record in the block. If this is greater than the number of lines actually needed, there will be empty lines between rows.

To leave the SPECIFY BLOCK OPTIONS window, press [Accept] to save the changes you have made, or [Exit/Cancel] to discard them.

15.13 HOW TO CREATE AND DEFINE A FIELD

When you create a field, the DEFINE FIELD window is invoked automatically. To change a field's attributes, place the cursor on the field, then press DEFINE. The DEFINE FIELD window allows you to define or change:

- The sequence number of the field, i.e., the order in which it will appear when you press NEXT FIELD or PREVIOUS FIELD while running the form.

- The name of the table column associated with the field. This column becomes the name of the field. SQL commands in triggers will refer to the field by this name. For a non-database field, including any field in a control block, you may use any valid name. But keep in mind that when you change the name of the field, the triggers referring to that field are not changed. You must find these and change the reference yourself.

- The field's data type.

- The field's trigger. To do this, select the SQL option from the DEFINE FIELD window.

- The field's attributes. To do this, select the ATTRIBUTES option from the DEFINE FIELD window. (See Section 15.14 for more about field attributes.)

- Validation properties of the field. To do this, select the VALIDATION option from the DEFINE FIELD window.

15.13.1 Field Validation

There are several provisions for validating the values entered in fields before those values are committed to the database. These are:

1. Field type on the DEFINE FIELD window. This prevents the entry of invalid characters or sequences, such as letters in a NUMBER field.

2. Field attribute on the SPECIFY ATTRIBUTES window: *Update Allowed* and *Update if Null* prevent existing values from being changed, *Fixed Length* prevents non-null values that don't fill the field, and *Mandatory* prevents null values.

3. Field value checks on the SPECIFY VALIDATION window: *Field Length* prevents values that are too long, and *Range* prevents values not falling between the specified minimum and maximum.

4. Field-level triggers on the CHOOSE TRIGGER window. These can be used for many other kinds of validity checking.

If field validation fails for any field, the entire commit process is halted. Changes already committed to the database are rolled back. When this happens, you must correct the invalid field and restart the COMMIT process.

*SQL*Forms* validates fields in the following situations:

- When a field ceases to be the current field.
- When the current record changes, fields in the old current record are validated.
- When the current block changes, fields in the current record of the old current block are validated.
- When the workspace is committed to the database, fields in every record of every non-control block are validated.

Some types of field validation, such as field-level trigger steps containing SQL commands or user exits, can change a field's value in a form. When this happens, the field's trigger is not executed immediately; it is executed the next time the field is checked in the normal course of operation. This provides effective validation of field values, but it may create confusion for you when a trigger finds an error in a field that you have not changed directly. Consider this as you define trigger steps.

15.13.2 Field-Level Triggers

A *trigger* is a sequence of operations that are executed when a certain event takes place. Each field in a form may have a field-level trigger which gets executed in the course of field validation, and also when the value of the field is changed.

Validation that requires comparing the values of two or more fields is generally performed in a block-level trigger since it is unsafe to assume that a field-to-field comparison will be meaningful when just one of two or more interrelated fields has been changed. However, field-level triggers are used for validating the value of a field in ways that are not possible with the SPECIFY ATTRIBUTES and VALIDATION windows.

A trigger is executed in a series of steps. Each step of a trigger performs one of the following types of commands:

- A SQL command. SELECT is the only SQL command that may be used in field-level trigger steps. By contrast, in block-level triggers, any SQL command may be used.
- A *SQL*Forms* command. This is a special command intended only for use in trigger steps.
- A user exit. This is a user-written procedure in a programming language such as C or COBOL.

Triggers can be executed by (triggered by):

- Entry, i.e., when you first run a form, or when the cursor enters a new block, record, or field.
- Query, before or after records are retrieved.
- Change, after you change a value, or before or after you commit inserted, updated, or deleted records to the database.

- Exit, i.e., when you leave a form or when the cursor leaves a block, record, or field.
- Keystrokes, e.g., when you press function key.
- User-named triggers, i.e., common triggers or "subtriggers" that you want to reuse or call from other triggers.

15.14 THE SPECIFY ATTRIBUTES WINDOW

When you select the ATTRIBUTES option from the DEFINE FIELD window, the SPECIFY ATTRIBUTES window will appear. Use this window to define the attributes of the field. The options for this window name the attributes a field may have. To enable one of them, select the corresponding option as illustrated in the next Section.

Some field attributes are independent, i.e., the presence or absence of one attribute does not determine the presence or absence of any other. However, it will be clear from the descriptions below that in some cases enabling one attribute may require enabling or disabling another. These interdependencies are automatic. Each field in a form has some combination of the following *attributes* (sometimes called *characteristics*). Select ATTRIBUTES from the DEFINE FIELD window to see them.

Database. If a field has the Database attribute, it represents a column in the table associated with this block of the form. Thus, the value displayed in the field for a given record is fetched from (and/or may be stored in) the corresponding field of a row in the table. If a field does not have this attribute, it does not represent any column in the table. Depending on the design of the form, however, it may be calculated from (and/or may be used to calculate) values in one or more columns of one or more tables.

Primary Key. If a field has this attribute, it is part of the block's primary key, and it also must have the Database attribute. You can use the primary key to ensure uniqueness of the records in a form. For example, to ensure that no two records in an employee information form have the same employee ID, you could give the employee ID field the Primary Key attribute. Uniqueness is enforced across all of the fields that are part of the Primary Key, i.e., uniqueness is not violated unless every Primary Key field in a certain record has the same value as the corresponding field in another record. At least one field in each block must be given the Primary Key attribute, whether or not you enforce uniqueness of the primary key. If you do not enforce uniqueness of the primary key, the Primary Key attribute has no significance.

Displayed. If a field has this attribute, its value is displayed in the form. If a field does not have this attribute, its value is not displayed. If a field does not have this attribute, it may be used by a trigger to perform calculations and yet be invisible to the user. If an error occurs in the field, however, information about the field may be displayed by pressing [Display Error]. The user will not be aware that a field exists if it does not have the Displayed attribute.

Input Allowed. If a field has this attribute, a user may enter or change its value. If a field does not have this attribute, *SQL*Forms* may display it, but a user may not enter or change its value. If a field has this attribute, it must have the Displayed attribute.

Update Allowed and Update If Null. These attributes are listed together because they are very similar, and because a field may have either one of them, but it cannot have both. If a field has the Update Allowed attribute, a user may change its value in a record fetched by a query. If a field has the Update If Null attribute, a user may change its value in a record fetched by a query only if the value is null (empty). If a field does not have either attribute, a user may not change its value in a record fetched by a query under any conditions. If a field has either of these attributes, it must have the Input Allowed and Displayed attributes.

Fixed Length. If a field has this attribute, its value must be exactly as long as the field. If a field does not have this attribute, its value may be shorter than the field. If a field has this attribute, it must have the Input Allowed and Displayed attributes.

Mandatory. If a field has this attribute, its value may not be null (empty). If a field does not have this attribute, its value may be null. Note that Mandatory and Fixed Length are independent; if a field has the Fixed Length attribute but not the Mandatory attribute, then the value need not be present, but must be exactly as long as the field if it is present. If a field has this attribute, it must have the Input Allowed and Displayed attributes.

Uppercase. If a field has this attribute, lowercase letters are converted to uppercase as they are entered; if a field does not have this attribute, lowercase letters are allowed. This attribute only affects information as it is entered into the field through the form. Lowercase information may still be entered into the corresponding table column through another form, or through a program other than *SQL*Forms*. If a field has this attribute, it must have the Input Allowed and Displayed attributes. The attribute is meaningful only if the field's type is CHAR or ALPHA and the field has the Input Allowed and Displayed attributes.

Autoskip. If a field has this attribute, *SQL*Forms* automatically skips to the next field when a character is entered in the last position of this field. (If the Fixed Length attribute is not present, you can skip to the next field before reaching the last position by pressing [Next Field]). If a field does not have this attribute, *SQL*Forms* never skips to the next field until you press [Next Field]. If a field has this attribute, it must have the Input Allowed and Displayed attributes.

Automatic Help. If a field has Automatic Help, its help message will be displayed whenever the cursor is in the field (except when an error message is displayed). To take advantage of this attribute you must define the help message on the SPECIFY VALIDATION window described below. An Automatic Help field must also be Displayed and have Input allowed.

No Echo. If a field has No Echo, its value will always be displayed as blank spaces, even though the field itself is visible. You can select this attribute to hide passwords and other information. If a serious error occurs in a No Echo field, the value may be displayed when the operator presses [Display Error]. To truly protect a value, put the field on page 0 of the form as well as defining it as No Echo. A No Echo field must also be Displayed.

15.15 THE SPECIFY SQL STATEMENT WINDOW

The SPECIFY SQL STATEMENT window (previously called "pop-up" in earlier versions of *SQL*Forms*) no longer exists in Version 2.0. SQL statements are now defined in a trigger. See Section 16.4.

15.16 THE SPECIFY VALIDATION WINDOW

When you select the VALIDATION option from the DEFINE FIELD window, the SPECIFY VALIDATION window will appear. Use it to define or change field properties that will influence the way data are entered and validated in the field. The fields in this window are:

Field length—The number of characters that can be entered for the field. This window field defaults to the displayed length of the field. If set to a larger value, *SQL*Forms* will scroll the field horizontally to display its entire value. (Horizontal scrolling is not supported on IBM 3270 display devices, personal computers that emulate the 3270, or asynchronous display devices attached to synchronous communication lines through protocol converters.)

Query length—Number of characters that can be entered for the field during a query. This window field defaults to the displayed length of the field. If set to a larger value, *SQL*Forms* scrolls the field horizontally to display entire value.

COPY FIELD VALUE FROM—In these fill-in items, type the block and field from which you want the value to be copied.

DEFAULT—A fixed value to be used as this field's default value when a record is created.

RANGE—Minimum and maximum valid values for the field.

LIST—Fill-in items. Type the table and column containing a list of valid values for the field. Press [List Field Values] to display values one at a time in ascending order. If a LIST table and column are specified, the RANGE (if any) is ignored.

HELP—An explanatory message for the field which will be displayed when you press HELP.

15.17 KEY TRIGGERS

You can use a key trigger to redefine what happens when you press a function key. These can be defined at any level by choosing TRIGGER from the DEFINE FORM, DEFINE BLOCK, or DEFINE FIELD window. You must then fill out the CHOOSE TRIGGER window. Once it is defined, the new key definition will be in effect whenever the cursor is in the form, block, or field associated with that trigger (unless it is overridden by a trigger of the same type at a lower level).

Some function keys cannot be redefined. Your *ORACLE* system is already set up with about 30 function keys, not all of which can be redefined. Since this changes from time to time and differs with different systems, check the *Installation and User's Guide* for your system to find which you can redefine.

15.18 USER-NAMED TRIGGERS

User-named triggers are not triggered by an event, but are executed from within another trigger. Their purpose is to create modules of code that otherwise would have to be repeated in several different triggers.

There are no set types of user-named triggers. You give each one its name (following the naming rules) and then use that name to refer to it. You can use the EXETRG function from the list of function codes in Section 16.11.1 to call a user-named trigger from another trigger.

While you can define a user-named trigger at any level, and then call it from another trigger at that level or lower, it is most convenient to define it at the form level so you can use it at any level. A lower-level trigger will override a higher-level trigger with the same name.

Chapter 16

*SQL*Forms:* Triggers, Macros, and User Exits

A TRIGGER WAS DEFINED IN CHAPTER 15 AS "A GROUP OF SQL COMMANDS, *SQL*FORMS* commands, and/or user exits that are executed when a certain event occurs." This chapter will show how triggers work. It will also discuss macros and user exits.

*SQL*Forms* supports two types of triggers: A *block-level trigger* is associated with a specific block and is executed when an event related to the block occurs, such as the initiation of a query. A *field-level trigger* is associated with a specific field, and is executed at some point after the value of the field has changed.

The characteristics of triggers that are specific to blocks are discussed under Section 15.12.2, and characteristics specific to fields are discussed under Section 15.14, both in Chapter 15. This chapter will discuss characteristics that apply to both block-level and field-level triggers.

16.1 HOW TRIGGERS WORK

A trigger consists of a "step" for each command executed. Three types of commands can be executed in a trigger step. *SQL commands* may query or modify any table you are authorized to query or modify. SQL commands may also use and change the contents of fields in all blocks of the current form. *SQL*Forms commands* perform operations such as invoking a series of *SQL*Forms* functions. You normally invoke these functions by pressing function keys. Third, *User exit commands* invoke user exits written in a programming language such as C or COBOL. User exits may perform any kind of computation on form fields; they may access fields in database tables, and they may use certain services provided by *ORACLE* and by *SQL*Forms.*

The steps in a trigger are executed one at a time. If a step modifies the contents of a field, that modification is visible to the following steps. Normally, the steps in a trigger are executed in sequence, but this depends on the outcome of a step.

16.1.1 Possible Outcomes of a Step

There are three possible outcomes when a step in a trigger is executed: it may succeed, it may fail, or it may cause a fatal error. For example, a syntactic error in a SQL command will cause a fatal error. So will a SQL command that refers to a nonexistent table. (However, syntactic errors in *SQL*Forms* commands or user exit commands may not cause fatal errors.)

SQL*Forms does not do syntactic checking on a command entered in the course of defining a trigger step. If the command contains a syntax error (e.g., a misspelled keyword or function code), the outcome of the step depends on the type of command as discussed below:

- A SELECT, INSERT, UPDATE, or DELETE command succeeds if it retrieves, inserts, updates, or deletes at least one row and fails if it does not. (But see "Query Mode" in Section 16.2 for a situation where a SELECT command has a different result.) Other SQL commands cannot fail. If a SQL command contains a syntax error, it causes a fatal error.

- A *SQL*Forms* command suffers a fatal error if it causes *SQL*Forms* to run out of memory. It will merely fail if it can't be executed for any other reason, including incorrect syntax.

- A user exit command may succeed, fail, or cause a fatal error depending on its internal logic. If *SQL*Forms* attempts to execute a nonexistent user exit, the result will be a fatal error. If a user exit command contains a syntax error, it will fail.

16.1.2 Step Outcome Consequences

Normally if a step succeeds, the next step in sequence is executed. If there is no next step, the trigger succeeds. The normal consequence of failure or fatal error is failure of the trigger. No further steps are executed.

The consequences of success and failure (but not of fatal error) are influenced by the settings of the trigger attributes associated with each step. These attributes are discussed in Section 16.1.4 below.

16.1.3 Possible Trigger Outcomes

When a trigger is executed, there are two possible outcomes, success and failure. The consequences of each depend on what type of trigger it is, as follows:

- In a pre- and post-insert, update, or delete trigger, success allows *SQL*Forms* to continue committing changes in the workspace to the database. Failure stops the commit. Changes already applied to the database are rolled back.

- In a pre-query trigger, success allows the query to proceed. Failure aborts the query.

- In a post-query trigger, success allows the fetched record to remain in the workspace. Failure causes the record to be replaced by a record with all blank fields.

- In a field trigger performed in the course of query execution (in query mode), either success or failure allows the query to proceed.

- In a field trigger performed while validating a field whose value has been changed, success permits the requested operation (commit, change of current field, record or block, etc.) to proceed. Failure means the field is invalid. The requested operation is cancelled; you must correct the value in the field and try again.

16.1.4 Trigger Step Attributes

When you select ATTRIBUTES from the TRIGGER STEP window, the TRIGGER STEP ATTRIBUTES will appear. These attributes include what happens when the step succeeds or fails, and how much memory is allocated to the step.

*SQL*Forms* assigns default values to its attributes. You need to define attributes only if you want to change the defaults. This section presents the purpose of each attribute; Section 16.1.5 gives a complete description of the effect of each.

Abort Trigger When Step Fails. If this switch is selected (and a failure label described below isn't specified), failure of the step halts execution of the trigger. Whether the trigger succeeds or fails depends on the "Return success when aborting trigger" switch (described below). This switch is selected by default, since failure of a trigger step normally means that something has gone wrong and you want to stop processing. Note that the "Reverse return code" switch (described below) will affect how step failure is defined.

Reverse Return Code. If this switch is selected, the normal criteria for success and failure are reversed. It is most often used to (1) make sure a corresponding record does not exist (i.e., the SELECT statement fails) before carrying out an action, and (2) display a failure message when the operator presses a key you have disabled, even though the trigger itself succeeds.

Return Success When Aborting Trigger. This switch is meaningful only if "Abort trigger when step fails" is selected. If both switches are selected, the trigger itself will succeed even though the step fails and execution is halted. It is most often used in triggers that don't need to be executed if certain conditions are met.

Separate Cursor Data Area. Normally, each trigger step is assigned its own cursor (memory space) for processing. But if memory is scarce, you can conserve it (but slow down processing) by deselecting the "Optimize SQL processing" switch on the SPECIFY RUN OPTIONS window. If you do so, you can select this switch to reserve memory space for (and speed processing of) the SQL trigger steps that are executed most frequently. This switch applies only to SQL commands in trigger steps; it has no effect on *SQL*Forms* commands or user exits called from triggers.

16.1.5 How *SQL*Forms* Processes Trigger Steps

The details of *SQL*Forms* trigger step processing are as follows:

1. If the trigger is being executed in query mode, and the step contains a SELECT command with no INTO clause, or with INTO clauses that refer only to Database fields in the current block, the step is not executed. *SQL*Forms* goes to step 8 (as though the command were executed and had succeeded.)

2. The command in the step is executed.

3. If the command in the step is LOCK TABLE and the step succeeded, *SQL*Forms* goes to step 8. If there is already an incompatible lock on the table, LOCK TABLE places a WAIT LOCK on the table if NOWAIT is not specified, or succeeds *without locking* if it is specified. LOCK TABLE cannot fail, but it will cause a fatal error if it contains a syntax error or the table does not exist.

4. If the step succeeded, values retrieved by SELECT . . . INTO commands or supplied by EXEC IAF PUT statements in user exits are moved to their destination fields. If the step failed, no field values are changed.

5. If the step resulted in a fatal error, a message describing the error is displayed. This is a *SQL*Forms* or *ORACLE* error message, not the message specified on the TRIGGER STEP window. You may get more information by pressing [Display Error]. Any *SQL*Forms* functions waiting to be performed as a result of a key command or earlier macro commands, whether in this trigger or another one, are discarded. No further trigger steps are executed. The trigger fails.

6. *SQL*Forms* decides according to the setting of the "Reverse return code" whether the step succeeded or failed. If it failed, it continues with step 7. If it succeeded, *SQL*Forms* proceeds to step 8.

7. Failure processing is performed. The failure message is displayed and, if there is a failure label, *SQL*Forms* goes to that step. The "Abort query when trigger fails" and "Return success when aborting trigger" switches are not meaningful. If there is no step with that label, no further trigger steps are executed and the trigger succeeds. If there is no failure label, however, then:

   a. If "Abort trigger when step fails" is deselected *SQL*Forms* proceeds to step 8 (as though the step succeeded).
   b. If "Abort trigger when step fails" is selected but "Return success when aborting trigger" is not, no further trigger steps are executed. The trigger fails.
   c. If "Abort trigger when step fails" and "Return success when aborting trigger" are both enabled, no further trigger steps are executed. The trigger succeeds.

8. Success processing is performed. If there is a success label, *SQL*Forms* goes to that step. If there is no step with that label, no further steps are executed. The trigger succeeds. If there is no success label, however, *SQL*Forms* goes to the next step, if any. If there is no step, the trigger succeeds.

Note: The "Reverse return code" switch is evaluated in step 6. This means that steps 1 through 5 are not affected by this switch.

16.2 QUERY MODE

The post-change field-level triggers in the current block are executed before the post-query trigger (if any) when a record is fetched in the course of a query. When this happens, the triggers are said to be executed in *query mode*. Post-query triggers are executed in this context to give the application an opportunity to initialize functions such as non-database fields.

Trigger processing in query mode differs from ordinary field-level trigger processing in the following ways:

- Triggers are executed only in Database fields.

- A field in the current block having the Database attribute may not be changed by a trigger step. Any attempt to change a field in this manner will be ignored (and will not cause a fatal error).

- If a SELECT command has no INTO clause, or if it attempts to SELECT values only INTO Database fields in the current block, it is not executed at all. Trigger processing proceeds as if the command had succeeded.

- User exit commands are processed the same way in query mode as they are in other contexts except that they cannot change field values, as noted above. However, *SQL*Forms* will pass a "query mode" flag to a user exit. The user exit may perform different functions depending on whether or not the flag is set.

- A trigger step containing a SQL command other than SELECT will cause a fatal error.

- A trigger step containing a *SQL*Forms* command is ignored. Trigger processing proceeds as if the command had succeeded.

16.3 SUCCESS AND FAILURE LABELS

Trigger steps are usually executed in order. You can change the order by using step labels (defined on the TRIGGER STEP window). You can associate a label with any step in a trigger. Then you can have another step branch to the labelled step by entering the label in the other step's SUCCESS or FAIL field.

For example, you may want a trigger to execute Step 1, then execute Steps 2 and 4 if 1 succeeds, or Steps 3 and 4 if 1 fails. You would fill in the LABEL, SUCCESS and FAIL fields for the 4 steps like this:

Step	Label	Success	Fail
1			STEPB
2		STEPA	
3	STEPB		
4	STEPA		

The labels STEPA, STEPB, are arbitrary. You may choose any valid *SQL*Forms* name, but each label defined must be unique within the trigger. In the above, step 1 doesn't need a success label since you simply want to continue with the next step if it succeeds.

The "Reverse return code" switch will affect which label is processed and whether a failure message is displayed. However, if you enter success and failure labels, the "Abort trigger when step fails" and "Return success when aborting trigger" switches are both ignored.

16.4 SQL COMMANDS IN TRIGGERS

You can use SQL commands in triggers to put data in fields of a form, perform calculations on data in a form, reformat data in a form, check whether data exist in the database, and compare data in fields of a form. Enter a SQL command directly on the TRIGGER STEP window. Each SQL statement (a command plus any subsidiary clauses) constitutes one step of a trigger.

SQL commands in triggers use almost the same syntax as SQL commands in other *ORACLE* products (but see exceptions below). One major difference is that *SQL commands in triggers do not end with a semicolon* (;). Note also the following restrictions and warnings when using SQL commands in a trigger:

- You can only use SELECT commands in a post-change trigger.

- You can use data manipulation commands (INSERT, UPDATE, and DELETE) only in commit (pre- and post-insert, update, and delete) triggers.

- If you use INSERT, UPDATE, or DELETE commands to modify a base table for a block in the current form, make sure to update any data that might be on the form.

Only SQL commands—not *SQL*Plus* commands—can be used in triggers. (SQL commands are much easier to debug if you test each one by running it under *SQL*Plus* before you place it in a trigger.)

16.5 TRIGGER COMMAND OPERATION

SQL commands in triggers operate on database tables, just as they do in other *ORACLE* products. For example:

```
SELECT  *
FROM    ORDERS
WHERE   ORDERID =210
```

When this command is executed, however, query results will not be displayed on the screen. Its only consequence is SUCCESS if it returns at least one row from the table, or FAIL-URE if it does not, or if it causes a fatal error. You can use this type of command, for example, to find out whether or not data exist in a table.

16.6 DISPLAYING QUERY RESULTS

If you want to display query results on the screen, you must use the two *SQL*Forms* extensions to SQL to refer to form fields, as discussed below.

Use the syntax :*[block] field* to refer to a field in the form. The colon (:) identifies a reference as a form field instead of a table column. (For compatibility with older forms, you may also use an ampersand (&) in place of the colon, but the colon is preferred.) Use this syntax anywhere a table column or constant value can be used. Omit the block reference only if the field name you specify exists in only one block of the form.

In a SELECT statement, you can include an INTO clause to place retrieved values in form fields. It must directly follow the SELECT command and precede the FROM clause. Use the INTO clause only to select data into form fields. The form field must not be preceded with a : in an INTO clause.

The extended syntax of the SELECT statement is:

```
SELECT            {[table].[column__list]/:[block.]field/*}
   [INTO          [block.]field]
   FROM           table__list
   [WHERE         clause]
   [HAVING        clause]
   [GROUP BY      clause]
```

16.7 SELECTING DATA INTO A FIELD

You can select data into any field in a block. It can be a field corresponding to a base table column for the block (a Database field) or not. It can be a visible field (a Displayed field) or not. If Displayed, it may be a modifiable field (Input Allowed and/or Update Allowed) or not. If you select a field name that is used in more than one block, you must qualify the field name with the block name. Otherwise, an error will result.

SELECT with INTO selects only one row. If the SELECT command would otherwise select more than one row, SELECT with INTO will select the first row only. To select several rows into a multi-record block, use the *SQL*Forms* EXECQRY function to set up a query for the block.

A table column may have many values—one for each row selected from the table— but a *SQL*Forms* field has only one value, the one in the context record of its block. Thus, it is impossible to select records from a block as if they were rows in a table.

16.8 THE CURRENT AND CONTEXT BLOCK, RECORD, AND FIELD

The *current block, record, and field* are defined as the one the cursor is in. These are the objects that user operations can affect. The current record of another block is the record that the cursor was in when that block was last the current block. For a block that has never been the current block, the current record is the first record.

Triggers make use of similar concepts: the *context block* and the *context record*. The context block of a trigger is the block that the trigger is associated with. The context record of the block is the record in the block referred to by field references.

The context block for any trigger executed in the course of a query, is the block in which the query is being performed. The context record of the context block for a pre-query trigger is the "record" containing the search criteria. The context record of the context block for a post-query trigger or a field-level trigger executed in query mode, is the record being fetched into the workspace.

During a COMMIT, the context record is the record being committed to the database.

Thus, each block in turn becomes the context block. Each added, updated, or deleted record in the block in turn, becomes the context record. This rule determines the context record for pre- and post-insert, -update, and -delete triggers, as well as for field-level triggers executed in the course of a commit.

The context record in a block other than the context block is always the same as the current record of that block.

16.9   TABLE AND RECORD LOCKING

You should be aware of how *SQL*Forms* handles table and record locking when you modify tables in a trigger step. Otherwise, you may design forms that cause deadlocks when two users try to use the same table at the same time. *SQL*Forms* locking is treated in detail in Chapter 8 along with all other types of *ORACLE* locking.

As a general rule, a trigger modifying a base table of the form should include the SQL command LOCK TABLE IN SHARE UPDATE MODE as its first step.

16.10   USING ROWID

Every table in the database has a column named ROWID. During a transaction, each row in a table has a fixed and unique ROWID value. Every block in a form has an invisible, non-updatable field named ROWID. When a record is fetched into the workspace, the value of ROWID is fetched along with it. This enables some types of triggers to identify the table row corresponding to each record in the workspace. (Newly inserted records do not correspond to any row, and so have a null ROWID.)

You can use the ROWID to pre-update, pre-delete, post-insert, post-update, and post-query triggers. Do not use it to pre-insert or pre-query triggers, since the records in the block do not have meaningful ROWID values for these triggers. Do not use it in the post-delete trigger because the row in the table no longer exists.

To display ROWID for debugging purposes, use a post-query trigger to select it into a displayed field. The ROWID field must be at least 26 characters long to display the whole value.

Under no circumstances should an operator or trigger change the ROWID. *SQL*Forms* requires a valid ROWID when work is committed to the database; therefore updating ROWID in a form may interfere with the updating process.

16.11   *SQL*FORMS* COMMANDS IN TRIGGERS

*SQL*Forms* commands can be used only in trigger steps. You can use them in triggers to redefine function keys; carry out a series of actions on a form, as if the operator were pressing function keys; execute user-named triggers; call other forms; manipulate variables; and carry out operating system commands. You can enter a *SQL*Forms* command directly on the TRIGGER STEP window. Each *SQL*Forms* statement (a command plus arguments or function codes) comprises one step of a trigger.

*SQL*Forms* commands must begin with a #. There are four commands that can be used in trigger steps:

#EXEMACRO Used to execute a series of actions on a form.

#COPY Used to copy constant, field values, or global or system variables from a source to a destination.

| #ERASE | Used to erase global variables. |
| #HOST | Used to carry out operating system commands. |

In writing *SQL*Forms* commands in triggers, you can use any number and combination of spaces, tabs, and new lines to separate the individual elements (which are called *tokens*). However, you must use white space to separate two tokens when they would not otherwise be recognized individually. You cannot use white space to separate the components of a variable (GLOBAL.*var__name*) or field reference (*[block].field*).

A *constant* or *command__string* represents a character string of any length enclosed in single quotation marks. To include a single quotation mark as part of the string, enter two quotation marks, like this:

'Don't forget the extra quote.'

A *[block.]field* reference in a *SQL*Forms* command must *not* be preceded by a colon (:). (Since *SQL*Forms* commands cannot refer to database tables and columns, the reference will not be ambiguous.) The only time you can omit the block reference is when the field name you specify exists in only one block of the form.

16.11.1 The #EXEMACRO Command

A *macro* is a series of actions for *SQL*Forms* to perform. This may include operator functions (as if the operator had pressed a function key) or special *SQL*Forms* functions that can only be performed by triggers. You can use macros to reduce repetitive or complex typing by the operator; control the flow of an application (for example, by coordinating records in two or more blocks in a form); make sure several actions are always performed in sequence; and provide help (e.g., by calling another form on which the operator can query for a customer ID). Macros can be executed conditionally, and you can nest conditions within other conditions.

A macro is defined in a #EXEMACRO command. Following the command, you must enter the function code of each action, followed by its argument (if any), followed by a semicolon(;). You can add as many function codes as you wish. When the trigger step containing the #EXEMACRO is executed, all the function codes will be executed.

There are restrictions on the function codes you can use in pre- and post-triggers; these restrictions are detailed later in this section. Therefore macros are primarily useful in key triggers. Also, key triggers change the effect of a physical function key, not the function normally associated with that key. For example, a KEY-NXTFLD trigger redefines what happens when the operator presses [Next Field], but a trigger that includes the NXTFLD function still moves the cursor to the next field.

SQL*Forms recognizes the function codes listed in Table 16-1. Separate function codes by a space or spaces, just as you separate the clauses of a SQL command. They may be entered on any number of lines.

How Macros Are Processed. The following example of a macro command simulates the pressing of the [Next Block], [Next Record], and [Previous Block] keys, in that order:

#EXEMACRO NXTBLK;NXTREC;PRVBLK;

The function codes in a macro are applied in sequence, regardless of the results of previous

Table 16-1. SQL*Forms Macro-Function Codes.

Code	Function
ABTQRY	Abort Query
CALL	Suspends processing of the current form and displays the form specified. When terminated with an EXIT code or [Exit/Cancel] key, resumes the original form at the point of interruption.
CALLINPUT	Suspends processing of the current macro and accepts and processes operator input. When terminated with an EXIT code or [Exit/Cancel] key, resumes the macro at the point of interruption.
CALLQRY	Suspends processing of the current form and displays the form specified, where only queries may be performed. When terminated with an EXIT code or [Exit/Cancel] key, resumes the original form at the point of interruption.
CHRMODE	Change Character Mode
CLRBLK	Clear Block
CLRFLD	Clear Field
CLRFRM	Clear Form
CLRREC	Clear Record
COMMIT	Commit
CQUERY	Count Query Hits
CREREC	Create Record
DELCHR	Character Delete
DELREC	Delete Record
DERROR	Display Error
DKEYS	Display Keys
DUPFLD	Duplicate Field
DUPREC	Duplicate Record
ENTQRY	Enter Query
EXEQRY	Execute Query
EXETRG	Executes a User-Named Trigger
EXIT	Exit to Main Menu
GOBLK	Moves cursor to block specified in current form
GOFLD	Moves cursor to field specified in current form
HELP	Help
LISTVAL	List of Field Values
MENU	Menu
MOVRIGHT	Right ($->$)
MOVLEFT	Left ($<-$)

Code	Function
NOOP	No operation; does nothing but display a failure message (if step fails). Only used in KEY trigger.
NULL	No operation; does nothing; does not display a failure message. Used for specifying no action where at least one function code is required.
NXTBLK	Next Block
NXTFLD	Next Field
NXTKEY	Next Primary Key Field
NXTREC	Next Record
NXTSET	Next Set of Records
PAUSE	Suspends processing of the current macro and displays the message "Press any function key to continue" on the status line. When operator presses any function key, restores the status line and resumes the macro at the point of interruption.
PRINT	Print form
PRVBLK	Previous Block
PRVFLD	Previous Field
PRVREC	Previous Record
REDISP	Redisplay Screen

codes. For example, consider the command:

#EXEMACRO NXTFLD;NXTFLD;NXTFLD;

This command normally would move the cursor forward three fields. If the first field contains invalid data, however, the first NXTFLD would generate an error message and leave the cursor where it was. Three NXTFLDs would generate three error messages. This illustrates that in writing a multifunction macro, you should consider the effects of the function sequence under all foreseeable conditions.

The NOOP and NULL functions do nothing. For example, if you want to disable the [Delete Record] key, you can define a KEY-DELREC trigger as:

#EXEMACRO NOOP;

Then, when the operator presses [Delete Record], nothing will happen. However, if you select the "Reverse return code" switch and enter a failure message like "Can't delete order records," the step will fail and the failure message will be displayed. (If you use NULL instead of NOOP, the results will be the same, but the failure message will be omitted.)

The #EXEMACRO command always succeeds unless it contains a coding error. (A *SQL*Forms* command containing a coding error always fails.)

Nesting Macro Commands. When a trigger invokes a command, that command may perform a function causing the execution of another trigger, which in turn may invoke another command. This is called a *nested macro command*. In this case, the processing of the first (outer) macro is suspended at the point where the second (inner) trigger is executed. Processing of the outer macro is resumed when the inner trigger has completely executed.

Avoid nested macros which result in a macro invoking itself. Such an arrangement will cause the command to invoke itself over and over till the end of time.

Restrictions on the Use of Function Codes. There are restrictions on the function codes you can use in certain triggers, depending on the trigger's classification as a *program trigger* or an *event trigger* relative to the basic *SQL*Form* functions like [Next Field] and [Execute Query].

A program trigger is explicitly invoked by a function key for which a key trigger is defined. Program triggers are "synchronous" in that they are invoked between the execution of basic *SQL*Forms* functions. Program triggers include all key triggers, and user-named triggers invoked by program triggers. You can use any macro function code in a program trigger.

An event trigger is invoked by an associated event, such as a cursor movement, field validation, or an attempt to commit a transaction. They are "asynchronous" in the sense that they are invoked in the middle of the execution of a basic *SQL*Forms* function. For example, a post-change trigger might be invoked while a [Next Field] function is being executed. Event triggers include all pre-triggers, all post-triggers, and user-named triggers invoked by event triggers.

In an event trigger, the only macro function codes allowed are those that do not interfere with the basic *SQL*Forms* function in programs. These include:

```
CALL
CALLQRY
NULL.
```

You can also use CASE and EXETRG in an event trigger, provided that only the three function codes above are actually executed within the CASE statement or user-named trigger.

Calling One Form from Another. You can combine multiple forms into a complete, modular application by calling one form while processing another. The *form call* may attach forms designed by two or more developers. This eliminates redundant form development and maintenance. Some of the tasks form calls are used for include:

- Menus that present a set of choices from which the operator can select.
- Help screens.
- Queries for information needed by the operator.
- Sharing blocks and tables among several applications.

There are two macro functions that call another form: both CALL and CALLQRY temporarily suspend processing of the current form while another is being processed. *SQL*Forms* accepts input in the called form until it receives an EXIT function code (or the [Exit/Cancel] key is pressed). It then returns to the original form and resumes the suspended macro. Both CALL and CALLQRY can be used in either a program or event trigger. But there is no direct access to one form from another. You must use global variables to pass information back and forth.

If the screen shows an error message when the CALL or CALLQRY is processed, the operator must acknowledge it before the called form is displayed. The message will be gone when the calling form is resumed.

CALL and CALLQRY have slightly different functions, and require different commits. CALL allows the called form to be processed normally. If there are uncommitted changes in the calling form, *SQL*Forms* will ask the operator to commit these to the database first. A Y (Yes) answer commits changes and allows the call to proceed. A N (No) aborts the call and causes the trigger step to fail. Changes cannot be committed in an event trigger, however, therefore, if CALL is used in an event trigger, and there are uncommitted changes, the commit prompt will not be displayed, the call will be aborted, and the trigger will fail.

CALLQRY does not require changes in the calling form to be committed, nor does it ask the operator to do so. Changes remain uncommitted until the form is resumed. But operations on the called form are mostly restricted to queries, as follows:

1. The called form cannot change the database in any way. Any attempt to do so will result in an error message. Thus, only non-Database fields and fields in control blocks can be modified on the called form.

2. SELECT is the only SQL command allowed in a trigger. Any other SQL command results in an error message and terminates the trigger with a fatal error.

3. The [Commit] key or COMMIT function is not allowed and results in an error message.

4. The [Clear Form/Rollback] key or CLRFM function is allowed but has no effect.

5. A user exit should not perform a COMMIT WORK or ROLLBACK WORK command. *SQL*Forms* does not enforce this restriction, however, and the results of these commands are undefined.

16.11.2 The #COPY Command

The #COPY command in a trigger step will copy constants, field values, global variables, or system variables from a source to a destination. The name of the source and the destination both follow the #COPY keyword. This is the only way to assign a value to a global variable. You cannot use constants or system variables as destinations. For example, the following command assigns the contents of the SUPPLIERS.SUPPLIERID field to the variable GLOBAL.ID:

```
#COPY SUPPLIERS.SUPPLIERID GLOBAL.ID
```

16.11.3 The #ERASE Command

The #ERASE command only erases the value of a global variable whose name follows the #ERASE keyword. Once it is erased, the variable name is no longer defined and its memory is released. The following command erases the GLOBAL.ID variable assigned above:

```
#ERASE GLOBAL.ID
```

If the variable has not been assigned (or has previously been erased), the #ERASE command is ignored.

16.11.4 The #HOST Command

The #HOST command in a trigger step will execute an operating system command. The #HOST command must be followed with either a quoted command string or the name of a field or variable containing the command string. Processing of the current form is suspended while the system command is being run. For example, the following command starts *SQL*Plus* and runs a command script called CUSTRPT:

```
#HOST 'SQLPLUS@CUSTRPT'
```

#HOST commands that work with one operating system may not work with another. However, *ORACLE* commands like "SQLPLUS" are portable and should work with any operating system running *ORACLE*.

A trigger step containing a #HOST command succeeds if the system command returns a "success" or "warning" status, fails if the system command returns an "error severity" status, or causes a fatal error (and aborts the trigger) if the system cannot execute the #HOST command or returns a "fatal error severity" status.

16.12 USER EXIT COMMANDS IN TRIGGERS

A *user exit* is a function written in a programming language, such as C, which is invoked by a user exit command in a trigger step. A user exit can display messages and perform processing that is beyond the scope of SQL commands. It can also perform computations and table lookups with much more speed than a SQL command.

User exits are generally only used to do things that other trigger commands can't do, such as performing complex field validation, complex computations, updates initiated by values on a form, and to optimize the performance of an application. User exits can either succeed, fail, or cause a fatal error. The user exit program must return a value to *SQL*Forms* indicating the outcome.

16.12.1 Writing a User Exit

User exits are currently supported in C, COBOL, Fortran, PL/I and Pascal. But not all of these may be used with all operating systems; see the *ORACLE Installation and User Guide* for yours.

Regardless of the host language used to write a user exit, it may invoke *ORACLE* services with embedded commands written in *ORACLE*'s SQL language. If embedded SQL commands are included, however, a user exit must be processed by the Precompiler, Common (PCC) before it can be compiled; PCC translates the SQL commands into function calls expressed by the host language. The host language's standard compiler can then be used to compile PCC's output. When the program has to be modified, the modifications are made to PCC's input, and PCC is run again. (PCC does not have to be used if there are no embedded SQL commands in the user exit.)

PCC may be called with an appropriate command line parameter to support each host language. The host languages are named *Pro*C* for use with the programming language C; *PRO*COBOL* for COBOL; *PRO*FORTRAN, PRO*PL/I,* and *PRO*Pascal* for each of those languages. Oracle Corporation publishes a user's guide for each of these.

To run a form making use of a user exit, you must link the object code into a new version of IAP (the component of *SQL*Forms* that runs a form).

16.12.2 Calling a User Exit from a Trigger

Once you have written, debugged, precompiled, compiled, and relinked a user exit program, you can call it from a trigger step. Put its name in the trigger step, preceded by a # sign and followed by any parameters accepted by the program, like this:

#exitname parameters

For example, the trigger step:

#VALIDATE 10 24 A

invokes a user exit called VALIDATE with three parameters.

You must specify a failure message on the TRIGGER STEP window.

Appendix A

ORACLE Reserved Words

THE FOLLOWING LIST CONTAINS THE KEYWORDS USED BY *ORACLE*. THESE ARE NOT AVAILable to the user for use as names of tables, columns, or views. However, you may use a reserved word for a name if you enclose it in double quotes, e.g., "ASSERT."

New versions of *ORACLE* sometimes add words to this list. Check the documentation for the version you have purchased. (The list below is correct through Version 5.0.)

ACCESS	CONTAINS	EXISTS
ADD	CRASH	
ALL	CREATE	FILE
ALTER	CURRENT	FLOAT
AND		FOR
ANY	DATABASE	FROM
APPEND	DATEPAGES	
AS	DATE	GRANT
ASC	DBA	GRAPHIC
ASSERT	DECIMAL	GROUP
ASSIGN	DEFAULT	
AT	DEFINITION	HAVING
AUDIT	DELETE	
	DESC	IDENTIFIED
BETWEEN	DISTINCT	IF
BY	DOES	IFDEF
	DROP	IMAGE
CHAR		IMMEDIATE
CLUSTER		IN
COLUMN	EACH	INCREMENT
COMMENT	ELSE	INDEX
COMPRESS	ENDIF	INDEXED
CONNECT	EVALUATE	INDEXPAGES
CONTAIN	EXCLUSIVE	

INITIAL
INSERT
INTEGER
INTERSECT
INTO
IS

LEVEL
LIKE
LIST
LOCK
LONG

MAXEXTENTS
MINUS
MODE
MODIFY
MOVE

NEW
NOAUDIT
NOCOMPRESS
NOSYSSORT
NOT
NOWAIT
NULL
NUMBER

OF
OFFLINE

OLD
ON
ONLINE
OPTIMIZE
OPTION
OR
ORACLE
ORDER

PARTITION
PCTFREE
PRIOR
PRIVILEGES
PUBLIC

RAW
RENAME
RESOURCE
REVOKE
ROW
ROWID
ROWNUM
ROWS
RUN

SELECT
SESSION
SET
SHARE
SIZE
SMALLINT

SPACE
START
STATEMENT
SUCCESSFUL
SYNONYM
SYSDATE
SYSSORT

TABLE
TEMPORARY
THEN
TO
TRIGGER

UID
UNION
UNIQUE
UPDATE
USER
USING

VALIDATE
VALUES
VARCHAR
VARGRAPHIC
VIEW

WHENEVER
WHERE
WITH

Appendix B

INIT.ORA Parameters

Parameter Name	Default Value	OK to Alter	Impact on SGA	Description
AI_BUFFERS	3	no	none	Number of after image buffers. No effect in Version 5.0.
AFTER_IMAGE	null	yes	-	Name of AI files. Enables AIJ. Can appear more than once in INIT.ORA file if there are multiple journal files.
AI_FILE_SIZE	0	yes	-	Size of AIJ files in *ORACLE* blocks. If 0, then use files in AFTER_IMAGE; if greater than 0, is size in K-bytes to create journal files.
AI_WARN_PCT	0	yes	-	Message sent to operator console when AIJ file is this percent full [not enabled].
AUDIT_TRAIL	0	yes	-	Non-zero enables auditing; zero disables auditing.
BEFORE_IMAGE	O/S	yes	-	Name of before image (BI) file. Must be created on most systems via *ORACLE*'s CCF utility.
BI_BUFFERS	O/S	no	some	Number of before image buffers.

Parameter Name	Default Value	OK to Alter	Impact on SGA	Description
BI_HIGH	end of BI file	yes	-	Last block in BI file for instance using this INIT.ORA file. Used by shared-partition systems. Set during installation.
BI_LOW	start of BI file	yes	-	First block in BI file for instance using this INIT.ORA file. Used by share-partition systems. Set during installation.
BLOCK_SIZE	O/S	no	some	Bytes in an *ORACLE* database block. Value is 2048 for DEC VAX/VMS, DG AOS/VS, and many UNIX environments; is 4096 for IBM VM/SP or MVS environments.
BUFFERS	50	yes	high	Number of data buffers cached in memory. The more buffers, the more likely that data will be found in memory; thus the less I/O necessary.
BUFF_HASH_BKTS	8	no	low	Number of entries in hash table used to find *ORACLE* buffers. If you specify value, it will be adjusted to a power of 2. Value should conform to

$$4 < = \frac{\text{BUFFERS}}{\text{BUFF\_HASH\_BKTS}} < = 8$$

Lower values result in faster lookup at expense of randomness in caching of algorithms, but might be OK for very large systems. Greater values result in slightly slower lookup. Val-

Parameter Name	Default Value	OK to Alter	Impact on SGA	Description
				ue of 1 may be OK for very small system
CLUSTERS	20	yes	low	Number of cached cluster definitions. Set to number typically in use at one time. Larger cache reduces parse time. If you alter, set 1 extra for data dictionary.
COLUMNS	350	yes	some	Number of cached column definitions. Must be large enough for widest table. Default is 5 times the sum of CLUSTERS plus TABLES. If you alter, include 50 as overhead for Data Dictionary tables. Larger cache makes it easier for *ORACLE* to find column definition in memory; this improves performance.
CONSOLE				[Not currently used]
CONTEXT_INCR	4096 bytes	yes	-	Number of bytes by which context area will grow when it requires more space. Range is 1024-32768 bytes, but is O/S dependent.
CONTEXT SIZE	4096 bytes	yes	-	Initial size of context area. Range is 1024-131072 bytes, but is O/S dependent.
DATABASE	O/S	yes	-	Name of primary DB file. Corresponds to first file of SYSTEM partition. File must be created (usually via CCF) and a name specified to run IOR.
DETACHED_DUMPS	O/S	yes	-	Names the logical or physical directory where dumps for detached processes are written.

Parameter Name	Default Value	OK to Alter	Impact on SGA	Description
ENQUEUES	5 times PROCESSES	yes	some	Maximum number of total enqueue entries.
FILES	5	yes	some	Number of DB files open in SGA. Each partition and extent counts as a file. Maximum is O/S dependent.
FIXED__DATE	null	yes	-	Fixes *ORACLE*'s internal SYSDATE. Usually used for testing only. Format: YYYY, MM,DD, HH, MM,SS. Null default indicates that current date is supplied by O/S.
INSTANCES	16	yes	-	Number of instances per shared partition system at IOR I-time. Applies only to shared-partition operation. Maximum is 16; all need not be used or running.
INSTANCE__NAME	-	no	-	Name of instance running this INIT.ORA file. Applies only to shared partition operation.
OPEN__CURSORS	50	yes	some	Number of cursors each process is allowed to open. Range is 10-255.
PROCESSES	O/S	yes	some	Number of possible concurrent processes. Allow 1 process per *ORACLE* logon and overhead of 5 (1 for each detached process, if in multi-user mode, and 1 for IOR) Maximum and default are O/S dependent. Minimum for single-user systems is 2. Value set for PROCESSES is used to calculate several other parameters.

Parameter Name	Default Value	OK to Alter	Impact on SGA	Description
READ_BLKS_REQ	lesser of 10 or READ_BLKS_TOT	no	-	Number of blocks that may be requested in a single read request. Range 0-255 blocks. Does not apply to single-user systems.
READ_BLKS_TOT	1/2 of no. of BUFFERS	no	-	Number of blocks that may be in outstanding background read requests at any time. Does not apply to single-user systems.
READ_REQUESTS	greater of 5 or PROCESSES	no	low	Number of outstanding background read requests. Does not apply to single-user systems.
SINGLE_PROCESS	0	yes	-	Zero enables multi-user system. Nonzero enables single-user system.
SORT_AREA_SZ	O/S	yes	-	Size in bytes of real memory available for sorting. Larger size will only improve efficiency of large sorts. Default is OK for most systems, but may need adjustment if very large indexes being created, e.g., if one process doing full system import, then increasing this parameter may speed the import, especially CREATE INDEX statements. Range and default are O/S-dependent.
SORT_FINAL_RA	O/S	no	-	Readahead depth factor during final sort passes.
SORT_MERGE_RA	O/S	no	-	Readahead depth factor during intermediate sort passes.
SORT_POOL_SZ	-	-	-	[No longer used]

Parameter Name	Default Value	OK to Alter	Impact on SGA	Description
SORT_READ_FAC	-	no	O/S	Multi-block read factor for sorting.
SORT_SPCMAP_SZ	O/S	yes	O/S	Size in bytes of sort space map in context area. Default is OK for most systems, but if very large indexes are being created, you may want to adjust. Sort automatically increases its space map when necessary, but not necessarily when it will make best use of disk storage. Range and default are O/S-dependent. See Chapter 6 for optimal formula.
SQL	SQL.ORA	yes	-	Name of SQL file to run during initialization.
TABLE_ACCESSES	fn of PROCESSES	-	some	Number of distinct tables in use at one time. Range is 8-208.
TABLE_HANDLES	8 times PROCESSES	-	some	Number of simultaneous table uses on one table. Maximum is 24.
TABLE_HASH_ BKTS	1-32, depending on TABLE_ACCESSES	-	some	Entries in hash table used to find table access entries. If you specify a value, it will be adjusted to a power of 2. It should satisfy the following ratio:
TABLE_NAMES	80	yes	some	Maximum number of names (table, view, and synonym) cached in SGA simultaneously. If altered, allow overhead of 10 for dictionary

$$4 < = \frac{TABLE\_ACCESSES}{TABLE\_HSH\_BKTS} < = 8$$

Parameter Name	Default Value	OK to Alter	Impact on SGA	Description
				tables. The larger the value, the more likely that *ORACLE* will find requested table in memory, thus reducing parse time.
TABLES	50	yes	some	Maximum number of table definitions cached. If altered, allow overhead of 10 for dictionary tables. Should reflect max number of tables and views expected in use at any one time. The larger the value, the more likely that *ORACLE* will find requested table in memory, thus reducing parse time.
TEMP_TABLES	1/10 of lesser of TABLE_HANDLES or TABLE_ACCESSES	yes	-	Number of temporary tables *ORACLE* will maintain after a warm start. More can be created, but will be deleted as soon as possible. (A warm start drops all temporary tables, to be created as required.) Zero is a valid setting.
TRANSACTIONS	5 times PROCESSES	yes	some	Maximum number of concurrent transactions.
USERINIT	null	yes	-	Name of file to run after file specified by SQL parameter. Assumes that account running this file is SYSTEM/MANAGER. File may not contain any CONNECT statements. Can run CATALOG.ORA by specifying it here.
USERS	30	yes	some	Maximum number of user names cached, not maximum number of users concur-

Parameter Name	Default Value	OK to Alter	Impact on SGA	Description
				rently logged on. Reflects expected maximum number of users referenced in SQL statements. A user name is only stored once. The larger the number, the better the performance with a large number of distinct *ORACLE* user names, but there is no need for this parameter to exceed the value of PROCESSES.
USER_DUMPS	O/S	-	-	Name of directory where error trace dumps are written (e.g., for IAP, ODL, RPT, etc.)

Glossary

AIJ—After image journaling, a DBA utility. See *after image files*.

after image files—Files used to record committed transactions, for rollforward recovery in case of system failure; also called *AIJ files*.

argument—An expression inside the parentheses of a function, supplying a value for the function to operate on. Also, a datum following the command filename in a START command, which supplies a value for a substitution variable in the command file.

ARH—See *asynchronous readahead*.

ASCII—A standard for using digital data to represent printable characters; an acronym for "American Standard Code for Information Interchange."

asynchronous readahead (ARH)—A process for speeding query time, which reads data from the database into the SGA for queries doing full table scans.

attribute—In *SQL*Forms*, A synonym for "characteristic," as in "characteristic of a field"; appears in many screen painter pop-ups.

audit-trail—A table in the Data Dictionary table, called SYS.AUDIT__TRAIL, containing descriptions of audited operations.

autocommit—A feature of *SQL*Plus* that commits changes to the database at the end of each command; enabled by the command SET AUTOCOMMIT ON.

base table—Any "real" table in the database, as opposed to a "virtual table."

before image file—A file containing images of data before changes are made, used to insure that data are not entered into the database before they are complete and consistent; also called *BI file*.

block—The basic unit of storage for all *ORACLE* data. Number of blocks allocated per table depends on the space definition in effect for that table's creation. Varies by operating system.

block-level trigger—In *SQL*Forms*, a trigger invoked when a query is performed or when records are committed to the database.

box—In *SQL*Forms*, a rectangular enclosure in a form, containing a group of related objects such as the fields and constant text in a block. Created with the DEFINE BOX function; also may be created by entering sequences of text characters such as '-' and 'I.'

buffer—The location where *ORACLE* keeps a command or program being entered, edited, or executed.

CCF—See *Create Contiguous File.*

candidate row—A row selected by a main query, the field values of which are used in the execution of a correlated subquery.

chained block—A subsequent block set up to store table data when the originally allocated block has run out of space because rows in that block have expanded due to updates. Usually used for table data, but index blocks can also be chained. Many chained blocks will have an impact on performance; if this occurs, the PCT FREE space definition parameter may be set too low.

CHAR—A data type which stores character strings to a maximum of 240 characters.

CHAR field—In *SQL*Forms*, a field whose value is a sequence of characters.

cluster—A method of storing together data from multiple tables when the data in those tables contain common information and is apt to be accessed together; used to improve performance, it has no impact on wording of SQL statements.

cluster key—The column(s) that clustered tables have in common, and which are chosen as the storage/access key.

cold start—Term for starting an *ORACLE* database for the first time. Usually called "initializing a database." Executing the IOR.INIT.

commit—To make permanent changes to the database. Before INSERTs, UPDATEs, DELETEs are stored, both old and new data exist so changes can be stored or data can be restored to its previous state. When data are committed, all new data that is part of the transaction are made permanent, thereby replacing the old data in the database.

compressed index—An index for which only enough information is stored to identify unique index entries; a "truncated" index, which reduces storage overhead. Contrast with *noncompressed index.*

concatenated index—An index created on more than one column of a table, used to guarantee that those columns are unique for every row in the table. Can be either compressed or noncompressed on any combination of a table's columns.

consistency check—In *SQL*Forms*, a processing step which verifies that two pieces of data make sense together. For example: a check that the supplier number in a row being inserted in an order table is already in a row in a supplier table. Block-level triggers are often used to perform consistency checks.

constant text—In *SQL*Forms*, the fixed information in a form. Thus, everything except field definitions and trigger definitions.

context area—A work area where *ORACLE* stores the current SQL statement; if the statement is a query, the result's column headings and one row of the result are also stored here.

correlated subquery—Same as *correlated nested SELECT.*

correlated nested SELECT—A subquery that is executed repeatedly.

Create Contiguous File (CCF)—An *ORACLE* utility available on some operating systems, used by the DBA to create and ready the database and BI files.

current buffer—The buffer that *SQL*Plus* editing commands will affect at any given time.

current line—The line in the current buffer that *SQL*Plus* editing commands will affect at any given time.

current SQL command—The SQL command in the SQL buffer, usually the SQL command most recently executed.

custom form—In *SQL*Forms*, a form created with the screen painter, as opposed to a "default form" which is described by the designer and then created by an automated procedure.

database administrator (DBA)—A user authorized to grant and revoke other users' access to the system, modify *ORACLE* options affecting all users, and perform other administrative functions. See also *SYS* and *SYSTEM.*

database format—In *SQL*Forms*, the format *SQL*Forms* uses to store a form definition in the database. This format holds the version of a form that can be modified by IAD (the screen painter). Created and read by IAD and IAC.

database variable—A variable associated with a database by the EXEC SQL CONNECT command; used to refer to the database by the AT clause of the EXEC SQL command.

Data Control Language (DCL)—One category of SQL statements; these statements control access to the data and to the database, for example: GRANT CONNECT, GRANT SELECT, REVOKE.

Data Definition Language(DDL)—One category of SQL statements; these statements define (CREATE), alter, or delete (DROP) database objects, for example: CREATE VIEW, CREATE TABLE, CREATE INDEX, DROP TABLE, RENAME TABLE.

Data Dictionary—A comprehensive set of tables and views owned by the DBA users SYS and SYSTEM, installed when *ORACLE* is initialized. Also contains information available to DBA only about users, privileges, and auditing. A central source of information for the database itself and for all users. The tables are automatically maintained by *ORACLE*.

Data Manipulation Language (DML)—One category of SQL statements; these statements query and update the actual data, for example: SELECT, INSERT, DELETE, UPDATE.

data segment—Storage allocated to the data of a table, as compared to storage allocated to the index on a table. Made up of an initial data extent, and zero or more incremental data extents. Size and number of these extents is determined by the space definition in effect during table creation.

data type—Any one of the forms of data that *ORACLE* can store and manipulate. Major *ORACLE* data types are: CHAR, DATE, LONG, NUMBER, and RAW.

date field—A field whose value is a date; sometimes applied to a field whose value is a number representing a date. (This latter type of date field was used in early versions of *SQL*Forms* that did not support true date fields, and is retained in later versions for the sake of compatibility.)

datum—A single unit of data.

DBA—See *database administrator*.

deadlock—A situation where two users are each vying for resources locked by the other, and therefore neither user can obtain the necessary resource to complete the work. *ORACLE* resolves deadlocks by rolling back the work of the user with the least work pending.

default—The value of any option which is built into the system, and which will be used by the system if the user fails to specify a value for that option.

delete trigger—In *SQL*Forms*, a block-level trigger performed in the course of deleting a row in a table during a commit. There are two kinds, *pre-delete triggers* and *post-delete triggers*.

detail line—A line in a report presenting data retrieved from a single row of a table.

dictionary definition locks—A shared lock owned by users parsing DML statements, or an exclusive lock owned by users doing DDL commands, to prevent a table from being altered while the dictionaries are queried. Many such locks can exist concurrently.

display width—In *SQL*Forms*, width of a field in a form. A field's value may be wider than the field's display width; if so, the user can employ horizontal scrolling to view the entire value.

distinct—Unique.

dummy table—A table containing exactly one row, useful as the object of a SELECT command intended to copy the value of one field to another field.

empty command—A *SQL*Plus* command consisting of just a semicolon. The empty command is a way of letting the program do nothing in a context requiring a command.

enqueues—A resource that monitors lock requests. Each process requiring a lock on a database object must obtain an enqueue for it. Maximum number of lock requests is determined by the INIT.ORA parameter ENQUEUES.

equijoin—A join condition specifying the relationship "equals" (=).

exclusive mode locking—A mode of locking tables to insure that one process is the only process updating a table's data. No other process can obtain a lock on the table until the exclusive lock is released.

export—To transfer *ORACLE* database files into some other storage area.

expression—One or more data items combined with operators or functions in a command. When *SQL*Plus* executes the command, it computes the value of the expression.

extent—A run of contiguous blocks in a database file, allocated either for a table's data segment or index segment. The first extent allocated is the *initial* extent. Each subsequent extent of blocks is an *incremental* extent. The number of blocks per extent is controlled by a space definition.

extent block—The first block in the initial data or index extent, which contains administrative information about each extent allocated to the table. There are three blocks of overhead per table (two for data and one for index). The extent block is the first data and first index block.

failure—In *SQL*Forms*, one possible result of the execution of a step in a trigger.

failure label—In *SQL*Forms*, a label specified as part of one step in a trigger identifying another step that *SQL*Forms* is to execute if this step fails.

field—A part of a table that holds one piece of data; the intersection of a row and a column.

field length—In *SQL*Forms*, the number of characters that can be placed in a field during data entry.

field reference—In a SQL command, a *SQL*Forms* command, or a user exit, a word used to identify a field containing a function code.

field-level trigger—In *SQL*Forms*, a trigger invoked when the cursor leaves a field after the field's value has been changed, and when a record is fetched into the current block in the course of a query.

file—A physical file that constitutes either a whole partition or a portion of a partition; a storage area used to store all database data.

filetype—The part of a file's name that describes the type of data stored in the file, usually separated from the filename by a period, e.g., STORDATA.LIS, where LIS is the filetype. Often called a file *extension*.

foreign key—A column (or combination of columns) in one table which is not a key in that table, but is a key elsewhere (e.g., in another table). Used for relating data in multiple tables using joins.

form feed—A control character which causes the printer to skip to the top of a new sheet of paper.

FRM file—In *SQL*Forms*, a binary file representing a form, created by IAG and read by IAP; the part of *SQL*Forms* that runs a form.

FSF—A program that creates a default form; invoked through the CREATE A FORM option of the *SQL*Forms* main menu, or can be run as a separate program from your operating system's command line prompt.

function—An operation which may be performed by placing the function's name, followed by parentheses, in an expression. Most functions take one or more arguments within the parentheses, and use the value(s) of the argument(s) in the operation.

group function—A function operating on a column or expression in all of the rows selected by a query, and computing a single value from them. Example: AVG, which computes an average.

heading—Text appearing above a report column to name or describe that column.

hexadecimal notation—A numbering system using a base of 16 instead of 10; it represents the numbers 10 through 15 by the letters A through F. Often used to represent the internal (raw) values of data stored in a computer.

HLI—See *Host Language Interface*.

Host Language Interface (HLI)—A layer of subrouting call entry points into the data storage place and Data Dictionary; called *Pro*SQL* in Version 5.

IAC—See *Interactive Application Converter.*

IAD—See *Interactive Application Designer.*

IAF—See *Interactive Application Facility.*

IAG—See *Interactive Application Generator.*

IAP—See *Interactive Application Processor.*

index—General term for an *ORACLE*/SQL feature used primarily to speed execution and impose uniqueness on data; provides faster access to data than doing a full table scan.

index segment—The storage allocated for the indexes on a table, made up of one initial index extent and zero or more incremental index extents. Size and number of these extents is determined by the space definition in effect during table creation.

initialization—The initial preparing of a database, always done when installing a database system for the first time, and invoked by using IOR INIT. Initial database tables are set up, and any pre-existing user data are lost.

INIT.ORA—A database system parameter file containing several settings and filenames used when a system is started using the IOR program.

INP file—A character file representing a form; created by Fastform, IAG, and IAC, and read by IAG and IAC. Serves as a bridge between a form stored in the database and that form's FRM file, and between earlier versions of *SQL*Forms* and Version 5.

insert trigger—In *SQL*Forms*, a block-level trigger executed in the course of inserting a row in a table during a commit. There are two kinds, pre-insert triggers and post-insert triggers.

instance—A member of a shared-partition database system, as in an *ORACLE* cluster running on a VAX Cluster. Although the instances all share the same data in one database, they each run semi-independently, with their own parameter files and portions of shared before image files.

Interactive Application Converter (IAC)—A program that converts forms from INP format to database format or vice versa. Invoked automatically after you create or modify a form, it also may be run as a separate program from your operating system's command-line prompt.

Interactive Application Designer (IAD)—A program that performs the functions of the screen painter in *SQL*Forms*. May be invoked through the "Create a Form" and "Modify a Form" options of the *SQL*Forms* main menu, or may be run as a separate program from your operating system's command-line prompt.

Interactive Application Facility (IAF)—Consists of two programs, IAG and IAP.

Interactive Application Generator (IAG)—A program that converts forms from INP format to FRM format. Invoked automatically after you create or modify a form, it also may be run as a separate program from your operating system's command-line prompt.

Interactive Application Processor (IAP)—Permits unsophisticated users to interact with the database in a structured environment.

IOR program—A DBA utility program used to initialize an *ORACLE* system, and to start and stop it. Options include running *ORACLE* shared when there are instances sharing a database file and starting *ORACLE* so that only DBAs can access the database.

join—Retrieval from more than one table.

Julian date—A means of converting date data so every date can be expressed as a unique integer. Can be obtained by using the format mask 'J' with functions on date data.

kernel—The part of *ORACLE* performing user-requested SQL operations. Also coordinates activities in multi-user systems.

key—The column(s) in one table that can be used to uniquely identify a row. Column(s) forming a key are usually indexed.

label—In *SQL*Forms*, an identifying word associated with a step of a trigger. Separate labels are specified according to whether the step succeeds or fails. See *success label* or *failure label*.

logical block—The unit of database storage that *ORACLE* uses to allocate space to rows with common cluster-column values. By default, a logical block is the same size as a physical block. It may be made smaller with the CREATE CLUSTER command's SIZE clause; thus, two or more logical blocks may be stored in a physical block.

LONG data type—A data type that allows strings of character data up to 65,535 characters long.

LONG RAW data type—Similar to LONG data type, for byte-oriented data up to 65,535 bytes long, but which makes no assumptions about type of data (e.g., ASCII or EBCDIC).

main program—A program run by entering the CALL command interactively. A main program may run other programs by executing the CALL command.

main query—The outermost query in a query containing a subquery; the query that displays a result.

main variable—A variable that receives a field value in an EXEC SQL command.

nested SELECT—See *subquery*.

nesting—An arrangement of two processing steps in which one invokes the other.

noncompressed index—An index of one or more columns in which all the index data are stored in the index. Allows for faster query time if all the data requested are stored in the index. Contrast with *compressed index*.

non-equijoin—A join condition specifying a relationship other than "equals" (=).

null—Empty. Not a value, but the absence of a value.

NUMBER datatype—A datatype for numeric data.

object—Something stored in a database, for example: tables, views, synonyms, indexes, columns, reports, stored procedures, stored programs.

ODL—See *ORACLE Data Loader*.

ODS—See *ORACLE Display System*.

ORACLE Data Loader (ODL)—User utility used to load data from operating system standard files.

ORACLE Display System—A DBA utility to monitor user and *ORACLE* processes.

OPS$ logins—A type of *ORACLE* username in which OPS$ is prefixed to the operating system account or ID to simplify logging in to ORACLE from that ID.

outer join—The rows that do not match the join condition.

painting mode—In *SQL*Forms*, the mode in which you interact with the screen painter directly (i.e., not through a window).

parameter—A column name, expression, or constant specifying what a command should do.

partition—A logical storage unit of an *ORACLE* database. Every database contains a SYSTEM partition, and may contain additional partitions. Consists of one or more physical files.

pass number—The number of times that all the blocks in the BI file have been cycled through; appears in the BI screen in ODS.

PCTFREE—See *percent free*.

percent free (PCTFREE)—A portion of the data block not filled by rows as they are inserted into a table, but reserved for later updates made to the rows in that block. Actual percent is determined by the PCTFREE value in the space definition used at table creation.

pop-up—In *SQL*Forms* 1.0, a menu displayed by the screen painter, so-called because it "pops up" over part of the contents of the screen, sometimes over other pop-ups. When no longer needed, it is erased, and the information it covered on the screen is revealed again. Called *window* in *SQL*Forms* 2.0.

portability—The ease with which a computer program can be adapted to hardware different from that for which it was written.

post-delete trigger—In *SQL*Forms*, a block-level trigger performed just after deleting each row from a table during a commit.

post-insert trigger—In *SQL*Forms*, a block-level trigger performed just after inserting each row in a table during a commit.

post-query trigger—In *SQL*Forms*, a block-level trigger performed each time a record is retrieved into the workspace after a query.

post-update trigger—In *SQL*Forms*, a block-level trigger performed just after updating each row in a table during a commit.

precedence—The order in which *ORACLE* performs operations on an expression. For example, in the expression $2+3*\times$, $3*\times$ is computed first, then 2 is added because multiplication (*) has higher precedence than addition (+).

precompiler—A program that reads a source program file and writes a modified source program file which a compiler may then read. *ORACLE* supports a precompiler called PCC (Precompiler, Common) which processes SQL commands embedded in user exits and other programs. The precompiler may be used with an appropriate command line parameter to process each of the host languages supported by *ORACLE*.

pre-delete trigger—In *SQL*Forms*, a block-level trigger performed just before deleting each row from a table during a commit.

pre-insert trigger—In *SQL*Forms*, a block-level trigger performed just before inserting each row in a table during a commit.

pre-query trigger—In *SQL*Forms*, a block-level trigger performed when EXECUTE QUERY is pressed.

pre-update trigger— In *SQL*Forms*, a block-level trigger performed just before updating each row in a table during a commit.

predicate clause—A clause based on one of the operators (=, !=, IS, IS NOT, >, >=, <, <=) and containing no AND, OR, or NOT.

propagation—The process of copying a value from one field to another logically related field, or computing a value to be stored in a related field. For example: when an employee's Social Security number is entered in a block of a salary record form, it may be propagated to a block of a withholding tax form.

public synonym—A synonym for a database object which the DBA has created for use by all *ORACLE* users.

query—An instruction to SQL that will retrieve information from one or more tables or views.

query mode—In *SQL*Forms*, a mode in which field-level triggers are executed in the course of fetching a record into the workspace.

query trigger—In *SQL*Forms*, a block-level trigger performed in the course of a query. There are two kinds, pre-query triggers and post-query triggers.

RBA—Relative Block Address, the number of an *ORACLE* block within a partition.

RAW datatype—Similar to CHAR datatype, except that it stores uninterpreted bytes rather than characters.

read consistency—Feature whereby a SQL query always sees a snapshot of a table as it existed at the start of query execution, even while others may be modifying the table.

record—One row of a table.

relational database—A database which appears to the user to be simply a collection of tables.

Report Writer/Formatter (RPT and RPF)—A report generation program which includes two utilities: RPF, the *ORACLE* Report Text Formatter, and RPT, the *ORACLE* report generator.

reserved word—A word with a special meaning in SQL or *SQL*Plus*, and therefore not available to users in naming tables, views, or columns.

rollback—To undo changes made to the database during a transaction or logical unit of work. Opposite of *commit*.

row-level locking—Synonymous with Share Update mode locking; a type of locking in which updates to data occur through locking rows in a table rather than locking the entire table.

row sequence number—A number assigned to a row as it is inserted into a table's data block; also is stored as row overhead and forms part of the ROWID.

ROWID—A pseudo-column for each row in the database, containing the address of each row. It is unique for every row. The fastest means of accessing any row. ROWID contains three parts: the partition number, the number of the block within the partition, and the number of the row within the block.

screen painter—A *SQL*Forms* facility for creating custom forms and modifying forms, represented in the main menu by the CREATE and MODIFY options.

segments—The storage space available for a table's data or indexes. Every table has two segments: one for data and one for all its indexes. Each segment is made up of extents, which are made up of blocks. The space definition controls how many extents are possible and the size of the extents.

SELECT—In *SQL*Forms*, one of the generic function keys recognized by the screen painter, and one of its most important functions. SELECT is a way to point at the object at the cursor and say: "I want this one." Used to (1) choose a field to be defined, copied, moved, or deleted; (2) choose an option from a window; and (3) mark the place where an end-of-line or corner-of-a-box is to be.

SGA—See *System Global Area*.

share mode locking—Locking that guarantees that data will not change while a process is querying it. This mode must be invoked explicitly with LOCK TABLE in the SHARE MODE statement.

share update mode—Locking in which updates to data occur through locking rows in a table rather than locking the whole table; same as row-level locking.

shared-partition system—A configuration where *ORACLE* systems on multiple network nodes share the same database files; each node is called an *instance*.

space definition—A database object used to control space allocation for the data of a table. Contains two main parts: specifications for the data segments and specifications for index segments.

split-screen scrolling—A feature of some display devices which makes it possible to scroll data in a range of lines without affecting other parts of the screen.

spooling—Writing displayed output to the spool; controlled by the SPOOL command.

SQL—See *Structured Query Language*.

SQLCA—See *SQL Communications Area*.

SQL Communications Area (SQLCA)—A storage area used by functions in IAP to return useful information to user exits that call them.

SQL*Forms—An *ORACLE* program which uses forms to retrieve and enter information in tables, intended to look like and be used like a conventional paper form.

SQL*Forms command—A series of functions invoked by a step in a trigger, normally user-invoked by pressing function keys.

step—In *SQL*Forms*, one operation in a trigger. A step may execute a SQL command, a *SQL*Forms* command, or a user exit.

Structured Query Language (SQL)—The basic user interface for storing and retrieving information in the database.

subquery—A query used as a clause in a SQL command.

substitution variable—A variable name or numeral preceded by an ampersand (&), used in a command file to represent a value that will be provided when the command file is run.

success—In *SQL*Forms*, one possible result of the execution of a step in a trigger; for example, a SELECT command succeeds if it selects at least one row, and fails if it does not.

success label—In *SQL*Forms*, a label specified as part of one step in a trigger, identifying another step that *SQL*Forms* is to execute next if this step succeeds.

syntax—The linear order of words or symbols.

SYS—One of the DBA's created when *ORACLE* is installed and initialized (the other is SYSTEM). SYS owns most of the Data Dictionary tables; SYSTEM owns the views created on those base tables.

SYSTEM (user)—One of the DBA's created when the database system is installed and initialized (the other is SYS). SYS owns most of the Data Dictionary tables; SYSTEM owns the views created on those tables.

SYSTEM (partition)—The original and only partition existing in a newly installed system. Every database system must have a SYSTEM partition with at least one file allocated to it.

System Global Area (SGA)—A shared storage area in main or virtual memory (depending on your operating system) allocated by the IOR program. SGA is the center of activity while the database is running. Size of the SGA (and performance of the system) depend on the values of the variable INIT.ORA parameters.

temporary tables—Tables frequently required to order data, and to execute SQL statements including DISTINCT, ORDER BY, or GROUP BY clauses; created, maintained, and dropped automatically by *ORACLE*. The average number existing at one time is set by the TEMP_TABLES parameter in INIT.ORA.

transaction—A logical unit of work as defined by the user.

transaction processing—The processing of logical units of work, rather than individual entries, to keep the database consistent.

trigger—In *SQL*Forms*, a sequence of SQL commands and/or *SQL*Forms* commands that are executed when a certain event occurs. There are two types: block-level triggers, invoked when a query is performed or when records are committed to the database; and field-level triggers, invoked when the cursor leaves a field after the field's value has been changed.

unique index—An index (either compressed or noncompressed) that imposes uniqueness on each value it indexes; may be a single column or concatenated columns.

union—The union operator in traditional set theory. For example, A UNION B (where A and B are sets) is the set of all objects x such that x is a member of A or x is a member of B, or both.

update trigger—In *SQL*Forms*, a block-level trigger performed in the course of updating a row in a table during a commit. There are two kinds, pre-update and post-update triggers.

user exit—In *SQL*Forms*, a function written in a procedural programming language such as COBOL or C, invoked by a step of a trigger.

user variable—A variable defined by a user with a *SQL*Plus* command.

unit of work—Equivalent to a transaction, it is a logical unit of work that includes all SQL statements since you either logged on, last committed, or last rolled back your work. A transaction can encompass one SQL statement or many SQL statements.

UFI—User Friendly Interface, an interactive user interface supplied by *ORACLE* through Version 4. Replaced and extended in *ORACLE* Version 5 by SQL*Plus.

validation—In *SQL*Forms*, a processing step which verifies that a piece of information is at least potentially valid. For example: a check that a number representing a day of the week is in the range 1 to 7. Field-level triggers can be used to perform validation.

variable parameters—Parameters that are set in the INIT.ORA parameter file which will impact the size of the system global area (SGA). If these parameters are increased, the size required by the SGA also increases.

view—A table that does not physically exist as such in storage, but looks to the user as though it does. A part of a table that does exist in the database. A "virtual" table.

virtual column—A column in a query result the value of which was calculated from the value(s) of other column(s).

virtual table—A table that does not actually exist in the database, but looks to the user as though it does. Contrast with *base table*; see *view*.

warm start—The normal way of starting an *ORACLE* database every time but the first; also, to execute the IOR program with option WARM.

window—A menu displayed by the screen painter in *SQL*Forms*. It pops up over part of the contents of the screen, sometimes over other windows. When it is no longer needed, it is erased and the information it covered is revealed again.

wrapping—Moving the end of a heading or field to a new line when it is too long to fit on one line.

Index